Charles Wheeler Denison

Hancock

Charles Wheeler Denison

Hancock

ISBN/EAN: 9783742897572

Manufactured in Europe, USA, Canada, Australia, Japa

Cover: Foto ©Thomas Meinert / pixelio.de

Manufactured and distributed by brebook publishing software
(www.brebook.com)

Charles Wheeler Denison

Hancock

HANCOCK

"THE SUPERB"

ROLL·OF·HONOR

YORKTOWN, WILLIAMSBURG,
CHICKAHOMINY, ANTIETAM,
FREDERICKSBURG, CHANCELLORVILLE,
GETTYSBURG, WILDERNESS,
SPOTTSYLVANIA,

EX LIBRIS

HANCOCK "THE SUPERB."

THE

EARLY LIFE AND PUBLIC CAREER

OF

WINFIELD S. HANCOCK,

MAJOR-GENERAL U. S. A.

THE IMPOSING RECORD **OF A** PROGRESSIVE **AND** BRILLIANT
CAREER; A STRIKING **ILLUSTRATION** OF THE MARCH OF
GENIUS UNDER FREE **INSTITUTIONS**: WITH A FULL
AND GRAPHIC **ACCOUNT** OF THE PROCEEDINGS
AT THE CINCINNATI CONVENTION: THE PLAT-
FORM, TABLES OF BALLOTS, ETC. WITH
ANECDOTES AND INCIDENTS.

INCLUDING ALSO

A SKETCH OF THE LIFE OF

HON. WILLIAM H. ENGLISH.

Richly Embellished with many Fine Illustrations.

THE WHOLE PREPARED WITH GREAT CARE

BY

REV. C. W. DENISON,
LATE CHAPLAIN U. S. A.,

AND

CAPT. G. B. HERBERT,
JOURNALIST.

PUBLISHED BY

THE NATIONAL PUBLISHING CO.,

PHILADELPHIA, PA., CHICAGO, ILL., ST. LOUIS, MO.,
AND ATLANTA, GA.

The White House, the Residence of General Hancock from March 4, 1881.

PREFACE.

THE pure patriotism, brilliant military genius, sound civilian statesmanship, and dauntless personal courage of WINFIELD SCOTT HANCOCK, equally with his stainless social record in mature life, his affectionate obedience to parental commands in youth, and his reverential regard for and memory of his boyhood's preceptor, as shadowed forth in the following pages of an impartial biography, render him at once an ornament to this nation, an honor to his native State, and a glowing ensample to the boys, the youth, and the men of America. His name and fame are as inseparably interwoven with the history of this great Republic as are those of the immortal GEORGE WASHINGTON. It was the fortune of the latter to have consecrated the "Stars and Stripes;" it was the destiny of the former to preserve that glorious flag from being rent into tatters during the temporary aberration which, at a critical period, afflicted several States of the Union. The name of HANCOCK blazes brilliantly amid the galaxy of names on the records of Revolutionary days, and its present wearer has added to that lustre by deeds of daring, acts of gentleness, and proofs of high and spotless integrity. In dealing with the sad and stormy scenes of Secession's strife, we have endeavored so to tone and mellow the bitter memories of that epoch that even those, **to** whom such memories are especially painful, will admit that the facts we present are excerpts from the history of their nation and of ours alike, and join with us in accepting the fitness of the title we have adopted, " HANCOCK THE SUPERB." That a career so exceptionably perfect should be crowned by the highest gift at the disposal of the people, would seem to be but simple justice ; one of those episodes which sometimes demonstrate " *the eternal fitness of things.*" It is, therefore, in no partisan spirit, but with a sense of broad-viewed, national policy, that we trust one more title, that grandest of all titles, " Elected President of a Republic of Sovereigns," may yet be bestowed upon the noble man whom we now know and respect as Major-General WINFIELD SCOTT HANCOCK. With this brief preface, we submit this volume to the friendly criticism of his fellow-citizens North, South, East, and West.

G. B. H.

PHILADELPHIA, *Aug. 1st, 1880.*

View of the Capitol at Washington, the Democratic Head-quarters after the 4th of March, 1881.

CONTENTS.

CHAPTER I.

1 *   (v)

Wifd S. Hancock
Major Genl
U. S. Vol.

At the Age of 37.

CHAPTER XXII.

CHAPTER XXIII.

CHAPTER XXIV.

CHAPTER XXV.

CHAPTER XXVI.

CHAPTER XXVII.

CHAPTER XXVIII.

THE UNITED STATES TREASURY, WASHINGTON CITY.

CHAPTER XXXVI.

CHAPTER XXXVII.

CHAPTER XXXVIII.

CHAPTER XXXIX.

CHAPTER XL.

WILLIAM H. ENGLISH, OF INDIANA.

CHAPTER XLI.

"COLONEL! CAN YOU TAKE THAT BATTERY?"

HANCOCK "THE SUPERB,"

THE LAWYER'S SON.

CHAPTER I.

*Sketch of Norristown, **where** his Youth was Passed — The Glorious Memories of the Surroundings — Valley Forge — The Illustrious Pedigree **of** our Hero, Winfield Scott Hancock.*

ON the 14th of February, 1824, in a retired part of the County of Montgomery, near Montgomery Square, Pennsylvania, WINFIELD SCOTT HANCOCK was born. He is the son of BENJAMIN FRANKLIN and ELIZABETH HANCOCK, who were also natives of Montgomery County. His twin-brother, HILARY BAKER, is a resident of Minneapolis, Minnesota, where he has been for some years engaged in the practice of law. The only remaining brother, Major JOHN HANCOCK, was in the Army of the Potomac during the late unhappy civil war. These three are all the children of this branch of the Hancock family.

At the age of four years Winfield removed, with
his parents, to Norristown, Pennsylvania, a beautiful
borough, finely located on the sloping banks of the
Schuylkill river, about twenty miles from Philadelphia. It is the shire town of Montgomery county.
Last census it contained a population of 10,753.
The court-house is well situated, on a commanding
eminence, and built of the handsome gray marble
of the vicinity. Its spire, which resembles that of
some modern churches, is seen from a considerable
distance, and forms an attractive object in the central
portion of the town. There are several churches,
some of which are quite elegant in appearance. The
streets are nearly all wide, straight, and generally
laid out at right angles. Some of them are finely
shaded with trees. One of the principal thorough-
fares has beautiful rows, the clean trunks and shady
branches of which reflect credit on the common sense
and good taste of the citizens. The banks, newspapers, hotels, markets, and other town appliances, be-
token the activity and conveniences of the people.
There are eight newspapers, one a daily, which circu-
late widely through the adjacent country, while the
daily papers of Philadelphia and New York find
numerous and constant readers, in a few hours after
they leave their presses. The public schools, which

WINFIELD SCOTT HANCOCK.

WILLIAM H. ENGLISH.

have been established several years, are abundant and well conducted. There are some good seminaries, finely situated in the outskirts of the town, which afford the best facilities for male and female education.

Owing to its being favored with a court house, and the strong stone jail 'appurtenance thereunto belonging,' Norristown has a liberal supply of gentlemen of the legal profession. Their numerous signs give evidence of the things signified in all the most frequented places. A somewhat amusing instance of the abundance of this highly valuable class of the community, in this quarter, occurred with the author.

We were returning from a visit to the market, whither we had gone before sunrise, in order that we might note its peculiarities and its patrons' habits, and had just turned a corner by the court-house, when a countryman accosted us:

"Maybe you're a strenger in Norristown?"

"Yes, sir," was our reply.

"Maybe you was 'quirin' 'bout the prices in merket?"

"Yes, sir," we again answered.

"Maybe you're a lawyer?" said he, looking at us with great reverence.

"No, sir!" we replied, not a little surprised at the

2

question, and quickly adding: "**What** made **you
think** so?"

"Why, strenger," he concluded, continuing **to look**
steadily at us, "you've got such a honest **face!**"

Completely overcome, we turned away, **and** passed
hurriedly down Court House Hill. Ever since **that**
eventful moment we have had a most exalted **opinion**
of the lawyers **of Norristown. How** widely-known
and well-established **must be the** integrity **of these
champions of jurisprudence, when a** common stranger in **the streets is supposed to be one** of their num
ber **by the honesty of his looks!**

The **public bridge across the river** Schuylkill, at
this place, is **one of the longest and most** substantial
in Pennsylvania. It **leads to the neat village of**
Bridgeport, where the **canal** flows **along the banks,**
and where, just above, **a** dam spans the stream, **down**
the sides of which the waters pour their crystal flood,
like **a** thin sheet of transparent glass hung **over a**
parapet. **In the** centre of the river **is a** lovely island,
the green **summer verdure of** which **is** reflected **in**
the passing waters; **and** whose romantic reaches **be-**
yond **remind the beholder of the days when the**
Schuylkill was the **sporting current of** the Indian,
when **its** groves echoed **to his wild** halloos, and the
hill-sides and valleys smoked **with** his wigwams.

"JINEING THE PINT."

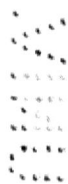

Now the dash of the water-wheel and the ripple of the canal-boat have taken the place of the paddling canoe. The savage shout has died away, and in its stead we hear the roar of engines on the railroad, and the clatter of machinery in the factories along the river. The smoke of the lodge has long since passed into thin air, and its space is supplied by the black vapor that rises from the tall chimneys of the busy iron forge, or the white steam of the lime-kiln. The Minie rifle has supplanted the bow; the axe of the pioneer has driven out the savage hatchet; the winding wild-wood path of the red man has become a country road, a turnpike, a railway; and a large town stands on the rude plots where the aborigines reared their solitary huts. The naked foot of barbarism has been lifted from the soil, and the shod step of civilization is in its place where beautiful Norristown flourishes to-day.

A few miles west from the Schuylkill is one of the most memorable spots in American revolutionary history. It is the Valley Forge. Here it was that the scattered remnants of the patriotic Continental army, under Washington, went into their scanty winter quarters. The British General, Sir William Howe, had vainly endeavored, with a much superior force, to draw the commander-in-chief into an unequal

engagement. His object was the complete conquest
of Philadelphia and the adjacent territory. But
Washington was too cautious to be allured from his
stronghold in these Pennsylvania hills; although to
remain there, through that unusually inclement season, was sure to cause him and his brave troops a
great amount of suffering.

The battle of Germantown had been fought by
Washington, with La Fayette and Pulaski, at that time
just introduced to our republican army. Germantown
is but a few miles east of Norristown, on the fine ridge
of country lying toward Philadelphia. The battle
took place on the 4th of October, 1777; and
although the American soldiers were enduring much
from sickness and privations, they attacked the invaders with such valor that they would have completely won the day but for an unforeseen withdrawal
of aid, for which it was impossible for Washington
to be prepared.

At the struggle of the Brandywine, which took
place not many miles from Norristown, on the
11th of September, in the same year, the Americans
fought equally well; but the smallness of their force,
and the wounding of La Fayette, had compelled a
retirement from the field. The determined will and
skillful strategy of Washington, fighting a strong,

"HOLD! WHAT ARE YOU ABOUT, FLOGGING THAT HORSE?"

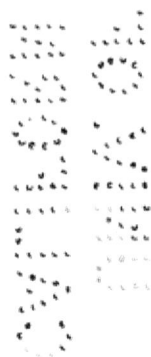

fresh force of the enemy, with disabled columns, kept
Sir William Howe at bay from Philadelphia. It was
not until the last extremity had come, that the revolutionary troops steadily and slowly retired to the
Valley Forge. Here was passed that winter of terrible trial. Without suitable food or clothing, worn
down by repeated marches and battles, deprived of
the comforts of home, driven into poor little shanties
for protection against the piercing cold, the patriots
of that day have gilded those hillsides and glens of
Pennsylvania with the glory of their deeds. It was
here that the selfish spirit of mean and cowardly men
added to the sufferings of the brave soldiers. At
the time when starvation seemed to be staring them
in the face, when their feet were yet sore and swollen
with their shoeless conflicts in the drifted snows, there
were wretches base enough to rush through the sad
and gloomy camp, crying "Beef! Beef! Give us
beef!" It required all the courage and force of character of Washington to check this unpatriotic outbreak, and convince the soldiers that to endure as
brave men should was finally to succeed in the great
struggle. In the 'dead waste and middle' of that
fearful winter, the Father of our Country retired to
the grove near his headquarters; and, spreading his
well-worn army cloak on the frozen ground, poured

2*   B

out the agony of his tried soul in prayer to the Deity. At that very moment treason was doing its worst against him. Attempts were being made to supplant him in command. Our oppressors abroad, uniting with traitors at home, were doing all in their power to scatter the Continental forces, and give up the country to the foe. It was not so to be! The Valley Forge, while it was the dark, icy grave to many of our early heroes, became, also, in the spring-time, the open door of hope, from which sprang forth new legions to do battle for Republican freedom. Well may it forever be a sacred spot. Pennsylvania has many glorious Revolutionary memorials; but the Valley Forge stands first among them all.

Surrounded by such associations as these, Winfield Scott Hancock was born. The name given him at his birth was indicative of the estimate put on love of country by his parents. That of Hancock is associated with everything that is noble and self-sacrificing in the early annals of the Republic. JOHN HANCOCK, the Massachusetts merchant, will be remembered with gratitude by patriotic Americans, as long as a page of the history of our land remains. He was one of the most determined champions of the Revolution that the American colonies contained. Of the fore-most men of his time, it was for him to say:

"Thy spirit, Independence! let me share,
Lord of the lion heart and eagle eye!
Thy steps I follow with my bosom bare,
Nor heed the storm that howls along the sky.
Immortal Liberty! whose look sublime
Has blanched the tyrant's cheek in every varying clime."

Hancock was among the first, while yet a young man and in the possession of a large fortune, to strike a blow against the royal oppressors of his native land. His life was declared to be forfeited, by a proclamation of the British Government. But he escaped the fury of a brutal soldiery, to enlist, with ADAMS, OTIS, and other patriots of that day, in the work of preparing for an armed resistance to foreign aggressions. Immediately after the battle of Lexington, he was chosen President of the Provincial Congress, in Massachusetts; and subsequently to be the successor of Peyton Randolph, of *old* Virginia, as President of the General Congress, which met at Philadelphia, and issued the Declaration of Independence, July 4th, 1776. On that immortal roll of worthies his name must ever stand conspicuous. The record there made was nobly attested all through his life, and in the hour of his death. Virtuous, modest, courageous, learned, dignified, rich, he gave up all for his country; and has left a name on the pages of history which every

American may well aspire to imitate and be proud
to honor.

Coupled with the name of HANCOCK, the subject
of our biography bears that of WINFIELD SCOTT.
It is a pleasure to be able to record here the fact that
the venerable Lieutenant-General acknowledged the
compliment paid him, and very often expressed his
deep personal interest in the career of the Pennsylvania boy, who still so worthily bears his distinguished name.

CHAPTER II.

The Schoolboy Days of Hancock — His early Military Predilections — His Youthful Friendships — The Permanent Impress of a good Home Moulds his Character — "Why, that big Boy out there Tried to Whip Me, and I was n't going to let Him."

WE must now introduce the reader to the home of Winfield, at Norristown. It was the year 1835. His father was at that time a school teacher, and engaged in fitting himself for the profession of the law. The home of the boy was a good one.

How much is included in these few short words! The true homes of America are its chief glory. They are the only sure social foundations of the Republican temple. In every such country the boys of to-day, when properly qualified, are the electors of to-morrow. As they decide the franchise, so the destinies of the nation may be decided. An American boy, rightly educated, may justly aspire to any position within the compass of man to attain, or of man to bestow. Hence the incalculable importance of early instruction in America; hence the immense interests

(21)

of society and government that cluster around the hearth and shrine of the American home.

Such was the home of Winfield. His parents were sincere Christians. The altar of worship stood like a sanctuary within their doors; and every day their family bowed with them before it. Morning and evening the incense of devotion ascended from that house. Nor did this hallowed home influence stop at the threshold. Impressed on the memory and heart, it went out into the duties of life. It made itself a motive in their thoughts, heard in their voices, and felt in their actions. It was not irresistible; it was not all-controlling; but, like the subtle air, it penetrated to every spot; and even if its presence could not always regulate, it was always acknowledged as able to do so, if its inherent power for good should be allowed free sway.

It was in the domain of such a home as this that Winfield received his earliest impressions of character. The uniform record of him, in his boyhood, is, that he was obedient to his parents, truthful and courteous, cheerful, sociable, and manly.

A gentleman sitting in the office of Winfield's father, heard quite a tumult among the boys in the street. There were shouts and other signs of personal conflict, which drew Mr. Hancock and his friend to the door.

"Come here, my son," said the father, calling out Winfield from the crowd.

The boy immediately obeyed, and came marching directly to the office door, his flushed face turned full on that of his father.

"What is the matter, Winfield?" inquired Mr. Hancock.

"Why, that big boy, out there, tried to whip me; and *I wasn't going to let him!*"

"But he is a great deal larger than you are, my son."

"I know he is, father; but he shan't whip me, for all that!"

It required some skill on the part of Mr. Hancock, aided by his visitor, to convince the lad that it was not his duty to go out and resume the fight, against all odds.

Another domestic scene, of an entirely different character, serves further to illustrate the boy.

Winfield and Hilary had come in together in the evening — for, being twins, they were then very seldom separate — and found their mother engaged in family affairs that would require her to remain up to a late hour. The father was necessarily absent, and she was alone with the children.

The two little boys moved about the house, attending to their tasks, as usual, until the time came to retire. The rooms were all still, save that in which the mother was engaged. The streets were almost vacant, and nearly quiet. The boys stood and looked at each other. They were tired of play. They had finished their studies. They had done their home errands. Both of them saw at a glance the state of the case; and, simultaneously, they hit on a happy expedient. They immediately called a council of two — a twin council of twin brothers — and unanimously decided the following propositions:

First. It is the decision of this council that mother is not to be allowed to sit up alone.

Second. The council will sit up with her.

Third. The council shall divide the time into watches of one hour each.

Fourth. Each member of the council shall keep awake one hour, and sleep one hour, watch and watch, until mother puts us to bed.

These articles of agreement, having been duly assented to by both the high contracting parties, were faithfully carried out; until both members of the council, at a late hour, were tenderly led to their youthful slumbers.

The attachment existing between Winfield and his schoolmates developed itself in a great variety of ways, reflecting credit on his juvenile propensities. He was always regarded as a leader among the boys at Norristown. When the time came to organize the occasional village accompaniment of an amateur boy militia, he was at once selected, by common consent, to hold the distinguished post of captain. The memory of this little body of Home Guards is cherished with pride by many of its members, to this day. The matrons look back with pleasure on the fact that their hands helped to equip the juvenile soldiers; and that when they appeared on parade, with mimic colors and music of tiny drum and flageolet, they cheered them on their marches, and served them freely with the required rations of lemonade and doughnuts.

The haymows and orchards in Norristown and vicinity will bear witness to the innocent raids of these budding patriots. In justice to them, it must be added that their depredations were never of a very serious character. They were generally welcome whenever they entered their temporary barracks, or camp-grounds; and usually found ample

3

opportunities to display their imitation martial deeds. Captain Winfield — perhaps owing to the significant fact that he bore the name of the then principal general of the United States army — always 'ruled the roster,' whether it assumed the form of a brigade, a regiment, or a battalion. His military experience, at the ripe age of twelve years, carried him triumphantly through every duty, — muster, parade, drill, inspection, and review. His personal appearance always commanded respect, at the head of his little troop. One peculiarity of paternal reverence often saved him trouble in the way of discipline. He always handed offenders over to their mothers. This was a capital idea of Captain Winfield's. It not only enabled him to avoid all the vexations of a court-martial, but it gave satisfaction to all concerned; for if a good mother cannot bring a soldier to terms, who can?

The boy-circle of Winfield in Norristown had its social singing-school. Here, again, his companions clustered around; for he was as popular in musical as he was in military affairs. His aid was especially valuable in this association, for its general management was conferred on his father, as chairman of a committee. On one occasion, when the singing-books were being given out, it so happened that a soiled copy fell into the hands of a playmate of Winfield. Before he was aware of the defacements, the lad had written his name in the book, and thus it was too late to change it.

"Leave this matter to me," said Winfield; "I'll see what can be done. You shall have a good book in the place of this."

"Thank you," replied his school-fellow; "but how will you do it?"

"Let me manage that," Winfield quietly added—"you may be sure I will do it right; for father, you know, is committee-man."

Without saying more, he took the soiled volume, and carefully erased the name his fellow-scholar had written in it. He then placed the book back in the pile, where he knew it must pass through the careful hands and under the scrutinizing eye of his father.

The time came. The school was all assembled and seated. The books were again to be given out. Mr. Hancock passed them, as usual, giving to each scholar his book, with his name in it. Directly he came to the soiled one. The name was erased!

"Who erased this name?" quietly asked the dignified chairman of the committee, holding up the book, and showing the defaced page.

"I did it, sir," promptly replied Winfield, standing up in his place.

"What did you do it for?" continued the father.

"Because I didn't want that boy to have a soiled book, when I knew there were plenty of good ones, not used."

Mr. Hancock looked an instant at Winfield, and, with a calm smile, put back the soiled book in its place behind him. Giving the school-mate a perfect copy, he added:

"Take your seat, Winfield."

That simple act of the lawyer's son spoke volumes. His attachment for his comrade determined his purpose to do him a favor. He was ready to do it, even if he had to ask it publicly of his father — a commanding gentleman, the personification of dignity, especially when presented to a school of youth, to supervise their treatment of books. The promptness of his response to the question of his father, in the presence of the school, resulting in the protection of his school-fellow and obtaining him the desired book, strikingly illustrates, through the boy, the genius and energy of the man.

CHAPTER III.

IT is the opinion of those who knew Winfield best
in his boyhood, that he chose the military life
from an inherent love of it. At that early period of
which we are now writing, he could, of course, have
no idea of what was before him. His parents had
not the slightest intention of devoting him to the
profession of arms. When, on pleasant Saturday
afternoons, released from the confinement of the
school-room, he gathered his fellow-scholars around
him, and, with music and banners, marched and coun-
termarched with them through the streets of the then
comparatively small village of Norristown, little did
his family or those who looked on the mimic parade
imagine that the modest, cheerful, amiable youth before them would rise to the dignity of a Major

3*   (29)

General in one of the greatest armies of the world.
When the miniature battles followed, the snow-ball
engagements, the hay-bank barricades, the wooden
swords clashing, the corn-stalk guns charging, the
scantling embankments were carried by stove-pipe
artillery, it was hardly supposed by the curious spectators that they were but the preludes to grand and
gallant realities, in which that youthful commander
should bear so conspicuous and enduring a part.

In the juvenile band he met for other purposes,
he was as affectionate and social as he was energetic
and commanding in military matters.   It was here
that his genius shone in a beautiful sphere.   He was
very fond of scientific experiments.   There are portions of his father's house that contain good illustrations of his taste in this particular, — the original
home-made electric battery, the collections of geo-
logical and mineral specimens, the drawings, sketch-
ings and paintings.

In the prosecution of his scientific studies, he was
happy in opportunities to administer or to witness
the administration and effects of nitrous oxide, or
exhilarating gas.   He was in the habit of gathering
with his twin brother, an amateur class of students,
to whom these and other experiments always afforded

pleasure. Winfield was invariably selected to be the grand lecturer on these august occasions.

> "And still they gazed, and still the wonder grew,
> How one small head could carry all he knew."

With him, however, it was a serious matter. He entered the arena of science with a keen relish for it, and a firm purpose to excel in it. He was amused, with the rest; but it was the amusement that rejoices in scientific combinations secured, and a prognosis chemically fulfilled.

On one of these occasions, a playmate whose given name was Washington, well known to be a good singer, was desired to take the gas at the hands of Professor Winfield. The attempt to induce him to sing, while under the influence of the exhilaration, had been repeatedly tried by others, but always failed. At length the juvenile Professor determined to try his own skill in the case.

Proceeding to administer the gas slowly, at regular intervals, he placed his mouth near the ear of the pupil, and breathed, in a clear, distinct whisper:

"Sing, Wash!—sing!—sing!—sing!"

In an instant the effect was produced. The lad sprang forward, and throwing himself into the attitude of a singing master, with arm erect, as if beat-

ing time and tuning-fork in hand, he began, in the
old tune of St. Martin's :

<blockquote>
"On Jo-ordan's sto-ormy **ba-anks I stand,**
   And ca-a-st a wi-i-shful eye
To Ca-na-an's fai-i-r and ha-a-ppy **land,**
   Where my-y posse-e-ss-ions lie."
</blockquote>

" Well done !" exclaimed the delighted young **Pro-**
fessor, as he saw his scientific victory; while all the
company joined in the applause.

It now came the turn of Professor Winfield himself.   What trait would the gas make him display?
We shall see.

A powerful charge of the subtle element was administered to him.   On the removal of the stop-cock, he
stepped gravely forward, like a clergyman in a pul-
pit, about to lead in some part of divine service.
There was a general disappointment, for a moment.
Pausing, slowly, he remained motionless, his eyes
fixed steadily on the floor, his right hand placed
firmly beneath his chin, his left foot slightly advanced.   In this position he remained an instant, as
if he were a statue, when, springing up, like an eagle,
he swept across the area, stretched out his arms to
their full extent, clenched his fists, and prepared for
active battle.   The nearest portion of the audience

incontinently fell back, or the threatened blows might have caused 'somebody to be hurt.'

Instantly, as the living effect passed off, he resumed his wonted habit of mingled dignity, courtesy, and energy.

These characteristics of the practical student were well developed in Winfield. At the village academy he acquired and maintained the position of an honest, truthful, obedient, courageous boy. It was his character, also, in the community. While popular with his fellow youth and fond of their society, there was something about this boy that led men of thought and reflection to take an interest in conversing with him. Many a time was he received with pleasure in the cluster of the citizens who were wont to gather in the store opposite his father's residence, and by whom the affairs of the day were discussed. It is worthy of remembrance that he loved to be among and listen to them. He was never known to intrude an opinion or to hazard a remark of his own; but as he stood there, with his modest, unassuming manner, the expressions of his face, as conversations progressed, clearly indicated on which side his convictions were, and that, if called upon, he was ready to enforce them by every means in his power. It was here, among these debating and enquiring free citi-

C

zens, that Winfield learned some of his best conceptions of the safeguards of our country. Here he saw, in the record of passing events thus laid before his opening mind, the practical application of those vital forces of which he had learned at school, and the relative value of which he now beheld wrought out into shape by those before him, in the movements of society. He learned the worth of freedom to all mankind by what he saw of its enjoyment among those immediately around him. Free himself, he longed in his young heart to give freedom, guided by law, to all the human race.

He was now fifteen years of age. His progress in his studies had been all that could be expected. As he advanced, new opportunities were presented for the development of his powers. The celebration of the anniversary of our national independence called him out in a new field. He was selected to read the Declaration in public on that day. It was an occasion of deep interest in the town. The largest church was crowded with people, and the schools were well represented. One of the pastors, who had always expressed pleasure in the marked genius of Winfield, when it was known that he was to be the reader of the Declaration, took him aside to his shady garden, and there taught him on what to lay the emphasis, where to pause, when to raise and how to lower his voice. It would be a graphic picture to witness that reverend divine now calling the Major General before him again, to hear how he would to-day delineate the immortal document he read in the grove, more than a quarter of a century ago, and which he has since so often and so bravely periled his life, on the field of battle, to maintain.

When Winfield was eleven years of age, there came to Norristown a poor little boy who was commonly called 'Johnny.' His father had died when he was but three years old, and he was placed in charge of a relative of the family. He grew up with the other boys of the place, and at the age of nine became one of the playmates of Winfield. By degrees there was formed an attachment between them. They saw something in each other that they liked.

As is too often the case, not only with children but older persons, this unfortunate child was neglected, and occasionally tyrannized over by his associates. This was one of the reasons why Winfield resolved to stand by him. Having ten pennies at his disposal where Johnny had one, he made it a rule, whenever occasion served, to divide with him. When they met, before or after school, and recreation was the object, Winfield would say:

"Come, Johnny, I have some pennies; let us go together and get something."

Thus the thoughtful generosity of Winfield and the affectionate gratitude of Johnny made both boys happy.

Sometimes larger boys would gather around Johnny, and tantalize and threaten him. He was the youngest and smallest among them. On all such occasions, Winfield, when within sight or hearing, would promptly and bravely come to the rescue.

"Look here!" he would say to the aggressor, "you are larger and older than Johnny, and ought to be ashamed to take advantage of him, on account of his age and size."

"What business is it to you, Winfield Hancock?" came the angry question.

"I will make it my business," was Winfield's decided reply. "Stand your ground, Johnny; they shan't hurt you!"

Occasionally, when this manly reinforcement brought threats on his own head, he would boldly add:

"If you want to take hold of a boy, why don't you find one of my size? Let little Johnny alone!"

His magnanimous courage always carried the day.

It was in this spirit that he obtained that control

over other boys, some of them older than himself, that distinguished his boyhood. Very frequently, when juvenile difficulties occurred, and it seemed impossible to adjust them amicably, the general cry would arise:

"Oh, leave it to Winfield; he'll settle it."

The young judge invariably accepted the office, and mounted the bench, on the spot. It is worthy of record that his decisions, whatever they might be, always gave satisfaction.

In after years little Johnny came as a carpenter's apprentice to the city of Philadelphia. He was still so poor that when he crossed the bridge, then standing at the head of Market street, he had but a solitary penny in his pocket. But he had a good trade; and immediately went to work. It was not long ere he was at the head of a gang of men. By continued industry he prospered in business, and became a rich man. Entering a new field, he was chosen a member of the Philadelphia city government, and took his seat in the Councils, respected and confided in by all who knew him.

In the same course of time, Winfield, his playmate, had become a Major General in the Army of the United States. But they who had thus been boys

4

together, did not forget each other when they became men. It was the pleasant duty of JOHN WILLIAM EVERMAN., Esq., for the government of Philadelphia, to introduce a series of resolutions commending the patriotism, courage, and skill of Major General WINFIELD SCOTT HANCOCK. These resolutions were passed unanimously by both branches of the City Councils, and it devolved on 'little Johnny' to be chairman of the committee that took them, elegantly engrossed, to the now distinguished friend of his early years.

The Councilman and the General met at the capital of the nation. How changed the scene now from that of their boyhood in the borough of Norristown! They came together, in the presence of the accompanying members of the delegation, in one of the parlors of Willard's hotel. With what cordiality the two playmates greeted each other!

At the close of a mutually agreeable conversation, the General said:

"We meet here, Mr. Everman, in our official capacities; but, sir, I desire to see more of you. I must leave, soon, for my post in the army. Come and visit me there, sir; and be sure and make my headquarters your home, during your stay."

This early friendship of boyhood continued for

several years. It has been repeatedly revived by
numerous pleasant memorials. When General Hancock visited Harrisburg, **Pennsylvania,** aiding, by his
powerful personal influence, in the great work of obtaining reinforcements for the noble Army of the
Potomac, he was waited upon by Mr. Everman, in
company with other gentlemen of the Philadelphia
city government. The pages of the records of the
past were often reviewed by the two friends on this
occasion. It was here the General was informed that
he was voted the freedom of Philadelphia, and that
the sacred area of old Independence Hall—the room
in which the Declaration of American Independence
was signed — had been opened to his use, for the reception of himself and his visits from the people.

The scenes of that occasion will long be remembered in Philadelphia. The honor is one seldom conferred on any American citizen. No one but a President or Ex-president of the United States, or a servant of the Republic similarly distinguished, has ever
enjoyed it. Here, within these consecrated walls, the
two friends — Winfield and little Johnny — enjoyed
the renewal of the friendship of their boyhood days.
As the crowd gathered around him, to do him honor
for his brilliant services on the field of battle, to uphold the Union our patriot fathers had met here to

establish, the General bent down close to his friend and whispered in his ear:

"You shall hear from me again."

A gentleman approaching touched on the political questions of the day.

"I know no politics," said General Hancock; "especially in such a presence as this,"—looking reverently on the portraits of the fathers of the Republic hung around the old hall — firmly adding:

"A good soldier knows no party but his country."

In receiving the Philadelphia resolutions, forwarded by Mr. Everman, the same noble impulse guided the pen of the General. By his direction they were enclosed to Mrs. Hancock, at her residence at Longwood, St. Louis county, Missouri, who acknowledged them from the friend of her husband in a beautiful and appropriate letter. A copy was placed in the hands of the parents of the General, and it ornamented the family mansion, overlooking a portion of the youthful playgrounds of Winfield and 'little Johnny,' at Norristown.

CHAPTER IV.

*An Interesting Episode which had much to do with Shaping the
Destiny of Young Hancock — The Ill-Treatment of a Horse by a
Drayman leads indirectly to a Cadetship for the Future General.*

AT the time of which we are now writing, there
resided in a populous part of Montgomery
county, Pennsylvania, a gentleman well known for
his extensive influence in political circles. His
deep interest in the arrangement of public matters
induced him to take long and frequent rides through
different parts of the county, and places adjacent.
He once represented that district in the Congress of
the United States. His type of character led him to
be strong in his likes and dislikes; to be decided in
his friendship and equally decided in his enmity.

For quite a number of years, in the prosecution
of his profession, he had employed one of the best
horses in that section of the country. With his
trusty steed, when a pressing occasion demanded, he

4*   (41)

was accustomed to start off, at times in the middle of the night, reach the dwellings of the members of his party he desired to see, rouse them from their slumbers, communicate the intelligence or counsel he thought of importance, and then, after driving or riding miles in his solitary routes of duty, to return to his office as the first beams of day gilded the surrounding landscape. Many a public movement has been announced in the papers, many a political event has controlled the party destinies of that district, and, to some extent, of the state and country, which had its unknown origin in the midnight journeys of this Montgomery county traveller.

Like other somewhat eccentric men, having no wife to love, he loved his horse. The noble animal was his companion in all these secret trips. It had become accustomed to his night approaches in the comfortable stables; it had sped for him, either bearing him on its back or drawing him in his vehicle, through highways and byways; it had patiently and quietly waited for him, through summer and winter, in sunshine and in storm, at the places selected by its master for his strategic interviews; and had thus, in many ways, enabled him to accomplish objects that were dear to his heart.

But, strong and enduring as is the horse, it cannot

last forever. There came a time when the good steed of our friend, while it retained all its wonted fineness of mould and form, gave signs of age. While suitable for short excursions, and as useful as ever for occasional drives, it could no longer withstand the long, and rapid, and repeated journeys to which for years it had been subjected. The owner, touched by the discovery of the fact, with a spirit that did him honor, decided to withdraw the animal from such active service. He took it to Philadelphia, and presented it to a professional acquaintance, then residing there, with the mutual understanding that the faithful creature should be employed only in light and easy duties — such as would especially benefit the recipient of the horse — until its death.

Time passed on. One day, when the lawyer was on a visit to Philadelphia, he discovered, as he stood near the Montgomery Hotel, a handsome horse, harnessed to a heavily loaded dray, quivering with excitement under his load, covered with foam, and a driver lashing him furiously with a large whip. Looking a moment at the suffering animal—panting there in the dry, dusty streets, in the middle of the month of July—he perceived it was his own former favorite! Rushing to the driver, and seizing his lifted whip, just about to descend on the lacerated back of the poor creature, he exclaimed:

"Hold! What are you about, flogging that horse in that brutal manner?"

The driver began to reply, when he again cried out:

"Where did you buy the animal?"

"Of ——— ———," (naming the party to whom the lawyer had presented it.)

"What did you pay?"

"Seventy-five dollars."

"And *he* took *that* money, for *this* horse!"

"Yes, sir; I paid him cash down"

"You did? Well; you may come down yourself, now."

The driver descended from his dray, and stood, looking with wonder at his questioner, while he, in turn, looked, with something rather different, at him.

"Now, tell me," he resumed, as calmly as possible, 'why did you strike such a handsome horse in that way?"

"I know it's handsome, sir; quick yet, in a light buggy; but, then, the critter ain't strong; its too old, 'squire."

"So, then; you cut and lash a noble horse because he's old, do you?"

"I've been cheated, 'squire, by the man I bought on."

"Been cheated, eh? I think you have!

"And you are not the only one who has been cheated about that horse.

"What will you take for the animal?"

"I'll take a hundred dollars; for it'll be some trouble for me to get another who'll *sell* as well."

"My friend! here are your hundred dollars. The horse is *mine* — again! I have always held that beautiful creature to be worth more than twice as much. I would not take five hundred, now!"

"Then you've made a good bargain, 'squire."

"Yes; a very good bargain; tho' I have been *sold*, myself; but this is the last time this horse will ever be.

"Take it out of that dray, as quick as your hands will let you! Go! get a dray horse, that will bear loading and thrashing better than this one!"

The still wondering drayman instinctively obeyed, and the horse, yet trembling and wet with fatigue and blows, was led to the stables of the Montgomery Hotel, where several days and nights of rest and care were required to restore the usual appearance and qualities. At the end of that time the revived pet was again in its old home, suitably enlarged for the purpose, and receiving its full share of wonted kindness.

———————

Now it happened that at the time this occurrence was taking place, the party who had thus summarily disposed of the present of our legal friend, removed a portion of his family into Montgomery county. His reason for doing so was that he heard a cadet was about being selected there for West Point, and he thought by that device to secure the appointment for his son. He had no right to solicit the favor. He was not a resident of the district, never had been, and never expected to be. His temporary location there was a subterfuge, a ruse; as mean an act as his selling the present of his friend, to be treated brutally in its old age.

The lawyer discovered the base trick, as he had discovered that practiced on him in the matter of his equine favorite; and, with his usual promptitude, determination and sagacity, he proceeded at once to thwart the trickster. We shall see how handsomely he did it. With the eccentricity and shrewdness peculiar to him, he determined that his horse, who had shared with him in suffering, should participate with him in his punishment of the wrong-doer. He at once mounted the animal, and proceeded to the house of the then member of congress for that district, the Hon. JOSEPH FORNANCE, **told him** the facts of the case, and took the steps necessary **to carry his** patriotic plan into effect.

Late that same **night he rode up to the door of** Mr. B. F. HANCOCK, **in Norristown.   Without** stopping to dismount, he at once began:

"Good evening, **Mr. Hancock!"**

"Good evening, sir," was the courteous answer, as Mr. Hancock, who had been roused from his sleep, came to the steps of his office.

"Mr. Hancock! would you like to have your son Winfield sent to West Point, **as a** cadet?"

"Really, sir, I hardly know what to reply to such a question.   It is a very sudden one to be proposed at this time of night.   I have not thought of the thing."

"Well, I wish you would think of it; for I have it in my power to send him."

"Winfield is rather young for such a position."

"He is as old as the boy who *another man* is trying to get in!"

"That may be."

"Yes, sir; I *know* it to be so!   Winfield is a smart boy, Mr. Hancock; a very smart boy; a great deal smarter than that other one; he has the talents for it, sir; just the talents; and, if you will say **the** word, he shall go."

"I thank you for the offer; but you must grant me time to reflect upon it.

"Call to-morrow morning, and I will **give you an** answer."

The family of Mr. Hancock are early **risers.** They were **up betimes; and** the cadet consultation was duly held. It is due to the mother of **Winfield** to record the fact that she took that active part in **it** becoming her position. Unintentionally to herself she had nourished some of the early military proclivities of the boy. She had helped to equip him in his juvenile uniform, when at the head of his miniature company of Norristown volunteers, while his father had been busy with other affairs. She knew well the bent of the mind of the boy. Winfield himself was consulted in the matter; and the decision was made.

The pawing hoofs of the venerable steed on the pavement in front of the house told that the applicant for Winfield was soon again at the door. The moment it opened, the clear voice of the still mounted lawyer made the earnest inquiry

"Well, Mr. Hancock! what do you say? I am all ready to complete the business. Shall Winfield go?"

" Yes, sir !" was the quiet response.

In an instant more the horse and rider were galloping down the street, across the adjacent bridge, to the temporary residence of the incumbent congressman.

The secret history of that early morning ride by that Pennsylvania civilian, on that petted old horse, of his interview with that member of congress, of their mutual conference and conjectures with regard to young Winfield, is all locked up in the past. What anticipations for the future of the boy glowed in the bosom of that rider are all buried with him in the grave. All unknown to us now are the hopes he indulged of the career of the cadet; how fondly he may have imagined him realizing all his expectations; succeeding in the admission; passing the ordeal of three years of study; receiving his commission and entering the army of the nation; serving the requisite term in subordinate positions, through drill, discipline, and the privations of camp, fortress, and march; encountering hunger, disease, fatigue and battle; perhaps rising to eminence among the sons of the Republic who should graduate with him from those classic and warlike enclosures; until, in bright perspective, the name of his youthful *pro-*

5   D

tege might be honored and distinguished in American military annals.

That solitary rider on that patriotic mission passed near the hallowed shades of the Valley Forge, and the vicinity of the sanguinary battle-ground of Paoli. The winding road carried him beside the silent grave of many a revolutionary hero, dying, unknown, in the early struggle of the colonies, for his God, for freedom and native land. The little hillocks were green with beauty as he galloped by them, and their sods seemed to whisper approval to him, in every bending blade of grass. Going in the light of the morning sun and returning in the cool shadows of the evening, the spirits of the heroic dead seemed to hover around him, as they ever do around all controlled by the loftiest purposes of the human heart. Beyond were the hillsides and gorges where Washington, like an invincible eagle at bay, gathered his chosen troops around him, and resolved to suffer, and, if need be to die, in all the horrors of an half-starved and half-naked winter camp, rather than surrender up the symbols of national liberty and hope committed to his hands by the American people. Here was the bridle-path he traversed, in his high emprise of duty. There he had his headquarters in the canvas tent. Yonder he counselled with the heroic Steuben and Knox, through the cold, dark nights, when the stars lighted up their vigils at the altar of freedom, and the fires of the bivouacs of her armed defenders glowed on the darkness of their lines beyond. Born in the entrenched mountain passes; sheeted in the towering drifts of snow; nursed at the breast of famine; shielded by the bleeding arms of patriots; soothed by the lullaby of the icy cradle of liberty, that rung with steel as it rocked in the stormy winds; guarded by brave hearts, warm with the noblest resolves that ever lived in the souls of men; and, above all, overshadowed by the outspread wing of an Almighty Protector, the infant Genius of American Independence here passed in safety its first fearful ordeal of the Revolutionary War. How bravely the native patriotism of our fathers arose from that gloomy sepulchre at the Valley Forge, and how sternly it renewed its proof of resurrection, history has abundantly attested. Immediately after these scenes followed the deeds of valor they performed in the ensuing spring, at Trenton, on the banks of the Delaware; compelling our enemies, with all their superior land and sea force, to retire from Philadelphia; and winning, against great odds, the glorious victories of Princeton and Monmouth, on the bloody sands of New Jersey.

On the return of that rider to Norristown, from amid such associations as these, in old Pennsylvania, the preparatory steps were completed with Mr. FORNANCE, the then member of Congress for that district, which resulted in making WINFIELD SCOTT HANCOCK a United States Cadet.

So singular was the cause of the beginning of his public career. The rider and the horse are long since dead; but how mysterious is the part they performed in thus preparing the way of one of the most distinguished of the military men of America!

> "This is **Thy work**, Almighty Providence!
> Whose power, beyond the stretch of human thought,
> Revolves the orbs of empire."

CHAPTER V.

.

AMERICAN history will always endorse the wisdom of the Father of our Country in the selection of West Point as a school for military purposes. Washington was deeply impressed with the vast strategic importance of that post during the Revolutionary War. The treasonable attempt of Arnold to betray it into the hands of the enemy, during the absence of the Commander-in-chief, at Hartford, Connecticut, to confer there with our French ally, Rochambeau, on a plan for the then ensuing campaign of 1779, has shown its relative position as a means of internal defence, in a very striking light. It was eminently fitting that he should early designate this stronghold as a suitable spot for the establishment of a school for the instruction of American youth in the great work of national protection. Located on the

5*   (53)

navigable waters of the Hudson river, in the midst of the most commanding hills, with a healthful and abundant country immediately surrounding it, having every facility for the construction of fortifications, the management of the engines of war and the movements of a sufficient number of troops, no military institution of its class in the world excels it.

WINFIELD SCOTT HANCOCK entered West Point as a cadet on the first of July, 1840, at the age of 16. At that time there were among his fellow cadets, most of them his seniors in age and entrance, such of our nation's military men as Lt. Gen. GRANT, Gen. JUDAH, PLEASANTON, HARDIE, REYNOLDS, ORD, INGALLS and AUGUR. His studies were of a nature to develop his talents in the right direction. Plans of fortifications, sections of embrasures, casemates, cannon and carriages, occupied his pen and pencil to advantage. Those who have seen the specimens of the skill and patient industry of Winfield, in works of this description, attest to their excellence.

The personal popularity which so marked him at home continued with the young cadet during the whole of his career at West Point. He frequently, after his graduation, expressed the opinion that he entered the academy too young; but it is not supposed that many agree with him.

While at West Point he was seen and conversed with for the first time by General SCOTT. It was the pleasure of the chieftain to express his satisfaction at the progress the modest youth was making. His kind expressions on that occasion will always be remembered by all who heard them.

The studies and service of West Point embrace a practical period of three years. During each term the cadet is regarded, as he was at his entrance, as a soldier of the nation, sworn to her defence by force of arms for four years after the time of his graduation, and then to be held as indirectly expected to do duty under her colors. As he advances in studies he increases his military drill and practice; passes through tests in the different arms of infantry, cavalry, and artillery; and learns, by actual service in amateur camps, the value of exercise, drill and discipline in the manual of arms, the camp, and the field. Experience has now abundantly proved the practical value of this national military school.

These are not the pages on which to record any additional testimonies in favor of the usefulness of West Point Academy to the nation. The war of 1812, through all its vicissitudes, attested the fact; it was repeated again in Mexico; and it has been frequently and strongly reaffirmed during the national conflict with the great rebellion of '61–4. If some of the sons of the Republic, educated carefully at her expense at West Point, have ungratefully turned against her, and cruelly stung the bosom that warmed them into military life, the great body of the cadets have been and still are bravely true to the glorious ensign of the Union.

The dry, quiet humor of Winfield developed itself at West Point, as it did in his boyhood at Norristown. In spite of all conventional rules, it would occasionally find vent in various ways. One of these humors of the cadets in which he took part was to welcome outsiders, who were sometimes under the impression that they had only to offer themselves at the gates and they would be admitted at once to enter the ranks. This delusion was humorously dispelled by the accompanying engraving, which was designed and drawn by Cadet Hancock. (See engraving, "JINEING THE PINT.") It is introduced here not merely to show one of the pleasantries of the Academy, but the talents of General Hancock, as a delineator. In the West Point Album, that has been politely placed at our disposal for the purpose, are several other original specimens of his genius as an amateur artist, while the large drawings of forts, navy yards, and arsenals, display in a favorable light his scientific attainments. Among these we have several elegantly drawn and finely colored outlines of public buildings, at West Point, and national works at other places, with sketches of nature, characters and scenes that do marked credit to his talents.

The youth of our country, who aspire to do her service—and what true American youth does not?—may well profit by the juvenile example and cadet experience of Winfield Hancock. He had no advantages over many a lad reading these pages. He had to contend with the same obstacles that beset others. The secret of his success, thus far, was that he was obedient to his parents; he was found in his place at school; he profited by the examples set before him by his Christian parents; he neither despised nor shunned the duties connected with the instructions of the holy day; he learned to prize honesty, virtue, truth, magnanimity, as above all price; and when, therefore, he entered the trying arena of a great national military institution, to contest for the guerdons of learning, self-control, position and power among men, he was in a good measure prepared for the ordeal.

Young American readers! the destinies of this great nation are soon to be committed to your hands. You are to frame and execute its laws; to raise, equip, and maintain its defences; to educate its masses, of which you yourselves are to be a part; to earn and manage its finances; to produce its crops, conduct its manufactures, display its arts, sail its ships, and represent it in all foreign lands. In a short time you are to fill the places of your fathers, who, in a single generation of thirty years, will have all passed away.

Be worthy, then, as WINFIELD was, of the high trust about to be consigned to your control. Be upright, be industrious, be obedient, be patriotic; and you will be fitting sons of the great American Republic.

CHAPTER VI.

A Brief Sketch of Montgomery County, Rich in its Revolutionary Associations — A County to be proud of, and a County that is proud of its Distinguished Son, the Present Nominee for the Presidency of the United States.

THERE is much of deep historical interest in old Montgomery county, Pennsylvania. Before young WINFIELD, one of her choicest native sons, had gone from her abode to his cadetship at West Point, before he had begun to reflect lustre on her name by his brilliant and patriotic career, the history of the county was well worthy of honorable mention.

The settlement of this county was one of the earliest in the central part of the United States. As long ago as 1640, nearly half a century before the grant of William Penn was given to the first English proprietors, there were settlers along the banks of the Schuylkill and its tributaries, beyond the present boundaries of Norristown. The Hollander, the Swede, the Welshman, the German, the Englishman, were its primeval colonists, following in the track of the Algonquin, who then held supreme sway over all

(59)

the land, from the Hudson to the Delaware, and from the Catskills to the Alleghenies.

Opened to civilization, it was separated from Philadelphia in 1784. It covered an area of 317,440 acres —the manor of Norriton, now the borough of Norristown, then embracing, in the grant of William Penn to his son, 7,482 acres. The whole of this town site was valued, in 1704, at a little over $3,000. The present extent of the county is 30 miles in length, 17 miles in breadth, and 490 square miles. Its population at the last census was 81,612.

No county in Pennsylvania has justly more pride of character than Montgomery. Its founders were men of tenacious religious faith, fixed purpose, great industry, and determined perseverance. In the interior townships there are many of the people who hold to the language which their ancestors brought across the ocean, with a tenacity that no changes of time, no inroads of progress, can relax. The tongues their fathers spoke centuries ago they speak to-day. A quiet, rural, thriving people, they are successful in their pursuits and hospitable to strangers. Around them, and all through the valley of the Schuylkill, the advance of the age has been steadily onward. The navigable streams; the manufacturing water-courses; the mines of iron, coal, and lead; the quarries of marble, limestone, slate, and sandstone; the foundries, kilns, factories, and forges, filling the railway, the river and the canal with their busy fruits of enterprise; all unite to present a picture of Montgomery which the historian is grateful to be able to record.

There are parts of this county that must ever be gloriously memorable in revolutionary annals. In 1777, after the defeat of the American army at Brandywine, the region of Montgomery was much frequented by Washington and his patriot troops. On the 17th of September, of that year, the Americans moved to the north, toward the Schuylkill, by way of Yellow Springs, and encamped on the Perkiomen. All this spot, from Parker's Ford to Norristown, from Norristown to Swedes' Ford, from Swedes' Ford to Perkiomen, from Perkiomen to Whitemarsh, from Whitemarsh to Paoli, from Paoli to the Valley Forge, is now sacred ground. It is to be remembered forever as one of the oldest battle-fields of liberty.

The encampment of Sir William Howe, when Washington was fighting him for the protection of Philadelphia, was at one time on the present site of Norristown. Washington was at that moment but a few miles above. The cruel massacre of Paoli might have been shared by the then little settlement of Nor-

6

ristown, but for the special interposition of the Almighty. An unexpected storm changed the whole nature of the campaign, and led the way for the withdrawal of the enemy from that section of the country.

The remains of the revolutionary breastworks at Swedes' Ford will always stand as a memorial of the stubborn defence made against invasion by our patriot fathers. It was here the foreign invaders were met, and the fording of the troops of Washington protected. Only a short distance from this line of the county of Montgomery, the Father of our Country passed, with his brave little army, to those terrible scenes at the Valley Forge, of which we have spoken in previous chapters. It was over this soil now forever made consecrate by their touch, that the patriot soldiers tracked their way in blood to their wintry quarters, and to their future achievements for American independence.

A fitting spot for the birthplace of WINFIELD SCOTT HANCOCK. From this historic point we now begin to trace his entrance on a more public career.

CHAPTER VII.

Winfield Graduates — His Gallant Career in the Mexican War —
Churubusco — Molino del Rey — Chapultepec — Toluca — The Com-
plimentary Resolutions of the Pennsylvania Legislature — The
Fleshing of his Maiden Sword.

ON the 30th day of June, 1844, Cadet HANCOCK graduated at West Point, standing number eighteen in his class. He was promoted to a brevet second lieutenancy in the Sixth United States Regular Infantry, July 1st, 1844, and on the 18th of June, 1846, received his commission as full second lieutenant in the same regiment.

His first posts of duty in the army were in the far West—in the region of the Washita, on Red River. The valley of the Red River borders on the Indian territory, and contains extensive prairies, among which are large tracts of fine timber. The soil is equal to any in the world for fertility and durability. At the time Lieutenant Hancock was stationed in

(63)

that quarter, the hostile Indian tribes were quite troublesome to the settlers on the frontier. It required skill and tact as well as courage on his part to discharge his important trust with propriety.

On being transferred from the Red River of the South, at Fort Towson, he was ordered to Fort Washita, our most western military station. He continued at this post in the discharge of his routine garrison duties until the spring of 1847, when, on the breaking out of the war with Mexico, he was ordered with his regiment to the front.

His first part in battle was taken on the 20th of August, 1847, at Churubusco. The army of the centre, under General Scott, had entered Mexico, via Vera Cruz, and was co-operating with the army of occupation, under General Taylor. The spirit of the Mexican government and people had been aroused, war having been formally declared against the United States. The victories of Taylor had signally prepared the way, and the movements of our troops were onward.

The Sixth United States Infantry, of which Winfield was now second lieutenant, was in command of Colonel J. S. Clarke, in this battle.

The severe defeat of Santa Anna at Buena Vista,

by General Taylor, had induced that Mexican chief
to make the most extensive preparations for opposing
the victorious advance of General Scott. Vera Cruz,
the principal Mexican town on the seaboard, had
fallen; and, after winning several other victories toward the interior, the army of the centre was now on
its way to the capital of Mexico. Two strong positions had to be taken before the city could be assaulted
—Molino del Rey, (the King's Mill,) and the castle of
Chapultepec. In the advance on this important point,
Lieutenant Hancock drew his sword in his earliest
fights for his country. He was under the immediate
command of Captain Hoffman, of the Sixth Infantry.
The assault was made on the works of the enemy
by the platoon in charge of Lieutenant Hancock, in
company with Lieutenants Armistead, Sedgwick,
Buckner, and Rosecrans—the last named having vol-
unteered for the occasion from the Fifth Infantry.

By order of General Worth, the battalion of the
Sixth Infantry, in command of Captain Hoffman,
formed in column and repeatedly charged the battery
of the enemy. Lieutenant Hancock was now under
fire for nearly the first time, like others of our officers
and men. The Second Artillery, under Captain
Brooks and Lieutenants Daniels and Sedgwick, aided
materially in our assault. The charge of our troops

6*   E

was continued until the enemy was driven from the field.

At three o'clock in the morning of the 8th of September, 1847, he moved with the troops on the assaulted batteries. The grey light of coming day had not yet tipped the heights around, when the two twenty-four-pounders placed in position opened on the solid stone walls of the enemy. No reply came; and it was at first supposed that the Mexicans had abandoned the post. It soon appeared, however, that they had only changed their place of defence, and were beginning, from a new and unexpected point, to pour grape and round shot on our advancing flanks. It is inferred, from some circumstances afterwards revealed, that the Mexican commander had been informed of the manner of our approach by foreign spies. The assault of the enemy was severe; cutting down our men in large numbers, killing and wounding eleven out of fourteen of our officers, and a like proportion in the ranks. On perceiving their temporary advantage, the Mexicans rushed on our lines with their usual savage ferocity, and murdered our wounded troops in cold blood.

Reinforcements were now thrown rapidly forward by General Worth, who resolutely attacked the Mexican flank. The Mexican General Leon, who headed a spirited sortie from the walls of Molino del Rey, was wounded, several officers of high rank were killed, and the enemy driven back. The access to the foe was sought in a variety of ways. The walls were scaled by our daring men, the top of the building reached by cutting holes in the solid stone, by means of their bayonets; the main gate was soon forced, and the troops rushed through with a shout that woke the echoes of the space beyond. A combat ensued, hand to hand. Door after door fell before the intrepid Americans; rank after rank of the Mexicans were swept before them; until a white flag of surrender appeared on the battered parapets.

It was a sanguinary battle — by many considered the most so of any during the Mexican war. The enemy had a very strong position, entrenched on a commanding hill, surrounded by massive stone walls, and outnumbered us three to one. But we carried the post against all these odds, capturing eight hundred prisoners, although at a fearful loss of life in our own ranks.

The next battle in which the young Lieutenant participated was that of the castle of Chapultepec. The edifice stands on a high, rocky promontory, nearly precipitous, and commands the entire country for miles around. The western slope is the only point where the approach is at all gradual, and this is covered by a dense chapparal and forest, where the ground is ragged with rocks.

On the 13th of September, of the same year, the battalion of the Sixth Infantry to which then Adjutant Hancock was attached, moved out from the conquered post of Molino del Rey toward Chapultepec. It was at the early dawn. The shadows hung deep from tree to tree, from rock to rock. A large force of Mexicans lay hidden in the darkness. Our men felt their way along, when, coming all at once into a comparatively open space, they found themselves confronted by the frowning battlements of the castle. The fight began instantly. An American color-bearer rushed forward to the ramparts, followed, with loud cheers, by a body of our men, who quickly placed ladders against the embattled walls, and began to scale them. Shout now followed shout as the soldiers sprang up the ladders and bounded over the wall, in the very face of the enemy. The Mexicans were taken completely by surprise. They stood a moment in suspense, astonished at the audacity of the Americans, and then dashed down, some of them headlong, over the precipitous rocks. Shot and shell poured in upon the works, like an iron torrent; and it was not long ere the strong castle was a mass

of ruins. A large number of prisoners surrendered
to our gallant troops — among them General Bravo,
and the surviving students of the Mexican National
Military School.

The part taken by the Sixth Infantry in this brilliant battle is worthy of special mention. It was all
the time actively engaged, including the command
of Lieutenant Hancock, moving out from Molino del
Rey by the left flank, and soon reaching the grove
at the base of Chapultepec. A portion dashed up
the hill in advance, of whom Hancock was one—the
remainder joining from the left base of the castle,
whither it had been detached to cut off the retreat
of the enemy — until the whole regiment, with a
grand huzza, swept into the thickest of the fight.
The colors of the command were advanced into the
enclosures of the castle, and the troops rallied gallantly around them. Entering the streets beyond,
they found themselves confronted by a breastwork
of masonry, and a large body of the enemy posted
behind it. From this barricade and the tower and
windows of the adjacent church, the street was
swept by the fire of artillery and infantry. But our
men moved steadily on. They passed to the rear,
flanking the Mexicans, and reaching a large building,
which they entered by force, and, commanding the

balconies poured their shot with telling effect on
the foe.   •

The Mexicans were forced back in disorder, aban-
doning every position they had held.   Our men now
seized new points, forcing their way with their bayonets and such missiles as could be used for the purpose, tearing holes in the houses with crowbars and
pickaxes, until they had formed a garrison around
them.   Every movement they made brought their
fire nearer the enemy.   The picked marksmen of the
Sixth, joined now by others of the Eighth, did terrible execution.   Officer after officer fell rapidly before
their deadly aim.   The two opposing forces at this
moment were not more than thirty yards apart from
each other.

Soon the disordered Mexicans began to waver;
then they broke and fled up the streets in dismay,
our men pursuing with all their speed.   It was literally a race for life.   The crashing of shells, the
tumbling of walls, the roar of cannon, the whistling
of bullets, the shouts of the advancing victors as
they rushed through the sulphurous clouds surrounding them, the flashes of their guns blazing like light-
ning from their serried ranks, gave the scene one of
the most thrilling aspects of the war.   The hard-

fought day was won; and the Sixth regiment rested, with their comrades, on their victorious arms.

Thus fell the castle, citadel, and town of Chapultepec. The Mexicans had barricaded their streets, intending to make secure use of the barricades and the adjacent houses to keep our men at bay. They supposed they would be able to destroy us all, by means of their protected fire. They had not calculated on our leaving these defences unattacked, thus preventing exposure in the open streets, and burrowing our way under cover, to their rear, through the dismantled walls of their own houses.

The enemy fought desperately during this terrible contest of four days. But it was all in vain. At the end of the fourth day the whole garrison was surrendered, the Mexicans, as some return for their acknowledged valor, being permitted to march out with the honors of war.

In the reports of the officers in command of the attacking force, the conduct of Lieutenant Hancock is repeatedly mentioned. In August, 1848, he was breveted first lieutenant for his gallant and meritorious bearing in these actions—his brevet dating from the 20th of August, 1847.

It was his privilege to be present when commissioners reached the American camp with proposals of peace. Terms of accommodation were proposed by them, but General Scott refused to listen to any but those of surrender. The morning following their arrival, on the 14th of September, 1847, the old hero, at the head of six thousand men, regulars and volunteers, marched into the conquered city, and the colors of the United States waved from the palace of the Montezumas. A treaty of peace was negotiated at Guadaloupe Hidalgo, on the 2d of February, 1848; and on its ratification at Washington, which occurred soon after, the Mexican war was brought to a close.

The part taken by Lieutenant Hancock in this war was further acknowledged in a series of resolutions adopted by the Legislature of his native State; in which his name, with those of other Pennsylvania soldiers, was mentioned with honor, and the document containing them placed in his hands.

He remained with the American army as it withdrew from Mexico, serving a portion of that time under Brigadier General Cadwalader, at Toluca. Before leaving, he was made Regimental Quartermaster of the Sixth regiment. He was among the last of our troops that left Mexico, and saw the Mexican flag take the place of ours, when the city was turned over to the Mexican government. He was next stationed on the Upper Mississippi, at Fort Craw ford, Prairie du Chien, Wisconsin, where he remained until the summer of 1849.

Fort Crawford is pleasantly situated on an elevated part of Prairie du Chien, on the site of the old French town of that name, overlooking the Mississippi river, flowing in front of it. The rapid settlement and extension of our Northwestern frontier having rendered this post of little value, in a military point of view, it was abandoned by the government of the United States, a few years after Lieutenant Hancock left it. The buildings still stand, all desolate and lonely, in view of the passer-by on the river. The silent spot is as quiet now as it was when the Indian first planted his foot on the shore, or his canoe had skimmed along the waters in front — an emblem, at once, of the advance of the power of civilization and the retreat of the wild savage before it. The descendants of the emigrants who first penetrated these once unbroken wilds will call to mind, as they look on the ruins of the old fort, the days when their ancestors roamed the forests beyond, or sped their way along the bosom of the Father of Waters. How changed the scene in the rapid march of years! The steamboat is on the river—the rail-car is on the land —but the Indian and the pioneer, where are they?

Prairie du Chien is a point of some importance in

7

the West. It has been for several years the western terminus of a railway, connecting the Mississippi with the East. It is now the starting point of another road, running still further West through the prairie land. The town is beautifully located, and the capital of Crawford county, Wisconsin. It is about one hundred miles west of Madison, the capital of that fine and growing State.

CHAPTER VIII.

DURING the year 1849 Lieutenant Hancock was promoted to the post of regimental Adjutant. This position he retained until the autumn of 1855, being stationed throughout the whole of that period, six years, at St. Louis and Jefferson Barracks, Missouri. The Barracks are on the Mississippi, about twelve miles below St. Louis. He was on the staff of Brigadier General N. S. CLARKE, an accomplished soldier and gentleman, then commanding the Sixth Infantry, and with whom he had served in Mexico.

On the 24th of January, 1850, he was married to Miss ALMIRA RUSSELL, daughter of Mr. SAMUEL RUSSELL, a much esteemed merchant of St. Louis. She is a lady of good sense and accomplishments, worthily filling the position she has been called to occupy.

(75)

Two children were the result of this marriage — a son named RUSSELL, after his grandfather, and a daughter, ADA ELIZABETH, who, to the deep grief of her parents, died on Governor's Island when just of an age to enter society. Her loving mother's heart is even yet in that grave, and many a silent tear will yet dim the lustre of her noble husband's advancement in life.

In the month of November, 1855, through the exertions of the Honorable JOHN CADWALADER, (then member of Congress for the district in which his birth-place is situated,) he was appointed an Assistant Quartermaster, with the rank of Captain.

In the summer of 1842, while yet a cadet, Winfield first returned home from West Point—a furlough of two months being allowed each cadet in the middle of the four years' term. It was pleasant to the young officer, now about eighteen years of age, to revive the scenes of his boyhood. He had not forgotten home. His father had accompanied him, two years before, as he entered the Academy, and he now greeted him, with the mother by his side, to the dear homestead of other days. Instructions and counsels were renewed. The worship at the family altar revived the sacred impressions of truth within his heart. Here, too, the proofs of his earlier devotion to science were reviewed; the specimens he **had** labelled were re-examined; the home-made galvanic apparatus he had helped to construct, and which had served to illustrate his private lectures before his classmates, and his more public performances in the old academy then on Airy street, was tenderly handled, and carefully readjusted, ere it was passed by in silence; and the whole paraphernalia of his incipient love of learning were more safely placed away in the recesses of the family mansion.

The large, two-storied brick building on Airy street, Norristown, will long be remembered as the spot where Winfield and his associates of early days went to school. It was situated at the end of DeKalb street, looking down the whole length to the bridge crossing the Schuylkill, half a mile in front. The site was commanding, and well adapted for such a purpose. The view on all sides was very fine. The town lay on the gentle slope beneath, with here and there a spire jutting up against the sky, in the foreground. At the sides and in the rear the cultivated fields and gardens spangled the landscape with grass and flowers, while overhanging trees skirted the edges with their variegated fringes of beauty. The lovely Schuylkill swept gently on in the distance, its surface dotted by an occasional boat, and its mirrored

7*

waters reflecting the multiplying and ever-changing pictures of earth and sky. The modest hills stood silent beyond, clad in their sweet robes of misty blue, as if reluctant to cast their shadows too long or too deeply on the quiet rural scene. Happy school-boy days! Who can forget them? Who would forget them, if he could?

The principal of the academy, in the period when Winfield was one of its scholars, was Mr. ELIPHALET ROBERTS—now living at 1516 Wellington St., Phila. His interest in his favorite, Winfield, was always strong and deep. We shall have occasion, in the course of these pages, to show with what propriety General HANCOCK recognized the teacher of his boyish years, when we come to speak of his public reception in that city, during his visit of the year 1863.

Mr. Roberts was succeeded in the academy and as a teacher to Winfield by Mr. WILLIAM HOUGH, who was himself deeply interested in scientific subjects, and who took peculiar pleasure in fostering Winfield's love of chemistry and electricity.

When the Norristown High School was established, under the superintendence of Mr. ASHBEL G. HARNED, Jr.—a gentleman who was very popular and successful as a teacher—Winfield was among his most favorite pupils. He remained at this school, making good progress in his studies, until just previous to his leaving home to become a cadet.

But with all these scholastic advantages, let it never be forgotten, especially by our young readers, that very much that Winfield was, and now is, he owes to the influence and instructions of home. Both his parents were deservedly much respected for their great moral and religious worth; for their useful and unselfish lives. Their part in life was an unselfish and an earnest one—whether for the benefit of their family or mankind at large. In the pursuit of business, in the performance of duties of every kind; superintending or teaching in the Sunday school, which was at the distance of a mile from their residence, across the river; attending to the intellectual wants, the spiritual aspirations of scores of these distant children, through the heat of summer and the cold of winter; visiting the sick, caring for the poor, relieving the oppressed; thus were the lives of the honored father and mother of Winfield ripening into the fruitage of holy deeds, and preparing for the awards of a glorious immortality. The chief characteristics of his father were energy, perseverance, caution, sound judgment, and good sense. His opinions have ever been highly valued by all who knew him. No man had been more frequently called to adjudicate

responsible cases, to allay exciting difficulties, to settle estates, or to manage the trust funds of the people.
The life of Benjamin Franklin Hancock is an honor
to his name.

Mrs. Hancock, the mother, possessed equally marked traits of character, of a different type. A kinder,
more benevolent, unselfish woman it would be extremely difficult to find. Her name was a sweet savor
of sincere Christian piety wherever she was known.

It is perfectly safe to say that many of the prominent traits in the distinguished character of General
Hancock may be directly traced to the moulding influence of his parents.

His military education and life, and the opportunity afforded by his influential part in the checking
of Southern secession, have developed in a remarkable degree the qualities that began to show themselves in his boyhood, and that were guided and fostered at home. His ability to command, his facility
in controlling great masses of armed men, his skill
in the use of means, his patient industry in overcom-
ing difficulties, his dashing energy to accomplish
great objects in the midst of danger, may all be
traced back, like living streams from the living fountain, to the hidden power of that one word—HOME.

The old two-storied school house near DeKalb street

has been swept away by the march of improvement. Not a vestige of it remains; and even its site is now hidden from view, being demanded by the extension of the street, for the purposes of travel. Here, where whole generations of children have studied and played together, where the hum of busy searchers after knowledge has sounded from the quiet walls, like the music of bees in and around the silent hive; where the gray-haired or more juvenile teachers have filled their tripod with alternate joys of victory and sorrows of defeat; where from this spot, once so sacred to learning in other days, have gone forth the boys who have filled their places in society, grown old as the teacher was, and passed, like him, away,—all now is given up to the rush of business, the passage of hurrying or tardy feet, the roll of wheels, and the tramp of horses. But, with all these and other changes, forever cherished shall be the memory of the old Airy street school-house in Norristown.

F

CHAPTER IX.

DURING the year 1856, when Winfield filled the post of Quartermaster, ranking as Captain, of the Sixth United States Infantry, he was stationed in Florida. A part of this time of service was spent near Saint Augustine. This is a commanding position, a city, port of entry, and capital of St. John's county. It is two hundred miles east of Tallahassee, and one hundred and sixty south of Savannah. It has the distinction of being the oldest town in the United States, having been settled by the Spaniards in 1565. Its location on the navigable waters of Matanzas Sound, only two miles from the Atlantic ocean, (from which it is separated by the island of Anastasia,) gives it a marked commercial and naval importance.

The city stands on a plain, only a few feet above the

level of the ocean. The streets are nearly all built
on the old Spanish pattern, being only from ten to.
eighteen feet wide. The houses and public buildings
are usually low, the former being not more than two
stories high, and all made of durable materials, the
stone or shell mixture of the sea shore. The upper
stories of the dwellings and stores project over the
streets, so that passengers crowd along the narrow
side-walks under the hanging verandas, while the
horses, mules, and cattle straggle and jostle their way
through the narrow avenues. Beside the county
buildings there are four churches, two newspapers,
and a United States land-office.

The harbor of Saint Augustine is safe and commodious, but the bar at the entrance prevents the
approach to the wharves of large ships, having
only nine or ten feet of water, at low tides. The
climate is mild and pleasant; the cool, refreshing
breezes from the contiguous sea rendering the spot a
favorite resort for invalids. Beautiful trees abound
—the olive, the palm, the orange, and the lemon.
The loveliest birds of the continent crowd the air,
while choice fish and game are in abundance. Navigation is carried on between St. Augustine and New
Orleans, Savannah, and other sea-ports, so that the
town has become one of the largest in Florida.

The location of Winfield was at Fort Meyers, in the vicinity of Saint Augustine, where he remained in active service until the year 1857.

It was at this place he occupied his talents as a delineator in making drawings of the ground-plans of the old Forts and adjacent surroundings — a work that proudly adorned the home of his parents — a worthy sign of his skill and industry as a draughtsman.

On the 7th of November, 1856, having been assigned to more active duties in the United States Quartermaster General's Department, for the Western District, he was ordered to the United States territory of Utah, on the slope of the Pacific ocean, and to accompany General Harney on his expedition to Kansas and the regions beyond.

Many persons, especially those abroad, who are aware of the existence of the crime of polygamy in Utah, are not conversant with the fact that it is several thousand miles distant from the national government, at Washington. Bad as the influence of that crime is on its immediate participants, and on the aboriginal tribes around, it should be remembered that those who practice it are mostly foreigners, and that the United States are no more responsible for it, in a governmental point of view, than is England for the superstitions of her colonies in India. There is a moral obligation resting on all Christian people to root out and scatter forever this disgraceful evil; but, so long as its upholders maintain an organization in unison with the national constitution, called a 'republican form of government,' they cannot be purged by force of arms. The time will surely come when this great violence to the civilization and Christianity of the nineteenth century will be removed.

From Utah Captain Hancock was transferred to California, and stationed at Benicia. He was for some time in the Quartermaster's Department there, in intimate association with that superior United States officer, General SILAS CASEY.

Benicia is located at an important point on the Pacific slope of the Union, and was at one time the capital of California. It stands on a commanding eminence, at the junction of the Strait of Karquenas with the Bays of San Pablo and Suisun. The waters of the vicinity are all navigable for quite large vessels, which extend their voyages up the river to Sacramento, the present State capital.

The appearance of the country around Benicia is remarkable. Not a tree or shrub is to be seen in all its borders. The high mountain called 'Monte Diablo,' or Devil's Mountain, presents one of the wildest

8

objects in the world. Its jagged sides, its black, **towering peaks**, its cavernous cliffs, where the spent vol-
canic action of bygone ages has left its deep lines
on the rifted chasms, where the thick clouds hang
their sulphurous vapors, where terrific thunders roll
and lurid lightnings flash, and where the upper winds
sweep with melancholy music the chords of the **lofty**
trees that crown the cold, barren summit, all **unite to**
render this mountain a prominent feature in the landscape to the traveller, as they have long caused it to
be a centre of superstitious reverence and dread to
the ignorant aborigines. On these awful and dreary
heights their wild imaginations have reared the
throne of the satanic presence, and surrounded it
with the spectral illusions of a spirit-land. The
voice of the raging winds on the towering peak is to
them the speaking of their infernal deity. The crashing thunder is the echo of his wrath, and the light-
ning's blaze is the glare of his kindled eye. For
ages past they have not dared to go up the sides of
their deified mountain beyond a certain point; and
here, like the children of Israel in the desert, around
the base of Mount Sinai, they have paused and stood
aghast with trembling awe. Even to this day, only
here and there a solitary pilgrim pierces through the
thick veil that hangs over these fearful heights; and,

casting aside the superstitions of the past, and gazing on the glorious picture of the handiwork of the true Deity that lives and glows on every hand beneath him, with Christian adoration

"Looks through nature up to nature's God."

To reach Benicia, Captain Hancock had crossed a large portion of our North American continent. He learned much of the country on the great plains, its people, its climate, its resources, its mineral treasures, its rivers and inland seas; until, leaving the almost extreme southern shore of our Atlantic possessions, he stood in sight of those on the almost northern verge of the Pacific.

From this post he was transferred to the old Spanish town of Los Angeles—or the town of the angels—located in the part of the West known as Lower California. Here he was stationed for two years, still occupying his responsible position in the Department of the Quartermaster General of the United States.

Los Angeles is located in one of the most beautiful regions in America. The coast ranges of mountains lift their breezy summits above its site, while teeming hillsides slope away toward the sea, and flowery valleys and fruitful plains skirt the scene beyond. The climate is one of the most delightful on the earth. The warm airs of the plains, cooled by those from the mountains as they meet and mingle together in friendly intercourse, produce an atmosphere which it is the perfection of refreshment to inhale. The soil around produces a variety of the most different seeds and fruits; potatoes and oranges, corn and figs, wheat and lemons, pears and pomegranates, melons and dates, wheat and rice, tobacco and grapes, cotton and buckwheat, sugar-cane and apples, grow and flourish side by side. The mountain breast of a bank may be painted white with dissolving snow, while the slope toward the valley is all variegated with the hues of flowers.

In this salubrious and genial clime Captain Hancock made his home for two years. The great mining interests of the rich region adjacent drew many American and other settlers around him, and his position required the exercise of much executive ability. His influence was sensibly felt, and became quite extensive through all that part of Lower California.

When the secession of 1861 took place in the United States, his voice and example were potential in arousing and extending the spirit of patriotism among the people. The peculiar character of a large portion of the immigrants to that section, especially those from the seceded and disaffected States of the Union, rendered them uneasy in the crisis that had so unexpectedly broken on the nation. Many of this class were Southerners by birth and education. Their kindred and their property left behind were in the South. They sympathized with secession; their hearts were with the Southron, and they longed for opportunities to take up arms in their cause. Popular outbreaks of the most violent nature were constantly threatened on every hand. There was the most imminent danger that the whole of that large and rich region of country would be swept away from its moorings to the Union, and borne down by mob violence into the vortex of violence to the old flag.

At this critical moment it demanded all the coolness, calmness, and courage of Captain Hancock to do his part in quelling the rising storm. Should it prevail to any extent, his own department would be the first to feel and suffer from its fury. The supplies and munitions of war his command was enabled to furnish, were tempting prizes to the ambitious bands that were forming and holding their gatherings all around him. Some went so far as to boast of what they would do in possessing themselves of the United States commissary articles and means of

8*

defence committed to his charge; while others, **more** openly rampant, threatened to **tear** down the national colors.

In the midst of all this tempest of passion and fanaticism, Hancock stood firm. His personal influence, as we have said, was great, and he exerted it now to the utmost. He rose to the emergencies of the occasion, and appealed directly to the patriotism of his countrymen. With the seditious aliens who were active in fomenting disturbances, who had nothing in common with the citizens who controlled the government by their votes, he was bold, strong, firm; yielding not an inch to their insolent demands, and presenting the courage of a patriot heart and the force of a gallant arm to their treasonable threats.

Thus Hancock met these distant and isolated seceders in one of their own strongholds. Thus he upheld, on that far-off Pacific slope, the flag of his country, the integrity of the Union, and the rights of man. His course in Lower California met the approval of the government and of all our countrymen who are conversant with its high merits. His name will ever be honored on account of it, not only on the shores of the Pacific, but those of the Atlantic, all through the United States. He had the happiness to witness the subsidence of this incipient rebellion, and to hear the cry awake and continue **to** resound on every hand:

> " Forever float that standard sheet!
>   Where breathes the foe but falls before us?
> With freedom's soil beneath our feet,
>   **And** freedom's banner waving o er us!"

CHAPTER X.

The Stars and Bars vs. the Stars and Stripes — Winfield Scott Hancock Rises to the Occasion — The Soldier-Statesman who Knew no Politics but the Policy of the Union, Earning the Right to become the First of American Citizens.

AT his own earnest request, Quartermaster HAN-COCK was transferred from his responsible but comparatively quiet post on the Pacific, to the more active scenes that stirred the pulses of the Atlantic coast, at the middle of the year 1861. His position in California was one of great relative importance, but the routine duties of a Quartermaster had never been suited to the energetic and courageous character of such a man as he has proved himself to be. As soon, therefore, as the necessary official preliminaries could be effected, he was on his way to the field of battle.

In the month of September, 1861, he landed in New York. Without stopping even a moment to visit his parents, at Norristown, although he had now

(92)

been absent from them over two years, in a distant part of the country, he pushed on, within a few hours of his arrival, to Washington, and immediately reported himself to the War Department, ready for active service. His mind was deliberately made up to the great issue. His life was again in his hand for his beloved country. His valuable services were at once accepted, and he placed in the front of the fight.

Here let us pause a moment, and take a survey of the field.

When, in the month of November, 1860, a large majority of the voters of America had declared the then incumbent was constitutionally elected President of the United States, it was clearly the duty of the minority to abide by the law, and yield obedience to the verdict. If they had been fairly outvoted at this election — and it is not pretended by any one but they were — the fundamental oaths, the democratic canons of the country, affirmed that the government should still be maintained, the laws administered, the powers and emoluments of office transmitted, until a new trial should confirm or reverse the result. The same sacred right of suffrage had been enjoyed by all the electors of the nation. Three parties, with distinct national issues, were in the arena; but all three openly swore allegiance to the same national standard, and vowed devotion to the same national Union. Secession, Disunion, Rebellion, were not in that presidential canvass. The election, with its greatly increased vote, with all the momentous and exciting issues at stake, was one of the most quiet ever held in the country. No one was molested in public or private discussions of the vast questions involved in the contest. There was not a life lost at the polls, where millions of men, each one as free and as good as another in the eye of the law, marched to the ballot-boxes of their voting precincts, and cast their votes for the candidates of their choice. No one, in all that vast host of qualified suffragants, of equal peers, yea, of reigning sovereigns, could with propriety rudely ask or threaten his fellow at the polls:

> "Under which king, Bezonian?
> Speak, or die!"

Every intelligent elector was his own king. Every responsible vote he cast was his own royal edict.

We have said the questions of Secession, Disunion and Rebellion were not in this great constitutional contest of voters. It is not to be understood by this historical statement, however, that the relative value of, and purpose to continue, the Union, were not passed upon by the people in that election On the contrary, they were so passed upon, and that, too, in the most decided, unequivocal manner. That vote of that large majority of the American people was, in fact, a strong, clear, emphatic constitutional endorsement of the Union of the States by the highest power in the land known to the laws. It was the sovereign verdict of the United States that the United States should continue. It was the constitution re-indorsing the constitution. It was the Union again pouring its own life blood through the living cycle of the Union. It was a national salute to the national flag, wherever it floated, around the world. Could anything of the kind be more nationally significant? Could anything be more nationally potential?

Thus stood the case when the final announcement of the decision was flashed along the electric wire, from the Atlantic, on the East, to the Pacific, on the West; from the inland seas, on the North, to the Gulf of Mexico, on the South.

What then? What became the duty of the majority? What became, also, the duty of the minority? It was the duty of the one to assume the reins of government, and conduct the public affairs of the country in the spirit and precepts of its founders; with becoming gravity to count and publish the votes of the different electoral colleges, in the consecrated halls of the several legislatures; to sign, seal, certify and forward the official ballot to the national archives, in the national capital, and make proclamation of the nation's choice; to inaugurate the man of that choice with all the solemn forms and rituals of law known to the constitution and established by the precedents of the fathers; to require that chosen man, and his associates in the offices in which, as the vicegerents of the people, the people had just placed them, to take upon their souls, in the presence of ALMIGHTY GOD and of all witnesses, the most sacred oaths ever administered from man to man, the record of which is to be forever on high.

Thus elected, thus inaugurated, by the virtue of the power they derived from their constituents, the people of America, what could any of these men do but obey their commands? Had a majority of this people declared by their votes that they held their Union to be a mere confederation of States? No. Had they admitted, for a moment, since they became a distinct nation, that they held their constitution to be a mere treaty between independent sovereignties? No. Had they delegated the powers invested by them in a consolidated nation, to be divided up between thirty-six or more distinct nationalities? No. Had they, at any time, given up their right, entrusted to their national rulers, to declare war and make peace, to negotiate treaties, to establish a currency, to regulate commerce between the separate States, or to punish treason, as a nation? No.

What then? The United States was a nation — a nation intact, sovereign, independent; composed of States that are separate as to their State rights, yet as to the Union in a nation,

" Distinct, as the billows, yet one, as the sea."

This was the view, and the only view, taken of our national existence by the great Father of our Country, and by all the patriots and statesmen who founded the Republic. To put in practice as a nation any other doctrine than this, is deliberately to commit national suicide, and lay the last hope of liberty and constitutional government on the American continent in the darkness and silence of the grave.

The election of a constitutional President of the United States having, then, been constitutionally declared, with all the solemnities of national law, what moral insanity, what political frenzy, what intellectual madness must have possessed those leading men of the Southern part of our Union, who, because they were actually defeated in a fair election, without waiting for the action of the government their fellow-

9   G

citizens of the Republic had thus chosen, lifted the dread standard of secession against the nation of their fathers and ours, and plunged the whole land, including millions of helpless women and little children, in all the horrors of a fratricidal war!

> "Patriot and faction,
> Like oil and water mix, when strongly shaken;
> But never can unite — disjoined by nature."

It was in this spirit that Captain HANCOCK enlisted in the war for the Union. He had seen in California, and in other parts of the country, the malign influences that began the war on the part of Disunion. He saw now that one or the other must perish. To refuse to fight under the flag that had made him all that he was as a military man, and that was sacred to him and all other patriots by all its glorious antecedents, was not only to prove himself the vilest of ingrates, but it was to participate in the follies of those misled men who, having failed in their attempts to continue to rule the country, were now madly bent on its ruin. As a patriot, bearing the honored names of a patriot soldier and statesman, his course was plain. He heard the trumpet call of duty, and hasted to obey the summons. His cadet vows were yet upon him, and gratefully and proudly he renewed them at the altar of the Union. He at once accepted the post assigned him, and entered with noble ardor on that career for the complete suppression of the rebellion, which we shall continue further to depict.

With all his brilliancy and dash as a soldier, HAN-COCK did not participate in the scenes of war we are describing, from a mere love of fighting. He chose the profession of arms in his youth from a conviction of duty. He now continued in it, in his manhood, actuated by the patriotic belief that 'resistance to tyrants is obedience to God.'

We put on record here his avowal of the princi-ples that guide him in all contests for our country. They are contained in a private letter of his to a friend, to whom we and our readers are deeply indebted for many of the important facts embodied in this volume.

These are his own words:

"MY POLITICS ARE OF A PRACTICAL KIND. THE INTEGRITY OF THE COUNTRY. THE SUPREMACY OF THE FEDERAL GOVERNMENT. AN HONORABLE PEACE, OR NONE AT ALL."

> "Far dearer the grave, or the prison,
>   Illumed by one patriot name,
> Than the trophies of those who have risen
>   On liberty's ruin to fame."

CHAPTER XI.

AT the time of his reporting for duty in Washington, in the month of September, 1861, Captain HANCOCK was thirty-eight years of age. He had served his country in the various positions assigned him in the army during a period of seventeen years. The most of this service had been rendered in Mexico, or west of the Mississippi river, and in the everglades of Florida.

In all the ranks of the army, among officers and men, he stood deservedly high. By his strict devotion to duty, his invariable courage, energy and patriotic enthusiasm, he had secured the confidence and attachment of all who knew him. Correct in his personal habits, polite, affable, friendly with all, unselfish and hospitable, he was a favorite wherever he went

He had his own opinions on all national questions, and was prepared to express and defend them. Although never a politician, and never having voted, his sympathies and convictions had always been with the Democratic party. But, like a true patriot, he never gave up to party what was due to mankind. He was firm and conscientious in the belief that Secession was Disunion; that Disunion was civil war—a crime against the honor, welfare and happiness of the American people. He had proved his stand on this issue by his patriotic course against the first dawnings of every attempt at Disunion, in California. By his personal presence and voice on that occasion, he had not only stemmed the incipient risings of the deep discontent, but he had rendered signal service to the Union by addressing the inhabitants in public on several occasions, and organizing and directing that public sentiment which exerted so potential an influence in maintaining the loyalty of that part of the Golden State in which he resided.

He proclaimed everywhere, and was always ready to maintain the opinion—if need be, with his trusty · sword—that no grievances of which the citizens of the Southern States might justly complain, could warrant or empower them to revolt against the constitutional government of the nation. His great-

9*

grandfather and grandfather had both fought in the war of the Revolution and in that of 1812, with Great Britain, to establish and perpetuate the Union of the States. It was not for him, who had sprung from such an ancestry, who had received such patriotic lessons in his boyhood, who had taken such obligations and acquired such a national education in the Military Academy belonging to all the Union, and who had already done valiant service under the time-honored flag of his country, basely now to prove recreant to all these inspirations of duty, with ignominious cowardice to sheathe his sword in ignoble ease, or with infamous treachery to wield it against the dear-bought liberties of his native land.

Acting on these high-toned convictions as an American patriot, he had offered his services, at the moment of the first avowal of a secession, to the Governor of Pennsylvania. As a native of the State, as a thoroughly-educated soldier of the regular Army, as an officer of established bravery and popularity with his troops, his valuable services would have been gladly accepted in such a command. But before the arrangement could be consummated he was on duty at Washington, in the service of the United States. Here he was immediately assigned to the post of Chief Quartermaster, on the staff of General

ROBERT ANDERSON, the hero of Fort Sumter, who had been placed in command of the Union forces in his native State of Kentucky.

While preparing to comply with this order of the War Department, only a very few days after his return from his post in California, he was proposed to the government by General McCLELLAN, then General-in-Chief of the army, for a commission as Brigadier General. This proposal was made unexpectedly to Captain HANCOCK, and without any solicitation on the part of his friends. The appointment was decided on his merits alone, and as such made by President LINCOLN, on the 23d of September, 1861. It was at once accepted, and the new Brigadier prepared himself for active service.

His experience in the cause of his country had already been varied and extensive. In Mexico, on the frontiers, among hostile Indians, in Florida, fighting the brave and wily Seminoles, associated with such commanders as Generals WORTH, HARNEY, Colonels CLARKE, BROWN, JAMES MONROE, and others, he had acquired a knowledge of military affairs, of strategy, and the best methods of commanding men that he was now enabled to turn to good account for his country. His campaign to Fort Leavenworth, in 1856–7, had been productive of peculiarly important results. From Florida to Kansas, and while remaining in the latter State, until the spring of 1858, he had signalized his skill and devotion as a soldier.

The expedition of General Harney to Utah having been abandoned by the government, Captain Hancock had been ordered to proceed, as Chief Quartermaster, to the occupation of Fort Bridger, one of the outposts of our Western frontier. From this point he accompanied his old regiment, the efficient and popular Sixth Infantry, through their long march across the continent to Benicia, California. This march was probably the longest continuous one ever taken by any body of infantry troops. It carried them through an immense tract of wild, savage country, where inimical Indians swarmed, at times, on every hand. The deep snows of the Sierra Nevada range of mountains—the highest summits of which have an elevation of sixteen thousand feet, and whose line extends all through the State of California, from the town of Los Angeles to the Cascades of Oregon—had to be encountered and overcome, the troops and horses supplied with rations, and the peculiar surprises and sudden dangers of that weary route of thousands of miles, constantly guarded against.

For the skillful management of the onerous duties of his department, all through this difficult march,

Captain Hancock received and justly deserved **great** credit.

It was now toward the close of the month of September, 1861. The army of the United States was not then fully organized. There was much inexperience and occasional demoralization among our raw troops. With all their patriotism and general intelligence, as citizen soldiers, they could not always be depended on in sudden emergencies and moments of critical danger. In the responsible work of their organization, drill, discipline, and setting in the field of action, General Hancock was called to take a prominent part. His remarkable traits of character, now ripened into full manhood, here displayed their worth in the service to the greatest advantage. He was at home, in his own chosen field. We shall see, as we progress, how worthily he continued to fill **his** role.

CHAPTER XII.

THE beautiful fall of September, 1861, dawned on the country. The national forces were now nearly organized. Troops were arriving at the front from all the free States, and gradually taking part in the conflict. The most busy fields of action at that time were in Missouri and Western Virginia. In the last-named region, especially, the confederated men were very belligerent, being constantly stimulated by their allies in civil life all around them. It was soon perceived that the contest for the supremacy of the Union in that section would be prolonged and severe.

Fighting had taken place early in this month at

several points along the Western Virginia lines. At
Boone Court House, Boone county—named in honor
of the old pioneer, Daniel Boone, of Kentucky—the
Union troops had encountered a body of armed "Secesh" and signally defeated them. This point is only
about two hundred miles, in a direct line, west from
Richmond. But the contest there speedily convinced
the Southrons the Union would not consent to allow
any part of the Old Dominion it could control to
pass, without a struggle, under the new flag Stars and
Bars. Our troops, fresh and comparatively undisciplined as they were, fought well on this occasion.
We drove the enemy at all points, routing them to-
tally, killing thirty, wounding a large number, and
taking over forty prisoners. None were killed on
the National side, and but six were wounded. The
town was burned during the engagement.

A picked body of the Charleston, South Carolina,
Home Guards, who had penetrated through the Shenandoah country to within a short distance of Harper's Ferry, Virginia, were attacked by the Thirteenth
regiment of Massachusetts Volunteers. The so-called
'Yankees' performed their parts so well on the 'chivalry' that they soon drove them, pell-mell, killing
three, wounding five, and capturing twenty prisoners.
These, with the wounded, were brought into camp by

the Massachusetts boys, who greeted them blandly
with the song 'Gay and Happy.'

Victories were being won by the Union arms in
different parts of the country. We had captured
Forts Hatteras and Clark, on the coast of North Carolina, possessed several important points on the Western waters, and done the enemy considerable damage
in Missouri, while he was pursuing the Fabian policy
of masterly inactivity by remaining in his trenches
in Virginia.

The patriotic feeling of the country was steadily
rising. Large popular meetings were held, presided
over by the civil authorities, and addressed in earnest
and courageous strains of patriotism by eminent men
of all parties. General Rosecrans—formerly, it will
be remembered, a fellow Lieutenant with General
Hancock, in Mexico—had won a decided victory near
Summersville, Virginia. The effect of this victory
was marked, through all that region to which Hancock was at that time assigned. The bold General
Floyd—notorious as the prominent secessionist who,
when the nominal Union Secretary of War, at Wash
ington, had very artfully sequestrated all the govern
ment arms and munitions of war under his control
to the special purposes of the South — was then in
position near the summit of Carnifax mountain, with

five thousand Secesh troops and sixteen pieces of artillery. The rear and extreme of both flanks of the enemy were inaccessible. The front was masked with heavy forests and a dense jungle. The brigade commanded by General BENHAM — one of the most accomplished and energetic of all our soldiers — was in the advance, and assailed the enemy with such skill and force that they were driven, on a number of occasions, from their guns. Several companies of picked Irish troops, led by Colonel Lytle, of the Tenth Ohio, charged the battery, in the face of the hottest fire that the enemy could pour from the heights. A German brigade, under Colonel McCook—son of the old patriot Judge DANIEL McCOOK, of Kentucky, who has given himself and four sons to the war for his country—followed in the assault with great bravery, and, for a time, silenced the battery.

Floyd, as usual with his consummate artifice, fled during the night; but the depth of the adjacent river over which he passed in his flight, and the obstructions thrown by him in his way, prevented a successful pursuit. He left his camp, however, as a trophy to the Union, including his own equipage, together with wagons, horses, large quantities of ammunition and fifty head of cattle.

In Hardy Co., Virginia, the gray coats had been
10

seriously worsted in several hard-fought engagements. A number of camps were captured from
them, containing large supplies of guns, uniforms,
ammunition, horses, teams, and grain.

On the 13th of September, of this year, the battle
of Cheat Mountain had been fought and won by the
Union forces. The Secesh had erected a strong fort
on the summit. This our troops succeeded in surrounding, where they cut the telegraph wire to prevent its being used by the enemy. This position
was deemed by the grays one of the most commanding in Western Virginia. But they could not stand
against the shells of the Union batteries; they precipi-
tately fled before our artillerists, leaving their dead
and wounded behind them.

The introduction of General Hancock to his new
field was the signal for continued activity. His best
energies were all taxed to prepare his command for
constant duty.

The army was now rapidly reaching its appropriate
proportions. The command of Hancock was consequently assuming a relative importance. His Brigade consisted of the Forty-ninth Pennsylvania, Forty-
third New York, Fifth Wisconsin, and Ninth Maine,
in the Division of General W. F. SMITH. On the

9th of October, 1861, his Brigade held the advance position on the Potomac, occupying Lewinsville.

The first battle at this point had taken place on the 11th of the preceding September. On the morning of that day a party consisting of several detached companies of infantry, a company of cavalry, and Captain Griffin's battery of light artillery, the whole in command of Colonel Stevens of the New York Highlanders, broke camp, and started for the enemy. The adverse pickets retired beyond Lewinsville as our troops advanced. Having accomplished the object of their reconnoissance, our men were about to return, when a large force of the enemy, consisting of two regiments of infantry and Colonel Stuart's regiment of Virginia cavalry, with a battery of four pieces, were seen approaching. The line of battle was immediately formed. The enemy commenced shelling in front, and were promptly replied to by Griffin. Every opportunity was now given the enemy to meet us in the open field; but they very prudently kept under the coverts of the woods, doing what execution they could at a respectful distance.

The national forces now brought into action a thirty-two-pound gun, which speedily and effectually silenced the batteries of the enemy. He was evidently glad to show signs of retiring. At this moment the gun was brought to bear on their cavalry, who now appeared in the open road, which sent them flying and reeling from their saddles in all directions.

The movement was a success, and the troops engaged returned to camp in good order, where they received the congratulations of the General in command.

These preliminary engagements with the enemy showed their near approach and constant activity. They were out in every direction, scouring the country for conscripts and supplies. Even at that early period of the war, Disunion began to feel its growing necessities for men, provisions, and munitions. Their forays became more and more frequent, as their wants steadily increased. At the commencement of the rebellion they had plunged into war with reckless ferocity, and their troops had all the advantage over ours of much greater experience, drill, and discipline. The whole Southern country had been transformed into one great camp. Every arms-bearing citizen was held to be a soldier; every crop was regarded as pledged to the warlike purposes of the time. In the cities of the South, especially, the dangerous character of the institution of slavery, where large masses of slaves were liable to assemble together under the influence of those of their class who had by any means obtained the boon of freedom, it had been the custom for years to maintain regular bodies of troops, many of whom were well-mounted cavalry, ready to be called out, at the tap of the drum, to put down a servile insurrection. The commanders of these drilled bands of men were the leaders, to a great extent, of the secession. Their seat of war had been transferred from their slave marts and plantations to the lines confronting the Union colors. They not only fought desperately, but they fought methodically. Their best men were soldiers by birth, by profession, and practice.

Against these chosen myrmidons of the slave power the nation had hurriedly assembled, at the call of duty, such regular troops as could be spared from important frontier and central posts, and the hardy volunteers who had rushed from their homesteads and farms, their shops and ships, from road-side and sea-side, to defend the national honor and preserve the national life. Is it any wonder that, at the first onset, our undisciplined ranks, fight as portions of them might, would show signs of precipitancy, and inexperience? Nay, is it not a wonder that at the commencement of this war, like our fathers beating back with their untried columns the serried veterans of England, we should have fought as well as we did?

At the time General Hancock engaged in his first fight on the lines of the Potomac, and in other parts of Virginia, spies and artful emissaries swarmed all around him. He was constantly on the alert for these decoys of the enemy.

A few weeks after he had gone to the front, three companies of the Cameron Dragoons, under Major S. E. Smith, commanded respectively by Captain Wilson, Company F, Lieutenant Stetson, Company H, and Lieutenant Hess, Company C, were sent out on a scout along the roads leading to Fairfax Court House and Hunter's Mills, Virginia. Arriving at a point about a mile distant from Fairfax Court House, these three officers, with eight privates, encountered an equal number of the adverse cavalry. They immediately attacked the enemy, but they fled in haste to a contiguous cover of woods. In the hurry of the chase they passed through a fruit orchard, when one of the pursued dismounted, and resting his five-shooter against a tree, fired three shots at Major Smith. All of them passed him.

The party now attempted to draw the enemy from their woody cover, but in vain. Soon after they joined their companions of the main body, and rode on to Hunter's Mills. When near the latter place, Captain Wilson and Lieutenant Stetson discovered a soldier — the same who had been trying to kill the Major with his carbine from behind the shelter of a tree—now endeavoring to escape. They dashed after the man, and soon returned with him as a prisoner to camp. He was immediately brought to the presence of General Hancock, who recognized him, by his appearance, to be a dangerous spy.

"Your name is Vollin, I believe?" said the General.

"Yes, sir," replied the captive, for a moment thrown off his guard.

"Ah! Vollin — or Villain — I am glad to see you. We have been looking for you for some time past."

Mr. Vollin, or Villain, was appropriately cared for. The General had dealt with spies before.

"You are aware of the fate usually awarded to spies, Mr. Vollin?" continued Hancock.

"I — sup — pose — I — am," stammered the guilty wretch.

"Then you will please prepare for it at your earliest convenience, Mr. Vollin! Good morning, sir."

The brigade of General Hancock was specially serviceable in the work of procuring supplies. On different occasions hay, corn, sheep, and beef cattle were brought in by his men, to the evident disgust of the losers and to the satisfaction of all who had the right to share in the spoils of war. The enemy soon found that their foraging parties were not the only ones in the field.

On the 21st of October he accompanied and took part in the reconnoissance made by the heavy detachment sent out from his camp to Flint Hill, Virginia. The party consisted of portions of Mott's and Ayres's batteries, and companies of the Fifth Regulars, and from Colonel Freeman's regiment of artillery attached to the Division of General W. F. SMITH. This timely movement resulted in discovering the position of the enemy, and the apparent number of his forces in the vicinity. It was one of the first reconnoitring parties in which Hancock participated in his new position of Brigadier General.

The spirit that animated the Union troops under Hancock, at the time of which we are now writing, is well illustrated by an incident. It is one of many of a similar character then taking place.

After the battle of Ball's Bluff, of the 21st of October, in which the gifted and gallant Senator EDWARD D. BAKER so nobly fell for his country and liberty, the brave soldiers who had borne themselves so steadily in that fight were publicly addressed:

"Soldiers!" said the speaker, "these are terrible gaps that I see before me in your ranks. They remind me, and you all, of our dead on the field of battle;

of our wounded comrades in the hospitals; of kindred and friends weeping at home for those who
filled the vacant places that once knew them, but
that shall now know them no more forever.

Soldiers! I ask you now and here, in full view of
all this, are you ready again to meet the rebellious
foe? Are you willing again to peril your lives for
the liberties of your country? Would you go with
me to the field to-morrow? Would you go to-day?
Would you go this moment?"

There was but the pause of an instant, when the
reply, "Yes!" "Yes!" "Yes!" came with a shout
from the thousands of the line.

The commander was answered.

CHAPTER XIII.

*The Campaign of 1862.— The Valley of the Shenandoah — Burnside at Roanoke Island — **Big Bethel** — A "Sick Man" inconveniently Captured — "My Husband's Aunt Betty."*

THE campaign of the Union forces in Virginia during the winter of 1862, with all its quiet, possessed a great relative importance. The public sentiment of the country, which had been almost wildly enthusiastic at the first outbreak of the civil war, was now beginning to settle down on a calmer basis. There was as much real patriotism in the land, but it was not so demonstrative as it had been.

Our contest was beginning to assume an overshadowing importance in the eyes of the European nations. The leaders of opinion there were evidently much surprised at the extent of the preparations so readily and continuously made by the United States. Our successes, notwithstanding the manifest disadvantages under which we fought, had more than

(118)

equalled our own expectations. The sentiments of the masses of the most intelligent people of Europe were turning strongly in our favor, although the aristocracy and their allies endeavored, by the most infamous falsehoods, to mislead and silence it. The wicked hope was indulged by the enemy at home and their sympathizers here and abroad, that the vast multitude of the laboring classes, who were suffering so bitterly for want of work in consequence of the famine of American cotton, would rise in revolt against their own rulers, and thus, on the plea of domestic revolution and anarchy, compel foreign governments to intervene in American affairs. This would have exactly suited the South. It was their constant inspiration, their unfailing aspiration, by day and by night. Such an intervention as they thus hoped, prayed and plotted for, would have brought us into war with England and France, compelled the opening of our blockaded ports, supplied the South with money and munitions of war, divided the North, and secured an ignoble peace in the certain destruction of the Union.

But the operations of this gigantic and nefarious plot were no sooner commenced than they were discovered and thwarted. By the special favor of that Divine Providence which, in the language of JEFFERson, 'ever manifests its interest in the affairs of nations,' our crops had been more abundant that year than ever before. We had enough not only to supply the wants of the people at home, to furnish the vast rations required for our immense army and navy, but we were able to begin to send those cargoes of food to the starving operatives abroad, the reception of which during that year, and the early part of the year following, by these victims of the foolish secession in America, at once opened their eyes to the true nature of our great struggle, and made the vast majority of them, as they are at this day, our firm and devoted friends. The threatened foreign revolt in favor of the aristocratic and slavocratic treason of America was thus nipped in the bud. It was literally choked in its very birth with the fulness of bread sent to its needy cradle by the American Union. The occupation of the alien and native plotters for the overthrow of our Republic like that of Othello, was all gone.

> "The cloud-capped towers, the gorgeous palaces,
> The solemn temples,"

which the charlatan oligarchs, the sham aristocrats and lying priests of American slavery had thus madly endeavored to rear on the ruins of the United States, were speedily dissolved;

"And, like an unsubstantial pageant faded,
    Left not a wreck behind."

This mistaken spirit of sympathy with the most serious secession the world ever saw, has since shown itself, and will probably continue to show itself, in various ways, at different times and places; but, like a serpent with its head crushed to the earth, while it may endeavor to 'drag its slow length along,' it must sooner or later die the accursed death it so richly deserves. Liberty must finally triumph. Man, everywhere. must yet be free.

The encampment of the great body of the Union force immediately in front of Washington, had the effect not only to afford complete protection to the national capital and to secure the mobilization, the drill, and discipline of large masses of raw troops, but it drove the enemy into positions they were poorly prepared to occupy. It was stated, on Southern authority, that some portions of the army under their General Lee, were reduced to the last extremities. On one occasion he was entirely out of provisions, not having the means to cook the next meal for himself, or to serve the next ration to his soldiers. His outposts were abandoned, one after another, and he made the best of his way to his winter quarters. In this expedient he was compelled to take the only

11

position he could maintain in all that part of **Virginia** he endeavored to occupy. This was the first lesson of the kind taught the haughty leaders of the rebellion; and it is evident that its effect was not lost upon them, nor on those they so madly led into danger in so bad a cause.

Several important skirmishes occurred during this winter. The South's foraging parties were frequently met by those of the Union, affording fresh opportunities to prove the mettle of our men. On one occasion, the active General Stuart, on whose dauntless prowess much dependence was placed by his associates and followers in the South, was met by the Union General Ord, and severely worsted. Stuart had with him in his foray four regiments of infantry and a six-gun battery; but he was completely routed, losing many in killed and prisoners.

The spring of 1862 opened on the country **under a** steady advance of the Union cause. Our limits confine us more particularly to those events in which General Hancock took an immediate part. The very important Confederate position at Port Royal, South Carolina, had been captured late the preceding fall. Several battles had been won in Missouri, Kentucky, at Fort Pulaski, Georgia, and on the Western waters, **and** a new impulse given to the navy by **the launching** of several of the new iron Monitors. The pulse of the people beat stronger than ever for the Union.

The Union forces under General BANKS were advancing through the Valley of the Shenandoah, and the general aspects of the campaign were favorable; but the first great movement of the spring of '62 was that made on the Virginia Peninsula, in the direction of Richmond.

The period of muster and drill in encampment had passed. The commanding General of that portion of the national forces known as the army of the Potomac, addressed his troops with the assurance that he considered them 'magnificent in material, admirable in discipline and instruction, excellently equipped and armed,' and led by commanders who were all that could be desired. Heroic exertions, rapid and long marches, desperate conflicts and severe privations were announced as before them.

It was now the middle of March, and the glorious news had come of the victory of BURNSIDE over the South at Roanoke Island and Newbern, North Carolina. By this victory we had captured three light batteries of field artillery, forty-six heavy siege guns, large stores of fixed ammunition, three thousand stands of small arms, and several thousand prisoners.

The important preparations for the contemplated

onward movement were completed in March, and near the close of that month the army was transferred from its camp, fronting Washington, to the Peninsular region extending from Fortress Monroe, in Virginia, up the waters of the James and York rivers.

Our first reconnoissance in that direction resulted in our occupying the commanding and somewhat celebrated position of Big Bethel. It was at this point, about a year before, that one of our first battles occurred with the enemy — resulting, in consequence of false information given by scouts, in the death of Major THEODORE WINTHROP and Lieutenant JOHN T. GREBLE — two of the most accomplished and gallant soldiers in the United States army.

The occupation of this post by our troops was a surprise as well as a disadvantage to the enemy. A strong detachment of infantry, cavalry and artillery was detailed for the purpose, accompanied by two companies of Berdan's Sharp-shooters, in the advance. Gray coats, as usual, were met at various points of the route. Every bush, and house, and fence was carefully watched for the peering eye or rifle of some hidden enemy. But only women and children were to be seen. If there were any secession belligerents about, they were too closely hid to be seen by our advance. Some of the Union yeomanry looked good-naturedly at us from their fields, door-yards and piazzas, as we passed silently on.

There are numerous comfortable and handsome mansions in this vicinity. The soil and climate are highly favorable to agriculture, and the associations of the route gave a peculiar interest to the march. But the most of the mansions and plantations were deserted, their late occupants having taken service in the opposing army.

As our troops passed from the open country into the woody interval occupied by the works of Big Bethel, they found that the enemy had deserted them. This was rather a surprise to us; for, after the boasting we had heard that the chivalry never would run, whatever might be the odds against them, we expected, of course, they would make a stand here — especially as their works were strong and well surrounded for defence.

There were five breastworks in the fortification, each a few rods in length. Three of them mounted one gun. The other two were of greater dimensions, mounting six guns each. On the right flank was a dense grove, which afforded material protection. The broad space in front, a part of which was marshy and miry, sloped toward the York river, and was fully commanded by the guns.

11*

It was soon perceived that there were gray soldiers on the opposite shore of the stream. A few shots sent among them by our sharp-shooters caused a speedy stampede. In their flight they attempted to tear up the planks of the intervening bridge; but a few more shots taught them to be more accommodating to travellers. The planks partially removed were soon replaced; but the enemy had gained so much the start, and ran so fast, our men could not catch them.

In one of the contiguous houses a trick was discovered, which, considering it was done by a chivalrous Virginian, is almost equal to anything of the kind achieved by a despised 'Yankee.' As our troops entered they were accosted by the lady occupant:

"What do yer want here?"

"We are looking for Secesh, madam."

"Well! there ain't none in this house! An' you'n better clear out, mighty quick!"

"It is our orders to search every house, madam; and we cannot leave until we have searched yours."

"Sarch *my* house, yer mean Yankees! I should like to see yer do it!"

"You will have that pleasure, then, madam; for we shall certainly look through your premises, from garret to cellar."

" Yer will? Well, if yer will, yer must. But'n yer won't find nobody 'yere but a pewer old sick un."

" Is it a sick man, madam ?"

" No ! yer 'quisitive critters ! It's my husband's aunt Betty. Been sick for goin' on ten yeres."

" Where is she?"

" Up charmber, there !"

Without more ceremony our troops passed into the attic, and there, between the sheets, half-hidden by a bed-rid crone, they found a gray uniform lying at his length, with his boots on! He had not even taken the trouble to brush them, nor in any way to arrange his dress as he sought his couch, being covered from head to foot with spatterings of mud and water. The 'sleeping beauty,' as our men called him, was tenderly rolled out on the floor, and made a prize of war.

CHAPTER XIV.

*Hancock at Yorktown — One of the Decisive Issues of the War —
"Wave, Richmond, all thy Banners Wave!" but still they Wave
in Vain — Hancock Breveted Major in the United States Regular
Army*

ON the 15th of April, 1862, the national troops
advanced from Old Point Comfort, Virginia,
where they had landed from Washington, toward
Yorktown. This memorable spot, it will be recol-
lected, is the site of the surrender of Lord CORNWAL-
LIS to General WASHINGTON, near the close of the
Revolutionary war. It is one of the oldest towns in
the country, the capital of York county, and situated
on the right bank of the York river, about seventy
miles south of Richmond. English settlers first
reached there in the year 1705. It was once quite a
flourishing place; but the deleterious influences at
work have been its bane for more than a century.
It now numbers only forty houses within its precincts.

The position is commanding, especially with refer-once to the passage of vessels, and the enemy had resolved to make the most of it. They threw up strong entrenchments, mounted some of the largest guns they could command, especially those stolen from the United States Navy Yard at the contiguous port of Norfolk, and garrisoned it with about ten thousand picked troops, under Magruder, one of their most energetic and undaunted commanders. This skilful soldier had served for many years in the Union army, had received his education at the national military school, at the expense of the American people, and, with all his crude vagaries, was considered one of our best artillery officers. He was one of those very peculiar men who keep up a seeming of war by means of bluster; who love to fire guns for the mere purpose of making a noise; and who hold a continuance of peace by a show of power which they do not possess.

It was emphatically so at Yorktown. But the Union army, not being aware how comparatively inferior the defences and small the garrison of Yorktown really were, passed on to its conquest with almost its entire strength.

The advance was begun on the 4th of April, with General Morrill's brigade, of General Porter's division, in the night; two companies of the Third Penn

sylvania cavalry and a portion of Berdan's Sharp-
shooters, who had just rendered such effective service
at Big Bethel, deployed as skirmishers. The advance
rested at a spot within six miles of Yorktown, and
at ten o'clock on the morning of the 5th they were
in front of the ramparts of the enemy.

Magruder, according to his invariable custom of
bluster, soon opened fire, regardless of consequences.
He was promptly replied to by the batteries of Captain Griffin, the Third and Fourth Rhode Island and
Fifth Massachusetts, who sent back two shots for every
one from the enemy. The cannonading continued
briskly until sunset.

The fight was resumed the ensuing day, the brigade of General Hancock being early in the field, and
taking an active part. The artillery firing was constant on both sides. Every attempt of the enemy to
make sorties and charges resulted disastrously. They
were always glad to retreat behind their entrenchments. The great body of our men had never been
under fire, but those in view of the vigilant eye of
Hancock were kept bravely up to the work, his experience in artillery practice being of great service.
As the sun of the afternoon, deflecting from the water,
glanced on our bright pieces, they afforded a good
mark for the enemy, who made the most of their

position behind their high ramparts. New troops coming on the ground, relieved the exposed and wearied gunners. The Sixth Rhode Island battery and Fifth Massachusetts, arriving in the height of this part of the engagement, rendered most important service. It was quite near sundown when the last gun was fired. Our men always took care to have the closing shot.

On a subseqent day General Hancock led in person a portion of his brigade into the open field in front of the enemy. It was one of the most exposed positions yet occupied by our army. His object was to drive a body of pickets from a piece of woods they occupied, in close proximity to the national works. The troops advanced through the open area, in the face of a deadly fire, drawing themselves directly toward the enemy, on their hands and knees. They were now within close musket-range.

The gray coats were cunningly secreted behind trees and stumps, and anxious to induce our men to rise to their feet in order that they might have a better chance to shoot them down, while they themselves were under cover. To accomplish this object one of their wily Captains shouted the word "Charge!"—in the vain hope that the Union boys would spring to their feet at the sound, and run. But he and his daring allies were very much mistaken. We did nothing of the sort; but, on the contrary, kept our recumbent position unchanged, every man with his gun loaded and cocked, his bayonet fixed, and steadily advancing on the foe.

Again came the plucky Captain's command:

" Charge bayonet ! "

This time his command rose to their feet, as if to rush forward upon us. But before they had moved an inch, a command came from Hancock's side:

" Fire ! "

The well-aimed rifles blazed in an instant in the very faces of the enemy. They fell back in dismay, leaving their dead and wounded behind them on the field.

During the skirmish a new hidden battery, which had been erected only the previous Sunday night, opened on our men, with the intention of driving off the advance. But the guns of Hancock soon silenced and dismantled it.

This was a sudden and severe lesson to the enemy. They had foolishly supposed, it seems, that the national troops were all, or nearly all, especially the volunteers, terribly afraid of the idea of being charged upon by cold steel. They even went so far in their folly as to suppose that if they should only cry to their men, in the face of our advancing columns, the word "Charge!" we should instantly take to our heels and scamper from the field.

This experience with the brave men under Hancock taught them a different and very salutary lesson.

It is evident from the history of the comments made upon it by the Southern press, that the position at Yorktown was held to be of the greatest importance to the continued success of the rebellion. One of the editors, speaking by authority, on the 15th of April, says:

"The issue at Yorktown is tremendous. When the battle does come off it will be a fearful one, for the stake is enormous. Confederate leaders and soldiers feel that the issue involves the fate of the country. The contest cannot long be deferred. The news of a terrible battle may startle us at any moment.

"Wave, Richmond! all thy banners wave,
And charge with all thy chivalry!

"Not only the fate of the temporary seat of government, but of Eastern Virginia, and even more than that trembles in the balance.

"We presume that President DAVIS himself will be on the field, as he has intimated."

Immediately after the appearance of this fiery outburst of chivalric eloquence, the enemy began the

12

construction of large fortifications on the Gloucester side of Yorktown. The works were in sight of the Union gunboats. About one thousand men were at work on the fortifications; but the arrival of the gunboat *Sebago*, with a hundred-pound rifled Parrott gun, soon dispersed the enemy. She threw her shot, at the distance of three miles, which were so well aimed that they could be seen falling in the midst of the foemen and exploding with fatal effect. The killed and wounded were carried off by the enemy in considerable numbers, and the remaining combatants were glad to hide themselves under the cover of the adjacent woods. At every attempt to renew their work they were driven back, and finally compelled to abandon it.

Our assaults on the Yorktown works now continued for several days in succession. The weather was favorable for operations, and our army made the most of it. Occasional attempts at sorties were made by the enemy—on one evening with a force of three thousand men — but they were invariably repulsed with severe loss to our opponents.

By two o'clock in the afternoon of Monday, April 17th, a section of Union artillery was planted within half a mile of the Secesh works, near the river, and well supported by infantry. Their outworks were assailed from this point with good effect.

On the morning following, the enemy advanced with a force of one thousand men, and commenced to strengthen one of their batteries located about three miles to the left of Yorktown. A battery was very soon brought to bear on them, when they were not only reduced to terms of quiet, but compelled to beat a very hasty retreat. A brisk fire was kept up by our guns for four hours; during which all their cannon were dismounted without the ceremony of being unlimbered.

The Union gunboats advanced nearer to the seat of the action as it progressed. On the 24th of April one moved up Wormley's creek, early in the morning, and threw her shells with force at the earthworks. At a distance of four miles, the shells exploded in the midst of the enemy.

A dashing movement was made on an advanced lunette of the enemy, early in the morning of April 28th, by company H, of the First Massachusetts regiment. The works were carried, and the enemy, consisting of two companies of infantry, driven back. Our men moved over open, soft ground, some six hundred yards, receiving the fire of the South at a distance of fifty yards; they did not return it, but rushed

over the ditch and parapet in the most gallant manner. The enemy were not prepared for so chivalrous
an act from the scorned Northrons. They broke and
ran in all directions the moment they saw the heads
of our men coming up the glacis and over the summit. We took a number of prisoners, and effectually
destroyed the works.

On the 2d of May the Union siege batteries opened
on the whole length of the enemy's line. The effect
was very severe. Our own works had been constructed with great care, and the guns placed in position were of the heaviest calibre suitable for such a
siege. The firing was kept up on both sides, for a
time, with great animation, although the loss of life
was comparatively small.

Our environment of the works had been complete.
The Union parallels and batteries had gone up day
by day, night by night, within point-blank range
of the enemy. His fire had been unceasing, and, at
times, vexatious. But it was not long ere we had
more than one hundred siege guns and mortars in
favorable positions for the reduction of the walls.

The sending of a war-balloon from our side on the
afternoon of the 3d of May, and the display of large
signal lanterns in the evening, gave the enemy certain ranges for their guns, which opportunities they

promptly improved. But at the hour of midnight the shelling from the fort slackened, and bright lights in the vicinity of the water batteries of the enemy attracted our attention. Near daylight followed a series of minute guns from inside the works. As the morning advanced, and they grey mist lifted from the waters of the river and the adjacent lowlands, floating away like gossamer in the breeze from Hampton Roads, it was discovered that the strategic opponents had deserted their entrenched post, and left us the works so carefully and solidly created. Yorktown was evacuated!

At six o'clock on the morning of the 4th of May, detachments of Union troops from Massachusetts, New York and Pennsylvania marched over the ramparts and occupied the deserted fort. In a moment more the national ensign, full and free, floated from the abandoned flagstaff, and the victorious troops greeted it with hearty cheers.

The victory was complete and a great one. The gray coats had held Yorktown with over ten thousand of their picked men. They had kept at work for months three thousand slaves, building fortifications and locating guns. The works were of the strongest kind then constructed in the country. They formed an immense connected fortification, with its

12*

numerous salient angles. The ditches were deep, the parapets lofty, and difficult to scale. The water battery below commanded the river on the Yorktown side, while that at Gloucester Point, on the opposite shore, was equally effective. The guns were the best that could then be obtained — a portion of them in most commanding positions being Dahlgrens, Columbiads and sea-coast pieces of good range. An immense area in front of the works, over which the Union troops would have been compelled to march, in case an assault had been attempted, was swept completely by opposing fires. Deep gorges, ravines and swamps were all around and inside the fortifications, presenting the most formidable natural obstacles to our advancing columns.

The occupation of Yorktown gave us possession, with the fort, of eighty guns in all, and a large amount of material of war. There were four magazines in a good state of preservation.

On arriving inside the fort, the enemy's tents were found standing in all directions. Some of these were daubed on their sides with clever caricatures of the Union troops; but, luckily for the artists, it was not quite convenient for them to stay and defend their characteristic specimens of humorous art. For urgent private reasons they preferred to leave their galleries to be admired by the eyes of their invading foes, acting on the impulse of the old distich :

> "He who fights, and runs away,
> May live to fight — another day."

It was rumored that Mr. DAVIS, the President of the insurgent Southern Confederacy, and the noted Generals LEE and BEAUREGARD, were present in Yorktown, while the closing part of the siege was in progress; and that, after much altercation, they ordered the evacuation. On the memorable night of that distracted council, while the Union guns were thundering at the gate for admission, the already defeated foe, with daring ingenuity, secretly buried percussion torpedoes in all the passages and approaches. It was not chivalry, but war. A single explosion sufficed to warn us of danger, and to thwart completely the artful plan.

But the works were ours. Another gateway to Richmond, the Mecca of our hopes, was entered and possessed; and it remains in the hands of the Union to this day. There, with all its sacred Revolutionary records, may it remain forever!

General Hancock was breveted Major in the United States Regular Army for his meritorious conduct at Yorktown, his brevet dating from the 4th of May, 1862.

CHAPTER XV.

THE battle of Williamsburg, Virginia, was fought on the 4th of May, 1862. The Union advance, leaving Yorktown in the possession of a sufficient garrison, reached the rear of the enemy, under one of their best leaders, General J. E. Johnson, on the morning of that day. The battle commenced immediately, and was continued, at intervals, until after sundown.

The march from Yorktown to Williamsburg had been made with much caution. It was a surprise to the enemy. He had no idea we would leave our entrenched works at the former place so soon after possessing them. White flags skirted the road as our troops passed on. The male occupants of the houses had nearly all fled, leaving behind their women, children, and servants.

In the vicinity of Williamsburg the enemy had

(140)

thrown up strong entrenchments. Their force had been materially increased by additions from Richmond and other camps. It was evident they were bent on making a determined stand.

The morning of our approach was dark and dreary. The rain fell in torrents. Hooker, Smith, Kearney and Heintzleman were among the first to enter the action. It raged during the day, and by four o'clock in the afternoon was at its height. Many of the officers and men were under fire for the first time, in the open field of battle. Several of the youngest of the former were subject to the most trying ordeals of their courage and presence of mind, as they rode, in the position of Aids, among the descending showers of shot and shell.

General Keyes came up with a divison of reinforcements at a critical juncture, aided by that venerable officer, General Casey. Couch, followed by a considerable body of cavalry and artillery, joined in the fight at this point, on the left, while Hancock was pressing the enemy on the right. Our troops fought with heroic valor. The vacancies rapidly made in the lines were as rapidly filled; and the surging columns pressed steadily on, meeting the enemy face to face, shot for shot, man for man.

General Hancock had called for reinforcements, and

the troops nobly respouded. Just as the sun was
going down, while the torrents of rain were yet falling, Hancock made that brilliant charge that must
forever associate his name with peculiar honor in
the battle of Williamsburg.   The enemy had massed
a strong force on his front, and had made several
fearful chasms in his nearest ranks.   Riding to the
centre, and quickly passing the words, " Fix bayonets!" he paused at the chosen point, and waving his
hat, gave the memorable order to his officers:

"Gentlemen! Charge!"

The brilliancy and effect with which that courteous
order was obeyed at that instant will never be forgotten. The Confeds were swept before it, like chaff
before a whirlwind. Officers, men, horses, artillery,
were borne back in confusion and dismay, rendering
the rout of the foe one of the most signal ever witnessed on any field of any war.   All the works on
the right of the Union line were captured at a blow.
The enemy were flanked on their left, and rolled up
over the earth like a parchment scroll.   The movement was masterly.   The success was complete. As
the news of it ran along the lines, and reached the
headquarters of the army, cheer followed cheer on
all sides, and the enthusiasm of the troops kindled
before it as a harbinger of victory. The most hearty

congratulations surrounded Hancock from all his
associates, and his character for brilliancy and dash
as a soldier took a nobler hue than ever from that
moment.

Reinforcements now continued to press forward.
As night closed in we had full possession of all the
fortifications on our front. Hancock passed the night
before them, on the field. The brave troops around
him rested on their victorious arms. Neither their
General nor they heeded that they were wet with the
drenching rain, spattered with mud, weary and hungry. Through the descending rain of that stormy
night, their watchfires were kindled only to show
them the conquered enemy beyond. They demanded
to be led again by Hancock in another charge. The
veterans among them thought of their bivouacs with
him in Mexico, when he was a young Lieutenant;
and they longed to follow him now as a General to
new fields of glory. The darkness could not hide
from their vision the dear old flag; the chilly night-
air could not dampen their ardor in its defence; the
presence of the enemy in force, just in front, could
not check their purpose to stand or fall for the Union
which those tremendous hosts had aimed to destroy.

Noble army of martyrs for American Liberty! It
required all the coolness and discipline, all the vigor

and persuasion of Hancock, to keep them that night within his lines. Had he but given the word, they would have rushed forward with him, again and again, in fiery onsets on their country's foes.

The following morning came with a bright and bracing air. Our troops were better prepared than ever for the renewal of the fight. But the word soon came from Hancock, still in the advance on the right, that the enemy had fled. They had availed themselves of the darkness and storm of the night to steal away, leaving their deserted fortifications for our advancing forces to enter.

This opening field fight of that campaign afforded many striking illustrations of the republican nature of the struggle on the Union side. Among our officers were several gentlemen of foreign birth, and some native born of great wealth and high position in American society. Of these, as the morning broke after the battle, Count de Paris could be seen ploughing his way knee-deep through the Virginia mud, with his bag of corn on his shoulder, which he had just filled at a neighboring crib, and with which he was to feed his horse. Mr. Astor, of New York, on the staff of the Commanding General, might be discovered washing the mud from his steed, and attending to grooming and culinary matters generally, on his own account. In the hospitals and on the field, officers and men were helping each other indiscriminately; together bearing the burdens as together they shared the honors of war.

The works captured from the enemy by the brave exploit of Hancock were found to be of a formidable character. The gallant charge he made was not a mere bloody display of valor. Its results were tangible, and valuable to the cause. The enemy had come upon him with a furious onset. They evidently calculated that he would fall an easy prey to their yelling assault. A man with less invincible courage, with less firmness of resolution than he, would have fallen back, and waited for still more reinforcements. But the moment the additional troops he sent for rallied around him, that moment he advanced — giving assault for assault, and closing the day with his steady charge of the deadly bayonet. Not until the enemy was close upon him, not until he could see their eyes peering into those of his own men, not until they had swept far across the open field that intervened between the opposing lines, did he give the memorable or der that has so honorably associated his name with the victory of that day.

It is admitted on all hands that the bearing of the foe was most gallant. His ranks were composed of

13   K

Virginia, Georgia and North Carolina troops, who literally strewed the ground with their dead ere they yielded to the impetuous valor of Hancock.   **Acres** of felled **and** tangled **trees, long lines** of **strongly-** built entrenchments, showed **the fixed** purpose of the enemy to hold their ground to the **last.** Their ammunition was abundant and their fire most gall- **ing.** But **for the unexpected** dash made on **them by Hancock, where, at the point of the** bayonet, **their works were wrested from them,** they would **have re-mained for a long time in a strong position of defence.**

Immediately **opposed to Hancock, leading the picked body of the enemy, was the active commander** Longstreet, **who had been a lieutenant with him in** some **of the** severest **fights in Mexico.   In his front,** almost **face** to face, was Early, **who had** been, **also, a** fellow officer with him on those distant fields.   What **a** place for such a meeting!

The brilliant success **of** Hancock **was gained with a loss of not more than twenty killed and wounded. His engagement decided the fortunes of the day. The falling back of the enemy gave the Union a thousand wounded and three** hundred uninjured **Confed prisoners. Thus far seventy-one** large guns **were captured, many tents, and a** great amount **of ammunition.**

With savage desperation the dismayed, demoralized, and hastily retreating foes signalized their defeat by placing torpedoes within their abandoned works, near their flagstaffs, magazines, and telegraph offices; and secreting them in carpet-bags, barrels of flour, provisions, boxes, and other available spots liable to be reached by our troops. Most fortunately, the horrible device was detected.

It is not pretended that the battle of Williamsburg partook of the nature of a great general engagement. It was more like a brilliant and successful skirmish of an army on the advance. The Secesh speak of it in their reports as 'a handsome affair.' In the official despatches of Generals Hooker, Smith, Couch, Kearney, Birney and Heintzleman — all of whom, with Generals Peck, Jameson, Devens, Casey, Graham, Berry, Stoneman, and others, won fresh laurels on that day — it is placed in its true light, as a preliminary fight of much importance, whose effect was as beneficial on the spirits of our own men as it was desponding to those of the enemy.

To the gallant and lamented General PHILIP KEARNEY is especial honor due for his great aid in the restoration of the fortunes of the day, on the hard-fought field of Williamsburg.

CHAPTER XVI.

THE advance of the Union army up the Virginia Peninsula, continued General Hancock at the front. He participated, with his accustomed gallantry, in the battles of Garnett's Hill, Savage Station, White Oak Swamp, and several skirmishes of an important character.

While thus occupied in the field of battle for his country, the General seized a moment to write a hurried letter home. It shows the heart of the true man, in the camp of the gallant soldier:

"U. S. CAMP, NEAR RICHMOND, 23d of May, 1862.

"MY DEAR MOTHER:

I wrote to father a few days ago. It has been some time since I heard from him or you. I presume some of your letters have missed me, in consequence of the changes of the field.

(148)

I am well; and so, also, is brother John. We are not in Richmond yet, but trust we shall be there, all in good time.

I hope that God, in his good mercy, will permit both your sons to reach that city, in safety and in honor.

I have not much time to write. Give my best love to father.

And believe me

Your devoted son,

WINFIELD S. HANCOCK."

" Mrs. Elizabeth Hancock,

Norristown, Pa."

This confiding tribute to his mother is of the same class with all his letters home. While at one of his Western posts, early in the service, at the age of twenty-three years, he writes to his twin brother:

"NEWPORT BARRACKS, KY., May 5, 1847

" MY DEAR HILARY:

I was exceedingly glad to find, on my arrival here from Fort Scott, two long and interesting letters from you. The only thing that grieves me is that I cannot get to Mexico. I made an application to-day to join the army going to the front. Whether the Adjutant General will favor it or not I do not know; but think it doubtful.

I am actively engaged as Superintendent of the recruiting service for the Western Division, and acting as Assistant Inspector General; but, though my services are said to be useful, I still want to go to Mexico.

Your affectionate brother,

WINFIELD."

How different might have been his career, had his

13*

going to Mexico continued to be 'doubtful'! But all his doubts on that subject were soon after removed. In a few weeks he was ordered to the front. From there he writes to his father:

"TACUBAYA, MEXICO, August 26, 1847.

"MY DEAR FATHER:

I feel thankful that I am able to write to you from this place. We have had to fight desperately to get here. It has been the theatre of a sanguinary battle. I left off my last letter to engage in preparations for it."

In the following October he writes from Mexico:

"I am exceedingly anxious to see you all. I send you some of the plans of our engagements."

Writing to his brother Hilary, under date of City of Mexico, December 6, 1847, he says:

"MY DEAR HILARY:

I am again made happy by the arrival of three letters from home. You ask me whether I have been in battle? I answer, proudly, yes! Beside being in several skirmishes, on the road from Puebla to Vera Cruz,—in all of which I can truly say I have endeavored to do my duty,—it was my part to participate in the battles of San Antonio, Churubusco, Molino del Rey, and the conquest of the City of Mexico. I only missed the fight of Chepultepec by being sick in my tent, and off duty, at the time. I shall always be sorry that I was absent. I was lying ill with chills and fever, directly under the fort, at the time the action began. I could not remain still under the firing; but, wrapping my blanket about me, I crept to the top of the roof of the nearest house, watched the fight, and had strength enough to cheer with the boys when the Castle fell. The balls whizzed around me, but I kept my post, doing what I could; and when I learned that the colors I saw hoisted on the conquered walls were those of my own regiment, my heart beat quick at the glorious sight.

The winter has set in here, and some chilly days are the consequence. The summits of lofty Popocatapetl are capped with more snow than is usual at this season. No snows, however, are on the plains. Here the roads are open and many of them beautiful. The Almada, or great Square of the Capital, is far superior to anything of the kind in the United States. The carriage road on the outskirts is splendid, and, at times, crowded with gay equipages. It is, also, a fashionable resort for walks. Its age is three centuries.

Give my love to father, mother, brother John, and all my other friends. WINFIELD."

He again writes his family from near Toluca, January 5th, 1848:

"We have another snow mountain overlooking us—the Nevindo. When the wind blows from that direction it is bitterly cold. But January is the end of the Mexican winter. The days begin to grow warmer as the month advances, although the nights continue chilly. There are no fire-places, and consequently no fires; as we more Northern-born find, to our great discomfort.

The Valley of Toluca is most beautiful, and very fertile. Like all the other Mexican valleys I have seen, it is perfectly level, as if it had once been the bottom of a large lake. Some of these wonderful areas look like the craters of extinct volcanoes. In the Valley of Mexico one of the remaining lakes is twenty miles long and fifteen broad.

The variety of fruits produced here is astonishing. On one of the market days, recently, over fifty different kinds were on sale. Think of opening a fine, fresh, ripe watermelon, in the month of January!

Love to all.   WINFIELD."

All his letters to his friends are written in this free and affectionate style. They contain, beside his descriptions of places and landscapes, his expressions of personal interest, full and correct accounts of his battles, and graphic drawings of the fields. It would be pleasing to give longer extracts, did the extent of our volume admit of it. These will suffice to show the character of the writer, inasmuch as he wrote without the remotest expectation that his letters would ever appear in print.

In what a pleasing light do these unstudied epistles present the subject of this memoir! His love of home, of kindred, of country, of the cause in which he has enlisted, his quiet devotion to duty in the midst of battle and danger, show the man as he is, and reflect new lustre on the niche of fame where his valor has placed him.

CHAPTER XVII.

The Terrible Struggles of Garnett's Hill, Savage's Station, and White Oak Swamp — Hancock as Major-General of Volunteers — The Return from the Peninsula.

DURING the operations of the Union army immediately before Richmond, in the spring of 1862, General HANCOCK had taken his usual active part. His brigade had continued in the division of General Smith, now a part of a new provisional army corps, in command of General W. B. Franklin. He was posted on the right of the main body, aiding in conducting the siege. His duties were peculiarly arduous in those pestilential swamps of the Chickahominy. He shared in all the dangers and fatigues of the principal attacks, and rendered important aid by his regular army experience in conducting the safe withdrawal of the men under his command.

At the fierce battle of Gaines' Mills, Hancock was

(153)

in charge of an independent body of troops, temporarily attached to his brigade.   His position was in
the extreme advance, his picket line extending across
an intersecting ravine.   At this point he met and
overcame a terrific fire of the enemy, massed in five
regiments; keeping them at bay, and thereby preventing them from pushing on to another part of the
field they were anxious to reach.

Late in the afternoon of the 27th of June, the
enemy, being reinforced, commenced to attack the
lines of Hancock more furiously than ever, from the
south side of the stream.   It was evidently their
purpose to force him back, and thus separate him
from the main portion of the army.   The attack was
opened with a heavy artillery fire of grape, shell,
round shot and shrapnel.   It was the most furious
onset made by the enemy in that portion of the field.
The cry ran along the lines of the Confederates:

"No quarter to the Yankees!   Into the river with
them!   Shoot them down in the water!"

This fiery assault was led by General Toombs, of
Georgia, formerly for several years a member of Con-
gress, and for some time a Senator of the United
States.   The enemy came forward with a yell and a
dash, calculating to drive everything before them.
There were five regiments of infantry, yelling and

surging to and fro, with desperate valor. The fight became, in places, one of hand-to-hand; and there was no spot where the opposing forces were more than ten paces apart. The attack was as short as it was fierce; but it ended in the complete repulse of the enemy. They were driven back, with all their yells and clatters, leaving nearly three hundred killed and wounded on the field.

This brief but sanguinary fight is known as that of Garnett's Hill.

On the following morning the enemy renewed the attack, with all the fury of armed men balked of their prey. But they were again signally repulsed, with loss; leaving a Colonel, Lieutenant Colonel, and other officers and men of the Seventh and Eighth Georgia regiments, prisoners in our hands

General Hancock continued to hold the enemy in check at this important point until three o'clock of the morning of the 28th of June, when he rejoined the remainder of the division of General Smith, and participated actively in the obstinate battles of Savage's Station, on the 29th, and of White Oak Swamp, on the 30th of the same month.

For his services at Garnett's Hill he was again recommended for appointment as Major General of Volunteers, by the commander of the army. He **was** recommended, subsequently, for three brevets in the Regular Army, for meritorious conduct during the Peninsular campaign.

On his return from the Peninsula, General Hancock prepared at once to take part in the defence of Washington, made by General Pope against the advance of the Southern foe, under Lee. But before he could reach the field of action, the Union army had withdrawn to a better position for the immediate protection of the city.

The particulars of the career of Hancock in front of Richmond, in the campaign of '62, are thus carefully narrated here, in order that it may be seen with what pertinacity, skill and courage he continued to act his part.

We must now go with him to the battle of Antietam; where the unusual honor was conferred upon him of being made a division commander, during the engagement.

CHAPTER XVIII.

Hancock a Colonel in the Regular Army — The Sanguinary Onset at Antietam — The Enemy driven back to Virginia — An Episode of Grim Humor — A Union Colonel in his First Fight.

ON the 27th of June, 1862, the brevet of Colonel in the Regular Army was bestowed on Hancock, for distinguished conduct in the Peninsular campaign. His next service was in command of his brigade at the battle of Antietam, in Maryland, which was fought on the 17th of September, of the same year.

This battle was one of the most baffling in its immediate character of any of the war; and yet its results have been eminently beneficial to the Union cause.

The transfer of the seat of operations from the front of Washington to the Maryland line had much enlarged the sphere of the Army of the Potomac. It became necessary not only to cover the National Capital with an adequate force, but Baltimore, Phila-

14   (167)

delphia, and important interior towns, even as far
west as Pittsburg, Pennsylvania, required protection.
The enemy were on the alert in all directions, de-
manding the most vigilant efforts of our patriotic
troops to meet and overcome them.

The first prizes to be fought for by the enemy and
to be defended by the patriots were Washington,
Baltimore, the Cumberland Valley, Harper's Ferry
and Philadelphia.

On the 16th of September the enemy were posted
on the heights in the rear of Antietam creek. This
stream rises in the southern part of Pennsylvania,
and pursuing a southerly course through a portion
of Maryland, empties into the Potomac. The country contiguous is broken, and beyond are the passes
of the South Mountain range. The principal roads
in the vicinity lead to and from Sharpsburg, Hagers-
town, Harper's Ferry and Baltimore. The body of
Southrons occupied strong positions among the hills,
commanding the valleys and plains below, for a considerable distance. Their artillery was well posted
on all the principal heights.

It was the design of the Union commander to
attack the enemy on their left. The Pennsylvania
troops were among the first to advance. The position of affairs, as our men swept into the areas before

the Secesh guns, was intensely trying; but their valor sustained them well to the close of the hard-fought engagement.   Our loss in killed and wounded, especially in officers, was large, several generals being carried from the scene of action.

In the valley of Antietam, where some of the hottest engagements of the battle were fought, we were crowded into a narrow space, and subject to a galling fire from the protected batteries of the enemy.   It was found to be almost impossible to enfilade them, in consequence of the abruptness of the hills.   These steep slopes were lined with rifle-pits and breastworks, from which the rifles and guns swept large portions of the whole of that part of the field.

As our troops continued to advance, determined to drive the enemy from their strongholds, the slaughter was fearful.   But they pressed on to every point where there was any possibility of meeting the foe on equal grounds.   They were now also strongly reinforced, battery being added to battery, as if they were determined, in return, to make a wholesale butchery of the brave men so exposed before their fire.

The battle over the entire field was much of it of this description.   It was one of the most unequal fights on record.   Our artillery was promptly filed into action, and handled with great courage and skill; but it lost immensely in every assault by the vast superiority of position held by the opposing gunners. Our batteries could not be brought into good point-blank range without the greatest difficulty; and, when they were, the Confed. embankments afforded them such protection that the most telling shots produced but little effect.

The first day closed on a conflict in which nearly two hundred thousand men had been hotly engaged for fourteen hours.

Harper's Ferry was disgracefully surrendered in the midst of the battle; thus cutting off a large supply of troops and munitions, at the same time furnishing a strong strategic point to the enemy, and materially interfering with the successful prosecution of the plans of the Union generals. But, with all these disadvantages on our side, the enemy were driven out of their entrenched mountain passes, compelled to fight and submit to defeat in the more open country, and to withdraw, subdued, thwarted, humbled, from Maryland to Virginia.

The part taken by Hancock in the battle of Antietam was characteristic of the man. He was prompt, vigilant, courageous in every portion of the engagements in which he participated. His own native hills of Pennsylvania were just beyond the field. The capital of the nation was liable to be assailed by an unscrupulous enemy. The large cities of Baltimore and Philadelphia were to be defended. The honor of the Army of the Potomac was to be maintained. These grave contingencies found him fully prepared.

On the night of the 17th of September, in the presence of a large and embattled force of the enemy, he slept on the field, with the brave troops who had won the day. By the morning of the 19th General Lee had withdrawn beyond the reach of pursuit, with an acknowledged loss of about fourteen thousand men, in killed and wounded.

During the height of the battle an incident occurred in his immediate command, which strikingly illustrates the character of Hancock. It took place on the night of September 16th. One of the new regiments, now for the first time in action, was in position on the brow of a commanding hill. The shots of the enemy raked it in such a way that the men were lying close to the ground, their rifles in hand, well loaded. They had done what they could on their line, and were now waiting additional orders. The commander of the regiment and all his officers were prostrate on the earth, with the men, among whom the balls occasionally ploughed deep furrows, scattering the soil and stones in all directions. The moon was riding high in the heavens; but the smoke of battle, which had not at that point ceased with the coming on of night, dimmed its shining rays. It was sufficiently clear, however, to distinguish persons and places with considerable readiness.

At this moment Hancock rode up to the prostrate regiment. Looking around for the Colonel, who could not be distinguished at once in the dim light of the moon, and through the smoke of battle, he enquired:

"Who commands this regiment?"

"I do, sir!" replied the new Colonel, bobbing up his head from its hole in the ground, and then, as an unfriendly shot whizzed by his ear, bobbing it back again.

Now, the Colonel was a truly brave man, with all the shrewdness of a Yankee. Having been bred to the law, and never under fire before, it took him some time to 'master the situation,' and to be able to 'define his position.' At that interesting period of his military novitiate, as one of his 'high privates' quaintly remarked, 'things looked kinder skeery.'

In his lowly posture, the Colonel had forgotten to rise and tender his superior the customary salute.

General Hancock, still mounted, and his staff around

him, at once saw the state of 'the case,' although he
did not then understand all its legal attitudes and
bearings. With his usual courtesy, he again enquired:

"How many men have you on duty, Colonel?"

"About eight hundred, I guess!" the Colonel replied, bobbing up his head, turning his face half-way
toward the General, and quickly bobbing it back
again to his covert.

"Are you *about* ready for an advance, Colonel?"
quietly continued Hancock, now beginning to smile
at the ludicrous scene.

"I rather guess we shall be," came a smothered
voice from the hole, "when we're ordered to."

"Perhaps General HANCOCK may order you to!"
politely interposed one of Hancock's aids, as he
pointed with his drawn sword to the commander of
the division.

"General Hancock!" exclaimed the Colonel, springing to his feet, and saluting in his best manner.

"I beg your pardon, General! I feel ashamed to
be caught in this position. It is my first fight,
sir. General! I await your orders. I will follow
you anywhere!"

The General and staff now indulged in a good
natured laugh, in which the Colonel heartily joined

As we have said, he was really a brave man, and had not the slightest idea of shirking his duty. But he saw, in a moment, how he and his new troops must appear in that position to Hancock. While the General and staff were sitting calmly on their horses, on the brow of the hill over which poured the Confederates' shots, he and his regiment had been lying on their faces, flat on the ground.

"Regiment!" he shouted, with a lusty voice, from which every shake and tremor had now fled: "Up, men! Front face! Present arms!"

The whole command rose at the word, sprang into position in line, in good order, and gave the salute in true military style. The General returned it with his accustomed grace; and, after giving the Colonel some additional instructions, passed with his staff along the front of battle.

It is due to that Colonel to state here that he repeatedly distinguished himself on that and other occasions; and, after being wounded in a hand-to-hand fight, he has received and now worthily wears the honors of his native State.

The scene will always be remembered by those who took part in it, as somewhat relieving with quiet humor the hard features of war.

In the light of an impartial history it is clear that

the South had not the slightest right to claim a triumph at Antietam. Our loss was a severe one, owing to the unassailable positions of the guns of the enemy; but their loss was much greater, and their withdrawal, under the circumstances, was a confession of defeat.

> "How sleep the brave, who sink to rest,
> With all their country's wishes blest!
> When Spring, with dewy fingers cold,
> Shall oft frequent their hallowed mold,
> She there shall press a fairer sod
> Than Fancy's foot hath ever trod.
> By hands unseen their knell is rung
> By lips unseen their dirge is sung
> There Honor comes, a pilgrim grey,
> To dress the turf that wraps their clay;
> And Freedom shall awhile repair,
> To dwell, a weeping hermit, there."

CHAPTER XIX.

Hancock at Fredericksburg — The Passage of the Rappahannock — Terrible Slaughter of the Union Troops — Hancock's Line Impregnable — His Care for his Wounded Men.

THE Army of the Potomac returned from its Peninsular campaign in the fall of 1862. In November of that year it arrived at Falmouth, Virginia, having made the march from Warrenton, a distance of forty miles, in two days and a half.

The ultimate object of the South was still the conquest of Washington. Encouraged by their allies in feeling, at home and abroad, compelled by the imperious demands of their necessities, they remained as long as possible in the vicinity of the national capital. A strong column of the enemy, under the justly distinguished brave General THOMAS J. JACKSON, had swept down suddenly on our rear, and placed the whole Union force, large as it was, at a temporary disadvantage. For many days the tide of battle had

(166)

beat furiously against the patriot army. Unac-
quainted with the country, surrounded by swarms of
active spies, exposed to those deadly malarias of the
lowlands and swamps to which the great majority of
them were wholly unaccustomed, the heroic valor of
our troops was suddenly called to encounter the most
fearful odds of any that had yet been forced upon
them.

The fights in which Hancock had participated at
Savage Station, Fair Oaks, and at other assailable
points, were bitter and sanguinary. But in every
encounter he came off victorious. He had hardly
received the message to prepare for action at the latter place, ere the enemy was charging all around
him. His vigilance was equal to the emergency.
The foe's artillery was most furious in its attack on
his extended lines. A strong brigade of picked men,
with a characteristic yell, burst on his pickets and
dashed headlong at his principal battery. The bullets showered on his devoted camp, from all directions. The smoke from the contending guns filled
all the air of the open spaces, and the sulphurous mist
of musketry hung like a cloud along the edges of the
dim forests. The Union men answered the wild
yells of the enemy with lusty cheers, and drove them

back at every onset. Two Georgia regiments were
nearly cut to pieces by Hancock's guns. He captured a considerable number of prisoners; among
whom was one of the most prominent of the Southern
secessionists, Colonel Lamar, of Georgia. He had
once been a member of the national Congress. A
Lieutenant Colonel shared his captivity.

The perilous fighting of those memorable days
must ever fill a bloody page in the volumes of American history. Men never fought more bravely, never
suffered more terrible privations from hunger, exposure, thirst and fatigue, than did those columns of
Union troops in all those closing scenes of that Peninsular campaign. The unflinching valor of our
men was admitted on all hands by the enemy.

One report of these battles states that the following
conversation took place between our own and some
Confederate officers. The Union officers asked:

"Did your men respect Yankee fighters?"

"Yes!" was the prompt reply. "They quite surprise us."

"You admit, then, there has been no faltering
among us on the Chickahominy?"

"Certainly we do! There never could have
been better fighting than yours in any part of the
world."

Among all these acknowledged deeds of valor, the name of Hancock must ever stand conspicuous.

The object of the enemy in following rapidly on after the Union army was, if possible, to intercept it, cut off its supplies, and then dash into Washington. They were perfectly familiar with all the Southern approaches to the capital. Their leaders in political affairs had been wont to rule it by approaches from the Southern side; why should they not possess it now, with arms, from the same direction? On all of their advances friends and allies surrounded them. There were plenty of false men in our own camps. In Washington they occupied some of the most lucrative posts of the Government; they swarmed through all the avenues; they chatted and whispered, they wrote and plotted in some of the most fashionable circles of society, and even in the obscure and detested purlieus of vice. Government plunderers were their secret counsellors; notorious characters were their ready spies. Men without a grain of pride or patriotism, all through the land, stood ready to aid them in the complete subjugation of the capital of the nation at the feet of the South. New England was to be sloughed off, as a pestilential plague-spot on the body politic. New York was to become a free city, and form a treaty of amity and alliance

15

with the confederated schemers. The West was to assume Mr. Calhoun's attitude of 'masterly inactivity' toward the rebellion; and, satisfied with its great interior empire and the free navigation of the Mississippi, was to be active only in fighting and keeping out of the new Confederation the loathed and hated East.

It was a boldly-formed scheme, with which to adorn the 'grim-visaged front' of a daring secession, in which the capital of WASHINGTON was to figure as the victor's prize. It was to be a triple crown of despotic power, emblazoned with the South, the Centre, and the West, which the bold hand of the Confederacy was to place upon the brow of some chosen chieftain.

The march of the Army of the Potomac to Falmouth, Virginia, in the middle of November, 1862, was one of the first of those strategic movements that resulted, ultimately, in the protection of Washington. In all that march, however, and while going into camp, our troops were seriously annoyed by the enemy. By making detours through by-roads, valleys and woods, we avoided those contests in which we must invariably have fought at a disadvantage.

The great object of the enemy — acting, no doubt, under the immediate orders of Lee — was to possess themselves of our guns. These, they well knew, would be eminently useful to us in the defence of Washington, and they were determined, if possible, to wrest them from us. Their most practiced sharpshooters were numerously detailed to pick off our gunners and horses, so that, in the miry roads of the fall season, the weapons might become an easy prey.

General BURNSIDE, at that time in command of the Army of the Potomac, completely deceived the enemy. They had **no idea he** would take the route he did. It was **their** expectation and hope that **he** would march for the defence of the capital by the way of Gordonsville, where they were prepared to assail him, in front and rear, from behind their strong entrenchments.

Our forces advanced in three columns — Hancock being on the extreme right of the line. His discipline of his troops was perfect, and his march made in good order. Few stragglers were anywhere to be seen; and he passed on rapidly in advance of the main body. The region through which he advanced was fearfully desolate. The fiery foot-prints of **war** had been there twice before.

Falmouth is one of the oldest towns in Virginia. It was settled as early as the year 1717. The houses have an antiquated appearance, and but little active

business is transacted within its precincts. There is
no public building in the town of any note. The
old-fashioned brick dwellings, with their quaint dor-
mer windows, carry you back to the days when Virginia was a colony of England, and when this ancient
town stood on the outskirts of civilization in the land
of Pocahontas.

The troops of General Hancock swept rapidly
through this region, fording rivers and ascending
high hills in their march. The soldiers were in good
spirits, singing gaily their army songs, and reposing
unbounded confidence in their leader. The head
waters of the Rappahannock soon came into view, then
the contiguous heights of the Blue Ridge of moun
tains, that put out their spurs from this region to the
shores of the Chesapeake Bay. The historic traveller looks in vain for the signs of the English Falmouth of Henry the Eighth, for the Castles of Pen-
dennis and Saint Mawes, and the opening view of
the British Channel.

The principal importance of Falmouth lies in the
fact of its close proximity with the larger town of
Fredericksburg, another of the old but more enterprising Virginia settlements. It is the county-seat
of Spottsylvania. Its location is on the right bank
of the Rappahannock river, and has some advantages

for manufactures and commerce. The tide water here terminates, at a distance of sixty-five miles north of Richmond. The railway from Washington to Richmond passes through Fredericksburg, rendering it an important point for the possession of an army in time of war.

General Lee had telegraphed to the inhabitants of Fredericksburg the fact of the near approach of the Union troops. We approached the town in four columns—infantry, cavalry, and artillery. Its surrender was demanded on the 21st of November, 1862, by General Sumner, then commanding the right division. A correspondence ensued between him and the civil authorities, at the termination of which preparations were commenced for shelling the town. The delay of the enemy in surrendering, for which every opportunity that courtesy could demand was afforded them, prompted an attack from the Union batteries. Meanwhile, General Lee had reached the spot, making it as defensible as possible, on his march toward Washington.

On the ensuing 13th of December the battle opened. It was fiercely contested on both sides, the Confederates having every advantage in position and massing of force.

The shelling of the two previous days, and the

15 *

landing across the river of bodies of picked men, had
done the enemy considerable damage. The passage
of the stream was repeatedly made, and under circumstances well calculated to test the valor of our
patriot troops. In consequence of the impossibility
of lowering the range of our batteries on the bank
so as to reach the town in front to advantage, the
houses and walls in that vicinity afforded protection
to the sharp-shooters of the enemy, who were busily
engaged picking off our gunners. Notwithstanding
this, the cannonading continued from a line of fire
supplied by one hundred and seventy-nine guns,
ranging from ten-pounder Parrotts to four-and-a-half-
inch siege guns, posted along the convex side of the
arc of the circle, formed by the bend of the river and
land opposite the doomed town.

The part of Hancock, in command of a division,
was everything that became him. His troops were
among those who performed the daring feat of crossing the river in open boats, scaling the opposite
banks, in the face of a deadly fire, and driving off
the enemy from their lurking places. They scattered
up the streets at our approach, throwing away arms
and accoutrements in their rapid flight. The shouts
of our men swept across the water as they witnessed
this gallant action, while returning cheers came back

from the brave fellows who at such imminent peril
had won the day.

Next followed the work of throwing pontoon
bridges across the river. Our men plunged waist-
deep into the stream, and worked as men do who are
under the sacred inspiration of patriotic duty. In
less than half an hour the first bridge was completed,
and a body of troops thrown across. The attempt
to shell them from the heavy batteries was a signal
failure.

The principal force of the enemy in Fredericksburg consisted of Mississippians, South Carolinians,
and Floridians.

A few months previous to this engagement, General
Hancock, being still in the advance, had reached
Bolivar Heights, on the line of the Potomac, early
in the morning, and driven the enemy before him.
He passed on to Charlestown, Virginia, which he
occupied. When at a distance of a mile and a half
from the town the enemy had opened their batteries
on him; but he used his guns to such advantage that
they were glad to retire.

Following up this success, he entered Snicker's
Gap, Virginia, still driving the enemy. A column
of their infantry advanced to retake it, but the fire
of the guns of Hancock rapidly dispersed them.

These reconnoissances discovered the whereabouts of the enemy, and prepared the way for the part which Hancock subsequently took in the battle of Fredericksburg. Ever on the alert, ever prompt at the call for action, he was in **every** part of the field occupied by his division, cheering **and** animating the **men** by his gallant bearing.

The passage across the Rappahannock was **made** by General BURNSIDE, then in chief command, under the greatest local disadvantages. Deceived by a feint of the enemy, who had purposely withdrawn a part of his force in front, apparently leaving his defences unprotected, Burnside threw his men over the river, only to be drawn before the batteries on the hills beyond Fredericksburg, from which the most deadly and continuous fire was poured into our unprotected ranks. It was placing them in the bottom of a great basin of land, to be fired upon by the shielded guns on the commanding ridges above. The crossing was hardly accomplished ere the hidden reserves of the enemy were brought rapidly to the front, and massed on our extended lines with terrific slaughter. The Union troops were swept down before the long files of protected batteries, like grass before the scythe of the mower.

The crests in the rear were reached by an ascending

advance that had to be fought, every inch of the way, in the face of a galling fire. The country and entrenchments beyond were nearly hidden by a dense fog, rendered more impenetrable by the clouds of smoke, belching from well-worked guns, that hung like a pall on the fortified hills. Every step was made by the men in uncertainty as to the numbers and positions of the enemy. It was only known Lee was before them, and that he was prepared at all points for assault or attack. Our own lines were more or less detached, being sent forward in separate bodies, whose means of communication were imperfect at the base, and liable to be fatally interrupted. If the enemy could have been outflanked and reached by means of an attack in the rear, the position would have been widely different, and the result, no doubt, equally so. The attack on our part was all that could be expected of brave men. It was steady, vigorous, dashing; but the exposure was too great for success. By the contingencies of the fog and our delay in throwing over the bridges, the enemy had ample time to mass his forces, to complete his defences, to bring up his reserves, and to place his batteries in such positions that they could sweep everything before them.

During the two days in which the Union army

stood in order of battle before Fredericksburg, advancing to the very front, and into the flash, and heat, and iron deluge of the ever-ceaseless fire, the courage of the men was admirable. Their stand was one of the boldest ever taken by any army; and bravely they maintained it to the last. The courage with which that contest was so long maintained against a numerous army strongly entrenched, the skill and strategy with which our troops were crossed and recrossed, in the face of the sweeping fire of the enemy, will ever reflect credit on the Army of the Potomac.

The course of General Hancock on that occasion exhibits his prudence as well as valor in a most striking light. He is generally associated, as he well deserves to be, with dashing deeds of brilliant valor but his course at Fredericksburg, as at other points, proves his caution to be equal to his courage. No officer is more careful than he of the lives of his men. He regards, as he should, these enlisted fellow-citizens as committed to his care, and that he is responsible that their lives shall not be thrown away. When, therefore, the whole army crossed the Rappahannock and drew up in order of battle before the entrenched legions of Lee, the first movement of Hancock was to halt as many of his troops as he could command in a sheltered valley. Here he gave them an oppor-

tunity, as a strict tactician, to pause, survey the field,
and prepare for the deadly onset. The arms were
stacked, and the men bivouacked for several hours.
They needed the rest. They fought all the better
for being granted it by the General.

The instant the time for decided action arrived, the
division of Hancock was advancing. He moved forward close to the river, and remained in that position
all night. In less than two hours from the time his
troops were in motion the head of the column had
crossed the river. When it reached the post assigned
it, directly in front of the enemy, the men were ankle-
deep in mud. It was toward the beginning of winter, and the chilly winds were sweeping through the
valley of the Rappahannock. But so perfect was the
discipline of Hancock, that, while camp-fires were
forbidden, the wet and cold ranks maintained their
positions in the line. Together officers and men,
with Hancock at their head, laid down on the wet
and frosty ground, with no pillow but the muddy
earth and no covering but the cloudy sky of a December night. With a fortitude and equanimity of
which history furnishes but few parallels, these heroic
men bore the privations of that dismal scene, planting
their colors in the darkness, and resolving to stand
by them to the last through every trying hour.

The battle began with the rising of the sun of the following morning. As soon as the division advanced, Hancock ordered skirmishers to be thrown out on the left flank, the column still advancing under a continuous fire of shot and shell. Regiment after regiment coming up and deploying in line of battle drew down a sweeping fire from the hidden foe. But our force remained at the front, and continued so, during the action. Every attempt that was made by the enemy to break through Hancock's line was immediately repulsed. The men halted on the march through the upper parts of the city only to form more perfect lines of battle, and do the more execution in the attack. His voice was heard above the roar of conflict, calling on the men who survived:

"Close up, men! Steady! Close up! Forward!"

In the midst of the fearful scenes of carnage that followed, the care of Hancock for the hospitals, and those wounded who could not reach them, showed the character of the man. The buildings selected for hospital service were watched over with tender care, and as safely guarded as the exciting circumstances of the moment would permit. While wounded himself, and remaining in the heat of the battle, he was constantly allowing sufferers to retire from the field and recross the river. But every permission of this kind was coupled with the firm command that every man whose wounds would admit of it, must return to the fight. Hundreds of his division, by his good management, were recruited and re-engaged in the action in this way. His troops fought well to the close, and were brought off in good order.

Such was Hancock at Fredericksburg.

16

CHAPTER XX.

IF the battle of Chancellorsville, Virginia, is to be judged by its immediate results, it was disastrous to the Union arms. If it is to be judged by its ultimate effects on the American army and people, it was a success to the Union cause. It was a fearfully bloody battle; in some respects one of the most so ever fought by any people, in any age.

The enemy had temporarily succeeded in the Napoleonic movement of massing large bodies of his troops in the centre of our most exposed position. He did not conquer us; he could not justly claim a victory; but he had, for a time, weakened a part of our power for offensive warfare.

This battle was fought in the first week of May 1863. The country in which it occurred is nearly

(182)

all wild and unfrequented. Parts of it are still a
dense, unbroken wilderness. The army of the Union
was commanded by General Hooker; that of Disunion by General Lee. The advance made by our
forces was among the tangled forests and dark jungles of the dismal wastes of Stafford. In some places
they were completely surrounded by hidden foes, who
peered upon them unseen from behind dark thickets,
and fired at their uncovered columns from their desolate refuges among the munitions of rocks.

Never was a country more capable in itself of being defended; never was one more difficult to overcome. It was like a woody Sebastopol in the wilds
of Virginia; an inland Gibraltar of the West.

The Union troops moved into these environed fast-
nesses, that bristled with hostile bayonets in every
thick-set wood, and frowned with heavy artillery in
every rocky pass. Their march was taken up at an
early hour in the morning, and by seven o'clock the
army was well massed in the outskirts of that gloomy
battle-field.

On the 2d of May General Hancock, then in command of a division, posted his men in the most
guarded manner. Surprises and ambuscades were to
be looked for, on every hand. The skirmishers were
thrown out by him in all directions, and abattis and

rifle-pits placed in front. The whole of his line was on the edge of a deep, dark wood, where it remained in battle array during the whole of that night.

Early in the morning of the following day the division moved forward. The attack on the enemy immediately began. Notwithstanding their protection in the woods, they were driven out of them, then from their rifle-pits, then along the rude plank road that lay beyond. A large column, massed in the distance, seeing the retreat, rushed backward with speed, and, for a time, fairly fled out of sight in the jungles. Rifle-pits were constructed rapidly along the enemy's lines, and skirmishing was kept up by Hancock, at a distance of only a few hundred yards in front of our works on the extreme right.

At ten o'clock that morning, the skirmish line extended some distance down the Fredericksburg road, directly fronting and close to the hidden position of the rebels. They had opened a brisk fire on our lines, at this point, on a previous occasion, keeping up their infantry volleys for four successive hours; but our resistance had been so general and so firm, it gradually slackened off, and then died away. Every attempt to break our lines had proved futile. Volley had been met by volley; battery by battery; our men growing more energetic and determined at each assault, until the rebels were satisfied they could not move us from our position, and sullenly withdrew. They did not yell once.

These men were in the immediate command of Hancock. He led them in person, placed them in the field under his own eye, and remained to take part in every engagement. His breastworks were well constructed as an offset to sudden assaults from the coverts of the woods, while his skirmishers, in rifle-pits, were well posted to prevent surprises. The men behaved well. Every attempt to enfilade them was promply met and repulsed, and every savage assault to capture our colors was hurled back in defeat. Much credit is due to the management of the Union batteries, on all these occasions.

A part of the way to the battle-field had to be pursued in open boats, where the navigation was tedious, and the line of march everywhere exposed to the wily foe. Arrived on the ground, our men took their positions with a coolness and courage worthy of the highest praise. They knew not the number of their secreted enemy; they could only tell by the rattling rifles and roaring cannon that they were near, and in strong force. Dashing on toward them in and through the forests, our men repeatedly captured their earthworks, and conclusively proved to them

16*

and the world what we could do, with anything like equal numbers and a fair field.

Hooker, Meade, Reynolds, Couch, Howard, Birney, Slocum and Sickles were **active in** this **engagement,** and were remarkable for the promptness **with which** their plans were carried out, even against the fearful odds that opposed them. In the position he occupied, **Hancock's part was not** neglected. His troops were **among the most valiant** and successful of any in **that bloody battle.**

In the height of the closing scenes of **this** terrible drama of carnage, the division was **ordered to** strike **directly across the front of an advancing column of** hostiles. **This column** came sweeping furiously **on,** with its famous battle yell, almost demoniac in **its** character, in the shape of one of **N**apoleon's wedges of war. **The design was** to thrust **it, with the** utmost **violence, in** the centre **of the Union lines favorably situated for** the **purpose. At this moment Hancock** dashed **directly across the field, in the face of the ad-vancing enemy, striking their iron** wedge with great **force at the designated point,** staggering its momen-tum, **laying** many **of them dead in** their impetuous march, **and breaking the effect of the** intended blow. In half an **hour** from **the time** Hancock struck the yelling **column,** it was in flight from the field.

The final result of Chancellorsville was a bitter disappointment to the enemy. They were not only foiled, disconcerted, cheated of their longed-for prey, but they found they had met a foe, even in the underbrush and rocky ravines, the briery wilds and lurking darkness of those dim woods, fully equal to their steel. Lee discovered, to his cost, that he might slaughter us from behind his ambuscades; he might entangle us in the forests and through the winding by-paths with which he was familiar; but he could not and did not conquer us in a hand-to-hand fight. The passage of our army across the river in the face of imminent danger, is admitted by the Southern authorities to have been well done; and the recrossing, with a furious enemy close in the rear, was as masterly a piece of military strategy as was ever performed.

The enemy lost in this battle five thousand prisoners, fifteen stands of colors, seven pieces of artillery, nine thousand wounded, and a large amount of commissary stores and munitions of war.

By the 6th of June our army was safely across the river, at Falmouth. In looking back from this point over the field, we find that the division of General Hancock, in its imminent position on the extreme left, did all that brave men, well led, could have done.

Their losses were among the severest of that scene of terrible carnage. He not only held his own, in the very front of the fight, but drove the enemy, at all points. No men, on any field of battle, could have been handled better than his were. His praise was on every tongue; and the despatches of those in superior command speak of his deeds with the highest satisfaction.

It was immediately after this engagement that President LINCOLN, as Commander-in-chief, assigned General HANCOCK to the command of his favorite Second Corps in the Army of the United States

The South now initiated new and yet bolder designs for the destruction of a Union that had never done them wrong; for the overthrow of a constitution that had ever provided ample protection for all their rights. They massed their scattered forces anew, and prepared for a raid further north — the domineering onset and fitting conclusion of which we now proceed to describe.

CHAPTER XXI.

The Invasion of Pennsylvania and Maryland—The Famous Heights of Gettysburg—"The Army of the Potomac" Confronts Lee's, and Prepares for Battle.

THE invasion of the States of Maryland and Pennsylvania, in the year 1863, by the large and picked force under gallant General Robert Edward Lee, must always occupy a conspicuous place in the history of the great American Rebellion. In some respects it may be regarded as the turning-point in the war. By a series of fortuitous circumstances the Southrons had won several important victories. Flushed with these temporary successes, pressed for immediate supplies by the brilliant conquests won over their western bases by General Grant and Commodore Foote, they turned, like hungry vultures in quest of fresh prey, on the tempting and comparatively unguarded lines of the more Northern border States. The successful invasion of these States would not only redeem what they had already lost, and

what they had serious premonitions of losing, at the
South and West, but it would supply them with
needed stores from the teeming valleys and fertile
plains and rich mountain mines of the central region
of the country; it would force beneath their tram-
pling feet, and yield to their clutching hands, eager
for the prize of victory, the stores and shipping, the
factories and dwellings of the populous cities of the
Union. What a splendid prize for the ambitious
Southron! With what fond delight the hearts of
the Confederacy gloated over the glorious prospect
that opened before them!

It was known to the invaders that large bodies of
the defenders of the Union had returned to their
homes, their terms of service having expired. They
entertained the belief that the force they might meet
would be composed exclusively of the undisciplined
yeomanry of the regions first to be ravaged, who,
they imagined, would fall an easy prey to their advancing veteran legions. They anticipated, and not
without reason, that many sympathizers in their
open and avowed purposes would hasten to meet
them, with open arms, as they crossed the border. In
the Atlantic cities, they knew, were large numbers
of aliens, sworn subjects of foreign monarchs, who
had sought our country only to witness or hasten its

dismemberment; who were ready to join, at a moment's warning, with anybody and everybody who would be most certain to secure its destruction as a Republic. These foreigners were led by one of the master military spirits of the age, who had gained his warlike knowledge in a national academy, and now turned that experience against the very parent of it. Brave but equally misguided men were with him in subordinate capacities, all of whom should have been inspired by nobler ambitions, since all owed equal fealty to the nation they were striving against so earnestly and so bitterly. One had occupied a seat in the Congress of the nation; and all of them, from the highest to the lowest in rank, who had shared the instructions of our national military schools, had been in part sustained there from the tributes paid for their education by the people of the commonwealths they were at that moment aiming to destroy. The United States cadets in that invading force were, at the instant of invasion, under the most solemn oaths to defend those States against all comers; to uphold the flag whose folds waved over them when they drank at the fountain of knowledge it guarded, and whose familiar stripes and stars now fluttered so reproachfully and yet so gallantly before their eyes, from the Union lines in front.

In spite of all this, in spite of the uncalled-for

nature of the rebellion, in spite of the fact that a
considerable proportion of the citizens about to be
outraged on the Pennsylvania line, and through the
contiguous region, were non-combatants, in principle
and practice, as their fathers had been before them,
on came the ruthless invaders. If, unlike the bar-
baric Assyrian, their cohorts were not

"gleaming with purple and gold,"

they were like him in coming

"as a wolf on the fold."

Early in June, 1863, this rampant force of invaders, followed by a long train of plunder wagons,
came sweeping down from the seat of war in Virginia to the doomed States of Pennsylvania and Maryland. The chief schemers in Richmond, in conjunction with their allies in the invading army and among
their fellow Confederates at the North, had blatantly
given out that the invasion, this time, was to be a
success. The free States were to be conquered; the
capital of the nation was to be taken and held. They
knew the country was comparatively unprepared for
it. They were as well aware as we could be that our
most reliable troops were nearly all employed on a
distant and dangerous service. They numbered,
when the invasion commenced,—they did not number quite so many when it ended,—an effective force

of 90,000 infantry, 10,000 cavalry, over 4,000 artil-lery,—an aggregate of 105,000 men, of all arms.

On the 28th of June, the Confederates, desperately determined to strike a heavy blow, formed their angry line of battle on the heights and among the passes around the town of Gettysburg. This now memora-ble place is situated on elevated ground, in the midst of a fertile farming country. It is one hundred and fourteen miles west of Philadelphia, and thirty-six south of Harrisburg, the capital of Pennsylvania. Its location gives it a peculiar importance. It stands like an interior gateway between the North and South. Its college and seminary, its churches, newspapers, banks, and manufacturing establishments, award it a controlling influence through much of the region where it stands. It contained a population of nearly 5,000.

The rapid and near approach of the enemy soon established the fact that this handsome and retired yet unfortified Pennsylvania borough was to be the theatre of a sanguinary fight. In the sudden emer-gency the most that could be done was to gather hastily such of the militia of the country as might be thrown forward to the field. This vast disparity between the character of the threatened attack and the means at hand for defence was startling to all

17   N

concerned. To the assailant it promised an early victory; to the assailed a fearful defeat. It is no wonder that alarm spread on every hand among the borderers. Unprotected families and property demanded the first care of the citizens, ere they could arm and prepare to march, all untried as they were, to meet the invaders. The only reliable hope for confronting and beating back the columns of Lee was in the Army of the Potomac; and that army, at the critical juncture of the first approach of the enemy, was supposed to be at a comparatively great distance. It was not until that noble host, then in command of General Hooker, and at the time of the action led by General Meade, came on the ground, that the work of defence assumed a definite shape.

The appearance of Meade was, to a large portion of the hostiles, like the coming of Banquo's ghost to Macbeth. Lee, of course, supposed that Hooker would pursue him; but he had not calculated on the alacrity with which our Potomac veterans flew to the rescue of the perilled border of the Susquehanna. He thought only of Fredericksburg and Chancellorsville. He had not heard, then, from Gettysburg or Vicksburg. As his bold troops moved down to the site of the battle and began to deploy in action, where they expected and hoped only to meet the raw volunteers, hurriedly brought against them, it was with ill-disguised astonishment they gazed on the dust-covered lines of veterans directly in front.

"'The Army of the Potomac!'" "The Army of the Potomac!" passed, in gasping tones, along the whole ranks.

" Ah! *they* are here!"

That splendid army was indeed there; and right bravely did it prove its presence through every day and hour of the succeeding battle.

The limits of our volume, and the space necessarily occupied by other topics of interest to the general reader, will not allow us to narrate all the scenes we should be happy to place in these pages connected with this signal action. It began on the morning of the 1st and closed on the evening of the 3d of July— the salvos of its glorious victory, in chorus with those of Vicksburg, appropriately ushering in the natal day of our nation's independence.

It is impossible, in this work, to do the justice they so richly deserve to all the parties who distinguished themselves on this memorable field. Meade, Reynolds, Sedgwick, Hancock, Slocum, Butterfield, Doubleday, Pleasanton, Couch, Gibbon, Graham, Sickles, Warren, and a host of others, are all worthy of honorable mention. The name of Reynolds deserves especial remembrance; for it was he who was first to withstand the surging horde as it swept over the heights; it was he who gave the enemy his first decided check; and he was the first general officer who fell on the Union side. All honor to his memory —and to that of the heroes who fell around him on that and succeeding days, and whose patriot dust has been so well enshrined in the National Cemetery at Gettysburg.

> The lightnings may flash, the loud thunders rattle,
>   They see not, they hear not, they're free from all pain;
> They sleep their last sleep, they have fought their last battle,
>   No sound shall awake them to glory again.

CHAPTER XXII.

The Furious Fight of Gettysburg — General Hancock, with the Second Army Corps, in the Centre of the Battle — Colonel Randall and the Gallant Thirteenth Vermont — "Colonel, can you take that Battery?" "I can, Sir!" — Hancock Severely Wounded.

THE position of General HANCOCK, in command of the Second Army Corps, was near the centre of the most active part of the field of battle. His right was near the Emmitsburg road, and his left extended toward the granite spur of Round Top. It was emphatically a post of honor, for the headquarters of the commanding General were immediately in his rear. The lines of Longstreet, under Hood, McLaw, Pickett, Garnett, and Anderson, were directly in front. Barksdale, one of the most active of the Southern generals, was in advance. Cemetery Hill — now so appropriately occupied as the site of the great National Cemetery of our Union heroes — was

17* (197)

on his right flank, beyond which was the rebel corps of Ewell, under Early and Rhodes. In the rear was a large body of cavalry, commanded by the energetic Generals Wade Hampton, W. H. F. Lee, and Jenkins, flanked by several batteries of the enemy. The brigade of Walker—formerly Stonewall Jackson's—extended, as the battle advanced, close to the rear, in front of the Twelfth Union Corps, under Slocum, aided by Geary, Wadsworth, and Steinwehr. Sedgwick, with the Sixth Corps, was on Hancock's immediate left wing, and Doubleday, with his splendid battery, on the right.

The plan of the field, prepared by Elliott, under the direction of DAVID WILLS, Esq., of Gettysburg, by authority of Governor CURTIN, contains a minute and correct sketch of every position occupied by both the contending armies, during the whole of the three days. The subsequent labors of Mr. Wills, in organizing and completing the measures that have resulted in the establishment of the National Union Cemetery, are well worthy of the high praise that is so generally bestowed upon them.

On the arrival of General HANCOCK the Union troops, composing the second division of the Eleventh Corps, under General Steinwehr, had been ordered by Major General Howard to occupy the commanding eminence of Cemetery Hill. At this time **Han-cock** was in command of the entire field, having been temporarily assigned to the post by General Meade, who had not then reached the lines. He at once stationed the troops so as to be prepared for any sudden assault the enemy might make. It was a critical moment. Our men were arriving rapidly, yet worn down with the fatigue of long and forced marches. But their valor was fully equal to the emergency. They repulsed the attack of the enemy, and, maintaining their strong position, were soon reinforced by the arrival of the Twelfth Corps, under Slocum, and a part of the Third, under Sickles.

The death of Reynolds, in the opening of the fight, while bravely leading on the old First Corps, checking the advance of the rested columns of the rebels thrown against the fatigued and smaller ranks of the Union, had cast a gloom over the scenes which closed the first day's battle. Early on the morning of the 2d of July, the Commander-in-chief arrived on the ground. He was pleased to recognize and approve the dispositions made by Generals Hancock and Howard, in the sudden emergencies of the hour. The positions taken by these Generals, and those of their associates in command, were regarded as favorable, and preparations were immediately made for a vigor-

ous attack on the enemy. The whole Union army
was at once concentrated at Gettysburg. By seven
o'clock in the morning of that day, the Second Corps,
in the immediate command of Hancock, was posted
at the front. The distance between him and the foe,
at this moment, was but little over a mile.

"The click of hammers closing rivets up,"

the clangor of trumpets, the roll of drums, the tramp
of armed men marching and countermarching, on
both sides, could be distinctly heard in the opposing
camps. The pickets of Union and disunion looked
each other in the face; and the flags of liberty and
slavery flapped defiance at each other. The great
battle was at hand.

It is but the just tribute of truth to history that
the fact be recorded here, that the position of General
Hancock on that memorable field, at that thrilling
moment, was one of paramount importance. The
arrival of the Second Corps, followed by the Fifth
and Sixth, was most opportune. But for that arrival,
it would seem that the day must have gone against
us. It checked the eager advance of the enemy,
gave our troops time for much needed rest, and rendered the numbers of the contending forces more
nearly equal.

At the hour of four o'clock in the afternoon of the

2d of July, the battle **was** resumed, **by the** opening
of the heavy batteries on our nearest lines. General
Sickles was wounded, and his command forced back.
At this perilous juncture Hancock, surrounded by
his associates, **came to the rescue. The enemy was
in turn driven from the field, and our success** ren-
**dered complete.   Every desperate attempt of the
enemy to** break our lines, **and, especially, to** possess
themselves of our ammunition and supply trains, was
bravely met and nobly overcome.

The morning of the third day broke over the field.
At early dawn our artillery opened fire, which con-
**tinued several hours ; but near midday no movement
whatever was made on either side.   At this hour,
following a silence more awful in such a spot than
all the thunders of battle, the rebel batteries directed
a** deadly **fire against the Corps of Hancock.   Lee
had vainly imagined this to be his most favored** point
of attack.   Dashing from behind the woods of Ceme-
tery Ridge, the flower of that part **of the** enemy's
force swept onward to the very muzzles of Hancock's
**guns.   His well-tried Corps, aided by Doubleday and
Stannard, met the** shock with all **their wonted coolness and courage, and hurled the foe back in con
fusion.**

It was at this moment the scene occurred **of which**

our artist has given the reader the graphic illustration that accompanies these pages. The Thirteenth Vermont regiment, **Colonel Randall,** was in a position to render assistance to one **of our endangered batteries.** General Doubleday, riding **rapidly up, drew off** a portion of **the** command. They quickly **obeyed his** summons, and rendered such support **to the artillery that the guns** were not only saved but enabled **to continue to supply** effective service. The remainder of **the regiment was in line of** battle, ready for **action,** at **a moment's warning, when a fresh battery opened in a new and powerful position, doing us considerable damage.**

General Hancock, perceiving the crisis **at a** glance, galloped to **the Vermonters,** through repeated showers of shot and shell from the enemy, **and** saluting and addressing Randall, **as he** pointed with **his sword to the** rebels **and** their guns, **enquired:**

"Colonel! can you take **that battery?"**

The Colonel lifted his cap, returning the salute, **and quickly replied:**

"I can, General!"

In a moment more came **the Colonel's order:**

"Thirteenth **Vermont! Forward!** Double-quick!"

The Green **Mountaineers** wheeled **at** the word, and, **with** fixed bayonets, **rushed on the** batteries **of** the

enemy. Colonel Randall, a gentleman somewhat
advanced in years, kept his cap waving in his hand,
his few remaining locks streaming in the wind,
as he rushed in front, cheering, at the top of his
voice:

"Forward! men! forward!"

Hancock was near them as they dashed on to within
firing distance of the battery, and poured among the
enemy ten volleys from their well-aimed rifles.

"Charge!" cried Randall, his tones clear and strong
above the roar of the Confederate cannon.

"Come on, boys! Now or never!"

Instantly the men sprang toward the gunners,
every bayonet fixed, and doing its work. They
rushed over the belching mouths of the guns, leaped
along the caissons, and, with a mountain shout, drove
the enemy from the hill, and brought off every piece
to the Union rear.

This gallant deed was scarcely achieved, ere General Hancock rode along the lines again, and enquired:

"What regiment is this?"

"The Thirteenth Vermont, sir," answered Colonel
Randall, still holding his cap in his hand.

"You have done yourselves great honor," continued Hancock. "The whole army will render you
thanks."

It was not long after this brilliant achievement that the General was wounded. He was laid bleeding on the grass, surrounded by anxious groups of officers and men. The breastworks of the enemy were but a short distance off, and the battle was still raging.

"Shall we not carry you to the rear, General?" enquired Colonel Vesey, who was near him.

"No, I thank you, Colonel," said Hancock, waving his hand gracefully, in the midst of his pain, calmly adding:

"Attend to your commands, gentlemen; I will take care of myself."

In connection with a preceding charge on Hancock's Corps occurred the death of the brave General Barksdale. Our forces had been pushed forward to meet the enemy, who were dashing furiously on our lines. After the enemy had been repulsed, some captured prisoners informed Colonel Vesey, then in command of the captors, that their General had fallen, and was lying in front, on the ground. The Colonel immediately advanced his line of skirmishers until they came to the place designated. There they found the dying General, stretched on the grass, weltering in his blood and writhing in agony. They raised him up carefully and carried him to the rear of our lines. He was speechless, and died about two hours after.

By the afternoon of **Friday, July 3d,** the storm of the battle had ended. The retreat of the enemy began immediately after his discomfiture. He literally stood not upon the order of going, but went — and that so rapidly, that he left nearly **eight thousand** prisoners, and sick and wounded, in our hands. The aggregate loss **of Lee was thirty-seven** thousand men — among whom were seven Generals killed in the battle, and **six** wounded. He lost in prisoners, including the wounded, thirteen thousand six hundred and twenty-one. Of trophies there were three guns, forty-one colors, and of small arms twenty-four thousand nine hundred and seventy eight.

Such was the battle of Gettysburg. Of the part taken in it, from its beginning to its close, by General Hancock, his friends may well cherish a grateful remembrance. The influence of this victory over the invaders of his native State will always be felt, and the gallant deeds of her son be cherished, not only through Pennsylvania, but in all the land.

During the severest part of the third day's battle, there was a period when the troops in command of General Birney were in imminent peril. A large force of the enemy, sweeping furiously down from

18

the contiguous hills, had nearly environed him in their deadly embrace. General Hancock, perceiving the danger from his centre, placed himself at the head of a picked division, and dashed rapidly forward to the scene. His gallant approach was noticed by all, and those who were nearest to him among the participants in the sanguinary struggle, felt sure that some important and brilliant movement was in hand.

Approaching the disordered lines, he bowed politely to the commander, and said:

"General Birney! you are nearly surrounded by the enemy."

"I know it, General Hancock," replied Birney; "I am doing my best against a superior force."

"I have brought you these reinforcements," continued Hancock, waving his hand toward the rapidly coming troops.

"You will place them, at your discretion, General Birney; and I will hold you responsible for their lives. General Willard, in immediate command, will fight the men."

The balls of the infuriate enemy, who had been bitterly disappointed at the reception given him by the lines of Hancock, were flying through the air like a driving storm of hail. General Hancock coolly maintained his seat on horseback, and watched, for a few moments, the dispositions made of the reinforcements he had so opportunely brought.

Bowing gracefully to the parting salute of the Generals and others in command, he turned the head of his horse toward another part of the hotly-contested field. At that moment a ball passed near him, and struck directly in the forehead of General Willard, who fell dead at his feet. The look of Hancock at that thrilling instant is indescribable. He gazed silently on his fallen and gallant companion in arms, and then glanced his searching eye to note its effects on the men. Every man was at his post, fighting bravely still, as the new commander stepped forward to the vacant place. Again he waved his hand as a signal of adieu to the heroic troops who were standing up so bravely for the old flag, and dashed onward toward the next post of duty and danger. As the two Generals, Hancock and Birney, rode rapidly along, reviewing the lines, giving orders and words of encouragement, the brave fellows who lay wounded in their path would raise themselves up from the crimsoned grass, and answer with cheers:

"General! we're driving them! Hurra!"

Regardless of their own sufferings, they rejoiced thus in the triumph of our country, some of them amid the very agonies of death.

"It was more than we could bear," said General Birney, relating the scene, as he remembered how his own tears, and those of the dashing Hancock, fell among those dying heroes.

> "What gem hath dropped and sparkles o'er his chain?
> The tear most sacred shed for others' pain;
> That starts at once, bright, pure, from pity's mine,
> Already polished by the hand divine."

It is no wonder to us, when we become familiar with such incidents as these in the career of General Hancock, that he should be so dear to the hearts of his men. When the roar of battle was the loudest, he was sure to be present, if in his power to be. Where his gallant soldiers fell the fastest, he was always certain to be near. The humblest man in the ranks never passed unnoticed. His manly, commanding presence acted like a charm wherever seen, and his well-chosen words passed like an electric force from rank to rank.

CHAPTER XXIII.

THE brief sojourn of General HANCOCK with his
parents, in Norristown, during a part of the
summer of 1863, was as agreeable as the state of his
severe wound would permit. On his reaching home
from the battle-field of Gettysburg, the citizens
flocked around to pay him their respects. His position in the railway car, where he was placed at length
on a stretcher laid over the backs of the seats, drew
to his side many sympathizing friends, who united
to testify their warm admiration of his character.
Arrived at the station, in Norristown, he was met by
a detachment of the Invalid Guards, who tenderly
placed him on their shoulders, and bore him through
the streets. The inhabitants along the route, as may
well be supposed, were deeply moved at the sight.

18*   O   (209)

Not knowing the extent of his wounds, and seeing him thus prostrate in the hands of soldiers, marching with a steady step on the side-walks, they watched the scene with peculiar interest. The boy of other days had now come as a Major General of the Army of the United States, bearing on his person a wound that attested the love he bore his native land. The door-ways and windows of the silent route were crowded with anxious faces, down some of which coursed the tears of sympathy.

What a change to WINFIELD from the days of his youth! How thickly the thoughts of boyhood, of school, of playmates and familiar scenes, crowded the mind of the gallant soldier! With what tender welcomes he was greeted at the threshold of the family mansion, and with what affectionate care he was borne to his quarters under the parental roof! Gentle assiduities, found only within the hallowed precincts of home, smoothed his couch of pain, and ministered to him there. Here let us draw the curtain, and leave him to repose.

His recovery was gradual, but sure. In a short time his active energies were again at work. His mind soon reverted from that sick-room, from his own physical sufferings, to the condition of his country, and his duties in the service. As he gained in strength, his fellow-citizens waited upon him, as opportunity offered, and testimonials of personal friendship were added to those of a public character. His fellow townsmen took immediate steps to testify their appreciation of his signal services. At the instigation of several of his **youthful companions,** and **others,** under **the direction, principally, of B. C. CHAIN, Esq., a service** of **gold and silver plate was** prepared, and subsequently presented to **him.** The set consists of nine pieces, elegantly embossed, and bears the following inscription:

TO

MAJOR GENERAL **WINFIELD SCOTT HANCOCK.**

FROM

CITIZENS OF HIS BIRTH-PLACE,

NORRISTOWN,

MONTGOMERY COUNTY, PENNSYLVANIA.

July 4th,

1864.

Crowning the inscription **on** each piece is the badge **of** the Second Corps—the Trefoil, or three-leaved clover—a peculiar plant, called by some the 'none-such,' indicative of rare honor, and a choice ornament in **the** architecture of the temple of fame.

The cost of this beautiful and appropriate testimonial **was** sixteen **hundred** dollars. Its value to **the**

recipient cannot be computed in silver **or** gold.   It **was** a pleasant reminder to him of the days spent as a boy in Norristown, and a proof, more precious than jewels, that his playmates had not forgotten them, nor the manly part he took in their youthful scenes. They had ever regarded him as a leader among **them;** **and this** valuable memorial was a renewed assurance **that they now held him** worthy to be a commander **in the patriot army of the** nation.

The moment the state of his health would permit, he resumed his labors for his country.   He had a good right to feel that the wound he bore was an honorable one; that he had won it bravely in a noble cause.   Every view taken of the part he bore in the battle **that caused it,** abundantly **confirms** this statement.

In reviewing the field **of Gettysburg,** the countrymen of Hancock must ever **be impressed with** the great value of his **services on that occasion.   On the** fall of the lamented REYNOLDS, HANCOCK had proceeded at once to Gettysburg, and assumed command of the three Army Corps then in that vicinity — the First, Third and Eleventh.   It had been contemplated to give the enemy battle at a place called Pipe creek; but, on arriving **on the ground,** Hancock was convinced that Gettysburg **was a much** better place for an engagement. The disposition of the whole army was made at that point, therefore, by his immediate direction. When he reached the field of action, at two o'clock in the afternoon of the first day, everything was in confusion. Our troops were prematurely retreating in all directions. He immediately put forth his utmost exertions; and, being well seconded by his staff, succeeded in restoring order, and posted the troops at those advantageous points which they continued to occupy during the fight, and at which they won the victory. Their positions near the Cemetery, connecting the lines with Culp's Hills and along the commanding ridges, to the base of Round Top, were the strongest that could be assumed by our side; and all of them were made by order of General Hancock. It was on this line that the crowning battle of Gettysburg was fought and won.

The reports of these positions were made in full detail by Hancock to General MEADE, when he came on the ground. Not one of them was materially changed, all through the succeeding battles. Their great advantages were at once admitted, and the success which attended them is a conclusive proof of the military skill of Hancock.

His subsequent part in the action of the left centre is well known to all. The repulse of the fierce

assault at **that point** was the **key** note of the day.
Victorious there, against the most desperate onslaughts
of the picked legions of Lee, **he** was prompt **to send,**
unasked, the support that was needed **in** other **direc-**
tions. It was while engaged **in a splendid** repulse
of the enemy, aiding the weakened columns **of the**
right wing against the fierce main attack, that he fell
seriously wounded. From this **spot** he was borne
from the field, when the victory was pronounced **com-**
plete, to his Norristown home.

The **wound was of such a nature as to compel him**
to employ an amanuensis, whom he directed **to write**
to his family and parents. Under the **kind** care he
received **he recovered** sufficiently **to leave Norristown**
for West Point. How natural **the transition!** On his
way thither, stopping **at the** Fifth Avenue **Hotel, in**
New York, he writes home, **under date of** September
15, 1863, requesting that **certain military documents**
should be arranged **and forwarded, in order that he**
might hasten his return to the field.

The **receptions that had** greeted **him in his native**
county, **in Philadelphia, and other places, were** followed **up in the Metropolitan City.** Public atten-
tions welcomed **him, on every side.** We can well
understand **how** cordial must **have** been his greeting
at old **West Point. What a** contrast was there between

his former and present sojourns in that national military school! His fellow cadets were all gone; some of the professors had followed them; but the scenes of other days came freshly back upon him, and he lived again in the haunts and studies of the past.

As soon as possible he reached his wife and children at 'Longwood,' near St. Louis, Missouri. Writing to his father from that city, under date of October 12th, '63, he says:

"I threw aside my crutches a few days after my arrival, and now walk with a cane. I am improving, but do not yet walk without a little 'roll.' My wound is still unhealed, though the doctors say it is closing rapidly. I find some uneasiness in sitting long on a chair, and cannot yet ride. The bone appears to be injured, and may give me trouble for a long time. I hope, however, I may be well enough in two weeks to join my Corps.

I am busy in trimming up the forest trees in the lawn of 'Longwood,' which covers nearly eleven acres. I know it is not the best time; but still it will do.

Alice and the children send their best love to you and mother.

Please give my best love to mother, and I remain, as ever,

Your affectionate Son,

WINFIELD S. HANCOCK."

"To B. F. Hancock, Esq.,

Norristown, Pa."

Every true parent in the land must prize such epistolary expressions as these from such a man as General Hancock. They show him as he really is.

Every youth, too, should learn a lesson from them, never to be forgotten.

The people of St. Louis united with their fellow-citizens elsewhere to do him honor. We shall speak in another part of this volume of the tribute they paid to his valor as a soldier and his worth as a man, in the elegant sword presented to him as a public testimonial from the Western Sanitary Fair in that city.

CHAPTER XXIV.

ON the 15th of December, 1863, Hancock was again ordered to Washington. His Gettysburg wound was not yet healed, but he obeyed the order with alacrity, and immediately reported himself for duty at the War Department.

It was during this period that he was talked of in influential circles for the command of the Army of the Potomac. There is no impropriety in stating that it was at one time seriously contemplated to place him in this position. He, however, did not seek it; neither did his friends seek it for him. On the contrary, he disclaimed all such desire; and the most active of his immediate counsellors were strenuous in their efforts to dissuade him from accepting the command. On all becoming occasions he expressed the opinion that General MEADE was the man

19   (217)

for the post; and that if he were continued in active command and properly supported by the authorities and the country, he would win great victories. Passing results have shown the wisdom as well as magnanimity of General HANCOCK in this matter. He well knew by experience the obstacles in the way to success with that army, at that peculiar juncture; and, therefore, as we have said, he did not seek the appointment, neither did he desire his friends to seek it for him. There is good reason for stating, however, that if General MEADE had made a request to be relieved, General HANCOCK would have relieved him.

He was soon detailed to the responsible work of increasing the ranks of the army, by his personal presence and exertions. Authority was given him to augment his Corps to fifty thousand effective men. His headquarters were established at Harrisburg, the capital of his native State, and he immediately proceeded to the work among his fellow Pennsylvanians. His language and measures on the occasion were well chosen, and to the point, his object being to recruit in all the States represented in the Second Corps.

Addressing the people of Pennsylvania, from his headquarters, at Harrisburg, under date of January, 15, 1864, he says:

"I have come among you as a Pennsylvanian, for the purpose of endeavoring to aid you in stimulating enlistments. This is a matter of interest to all the citizens of the State. I earnestly call upon you all to assist, by the exertion of all the influence in your power, in this important matter.

To adequately reinforce our armies in the field is to insure that the war will not reach your homes. It will be the means of bringing it to a speedy and happy conclusion. It will save the lives of many of our brave soldiers, who would otherwise be lost by the prolongation of the war, and in indecisive battles.

It is only necessary to destroy the rebel armies now in the field, to insure a speedy and permanent peace. Let us all act with that fact in view.

Let it not be said that Pennsylvania, which has already given so many of her sons to this RIGHTEOUS CAUSE, shall now, at the eleventh hour, be behind her sister States in furnishing her quota of the men deemed necessary to end this rebellion. Let it not be that those Pennsylvania regiments, now so depleted, that have won for themselves so much honor in the field, shall pass out of existence, for want of patriotism in the people.

WINFIELD S. HANCOCK,
Major General U. S. Volunteers."

His success in recruiting was equal to the expectations formed. Subsequent events have well attested the efficiency of his measures. Facilities for carrying out his patriotic design were offered him in the cities of New York, Albany, Boston, and other places.

At Philadelphia, in the ensuing month of February, public demonstrations of respect awaited him. The city government passed a series of resolutions, introduced by one of his former playmates at Norristown, then a member of the Councils, JOHN W. EVERMAN, Esq., of which we here present a copy:

Select and Common Councils
of the
CITY OF PHILADELPHIA.

WELCOME

TO

MAJOR GENERAL WINFIELD SCOTT HANCOCK.

Resolved, BY THE SELECT AND COMMON COUNCILS

OF THE

CITY OF PHILADELPHIA,

That the THANKS of the Citizens of Philadelphia are eminently due and are hereby tendered to

MAJOR GENERAL HANCOCK,

for his brilliant services in the cause of the UNION, during the present unholy Rebellion against the authority of the GOVERNMENT AND PEOPLE OF THE UNITED STATES.

Resolved, That the use of Independence Hall be granted to Major General HANCOCK, for the reception of his friends; and in order to afford the Citizens of Philadelphia an opportunity to testify their personal regard for him, and their appreciation of his gallantry and patriotism.

Resolved, That the Mayor of Philadelphia and the Presidents of Councils be requested to carry these resolutions into effect; and that the Clerks of Councils be requested to furnish a copy of the same to General HANCOCK.

ALEX'R J. HARPER,
President of the Common Council.

[CITY SEAL.]

JAMES LYND,
President of the Select Council.

Attest: WM. F. SMALL,
Clerk of Common Council.

Approved February 18th, 1864.

ALEX. HENRY, *Mayor.*

The reception of the General and his friends followed soon after, in Independence Hall. The papers of the day describe the scene as one of the most imposing that ever occurred within the walls of the sacred old Temple of American Liberty.

On the ensuing 22d of February, the anniversary of the birth-day of WASHINGTON, General HANCOCK reviewed the volunteer troops of Philadelphia and vicinity. The parade passed off in the most spirited manner. The appearance of the General on the field, surrounded by a brilliant staff, passing along the line with the troops arranged as if in battle array, was full of excitement, and called forth the loud plaudits of the immense throng of citizens who witnessed the display. Some idea of his presence in action could be formed by the gallant bearing of the General on this popular occasion.

At the close of the review an incident of a personal character occurred, which we narrate here, as in keeping with the man and the scope of our book.

The General had dismounted, at the close of the day, and was about passing up the steps of the La Pierre House, surrounded by the officers who escorted him, when his eye caught that of his early teacher in Norristown, Mr. E. ROBERTS, who was standing, with his daughter, near the entrance to the hotel.

19*

The General paused, and extending his hand to the two friends of his early years, expressed his pleasure at meeting them, and introduced them to the gentlemen present. It was a singular but agreeable meeting between the old teacher and the now distinguished scholar.

"Call and see me at the hotel, Mr. Roberts, when I am more at leisure," said the General. "When I am a little stronger from the effects of my wound, I will return the call."

At the appointed time, the teacher and scholar met again. As Mr. Roberts entered the private room of the General, at the La Pierre, he was lying on his couch, suffering from the fatigue to which the review of the previous day had subjected his wounded limb. But he rose at once to pay the respect due from a good scholar to a good teacher.

"Do not rise, General Hancock," said Mr. Roberts; "I feel, sir, that you are laying me under too much obligation by doing so."

"No, Mr. Roberts," the General replied, "I shall always feel, sir, that I am under obligations to you."

"It is sufficient honor for me, General, to have had you for a scholar."

"No, sir. I feel that my teachers have all honored me. Beside, sir, you are much the older man of the two; and my parents always taught me to reverence grey hairs."

"I did not have grey hairs when you first **knew** me, General."

"True, sir. Our mutual obligations were formed when we were both younger than now. But I cannot omit to use my anatomy now, even if it is impaired. Let me be ever so old, I can never forget my school-teachers. I feel that my experience in life has proved this to be true: as is the teacher, so is the school-boy; as is the school-boy, so is the man."

Other parties calling in, this interesting interview was closed. But not long after the General took his son Russell with him, and called on his old teacher.

"This gentleman, my son," said the General, "is one of the teachers of your father, when, like you, he was a boy. Remember always to respect the teacher of your youth; and, should you live to become a man, you will never regret it."

It is this spirit of the man that stamps the name of HANCOCK with peculiar honor. He was always the same among his soldiers. An officer of the staff of another distinguished General, in alluding to this attribute of Hancock's character, says of him:

"The attachment that he manifests for his brave soldiers is remarkable. While he despises a coward,

if the humblest man in the ranks should be the first
to enter Richmond, as a conqueror, General HANCOCK
would be among the first to do him honor."

Passing from Philadelphia to New York, he was
received in the latter city with much distinction. The
Governor's Room, in the City Hall, was placed at his
disposal, for the reception of his friends, and **every**
measure adopted that could be to aid him in procuring recruits for his Corps. A large number of his
troops were from the Empire State. They were so
much attached to his person, and their acquaintances
at home so participated in the feeling of attachment,
that when he presented himself to the people he was
claimed by them as a New Yorker. This impression
became so common, for a time, that one of the publish-
ers of that city announced a volume on his life, as a
New York General.

Passing to Albany, the capital of the State of New
York, the Legislature paid him an official tribute
of respect for his distinguished services to the
country.

The same honors were bestowed upon him in Boston, the capital of Massachusetts, where the General
Court invited him to their Representative Chamber,
and where the merchants and other citizens waited
upon him at the City Exchange. His agreeable man-

ners, added to his well-known courage and skill in
battle, created the most favorable impressions wherever he went on his tour of duty through New England.   Patriotic applause greeted him at every point,
and a considerable number of fighting recruits flocked
to his standard.

P

Hancock's Campaign with Grant — He is made Major-General of Volunteers — The Fight in the Wilderness — Our Hero again Wounded — Generals Stuart and Johnson, the Prisoners of his Command — Affecting Meeting with Old Companions.

ON the 18th of March, 1864, the General, while still actively engaged in recruiting his Corps, writes to his father from Harrisburg, Pennsylvania:

"I have just received an order from the Secretary of War, to report without delay to him for instructions, prior to rejoining my command in the field. I have but time to notify you of the fact."

Such was the modest announcement of his entrance on that great campaign with Lieutenant General GRANT, in which he has borne his part with so much propriety.

His position at the head of the Second Army Corps was one in which he felt at home. He knew the men, and they knew him. A large proportion of them were citizens of his native Pennsylvania, and had enlisted in the service of the United States under him as their commander. His presence among them

always excited enthusiasm, and his fearless exposures
of his person inspired them to deeds of valor. As
a leader he resembled Murat; but, while he had all
the dash and brilliancy, he displayed the attributes of
a true patriot enlisted in a far better cause than that
of any Marshal of France. His convictions of the
justice of the war for the American Union were firm
and resolute. It was, therefore, with the ardor becoming the great occasion before him, an occasion
on which he felt was staked the very life of the Republic, that he proceeded to the front and resumed
his command.

The army marched from Culpepper Court House,
Virginia, on the 3d of May, HANCOCK leading the
advance. This post of honor was eminently his due.
In all the previous battles in which he was engaged
he had won it by merit on the field. At the sanguinary fight at Fredericksburg, he had proved how wor
thy he was to occupy it by the skill with which he
fought his men. On that occasion, out of five thousand under his command, two thousand fell around
him, killed or wounded, including over one hundred
and fifty commissioned officers. He was much ex
posed on the field, and had three of his Aids wounded
by his side. When the report came in from a flag
of truce sent to the enemy to make arrangements for

the burial of our dead, it was found that the men nearest the earthworks, far in advance of the Union lines, were largely composed of the division of Hancock. No other troops but his, and those of Kimball's brigade, had ventured so close to the face of the foe.

It was immediately after these signal services, as a leader of the advance, that he was nominated by General BURNSIDE as Major General of Volunteers. His appointment to that rank dates from November 29th, 1862.

In the battle of Chancellorsville, where our whole army was so exposed to the hidden and furious onslaughts of the enemy, he occupied the advance of the extreme left wing. Through all the savage assaults made upon him he held his position firmly, and handled his command with such judgment and energy, as to elicit the admiration of all who witnessed his movements.

His position at Antietam and Gettysburg was precisely the same—in the advance. At the latter place his line of battle was thrown forward for a mile and a half in the immediate front of a large body of the centre of the enemy, composed of their best troops. It was on this position of Hancock that Lee opened his principal fire from his batteries of one hundred

and fifty guns. The whole of the left and of the
left centre withstood this tremendous cannonading
with unflinching valor, with Hancock at their head.
It was toward the close of this assault, that he, and
General Gibbon, temporarily commanding the Second
Corps, received their severe wounds.

It is not surprising, in view of such facts as these
and others like them in the history of General HAN-
COCK, that he should be assigned to an active position
at the front by so justly distinguished a man as Lieutenant General GRANT. Neither is it to be wondered
at that he should have filled his post so well in the
last campaign for the conquest of Richmond.

His first battle under Grant was that fought in the
Wilderness. This action took place on the 5th of
May. The scenes connected with it are among the
most exciting of any in military history.

Our troops had gone forward to the fight with an
ardor that was truly irrepressible.

> "Hark! I hear the tramp of thousands,
>   And of armèd men the hum:
> Lo! a nation's hosts have gathered
> Round the quick alarming drum.
>   Saying, 'Come,
>   Freemen, come,
> Ere your heritage be wasted!'
>   Said the quick alarming drum."

The scene of war was reached in a few hours' rapid
20

marching. The battle began on the 5th of May. On placing his troops in the field, Hancock found a strong force of the enemy massed against him. He immediately commenced the attack.

The spirits of the men were worthy at that momentous hour of their cause and their commander. The country around has been already described as among the wildest parts of one of the wastes of Virginia. Its surface is thickly dotted with densely wooded hills, interspersed with marshy lowlands, and sandy desert plains. It was settled as long ago as 1675, the county bearing the name of Old Stafford, in England. It is separated from the adjoining State of Maryland by the Potomac river, and supplied mainly by the Rappahannock.

Into this well-named Wilderness Hancock marched his patriot men, and pitched battle against the enemies of our country. At the first attack the enemy fell back; but, adopting their familiar Napoleonic tactics, they soon after massed their forces, and made a combined furious attempt to break our main centre, directly between the Second Corps, under Hancock, and the Fifth, under Warren. It was all in vain. They were hurled back in confusion.

On the following Thursday the battle was resumed with new vigor. Hancock occupied the extreme left

wing, with a cavalry support resting on a point between Parker's Store and Shady Grove Church.

The attack was commenced by the rebels on Friday morning, Longstreet striking with all his might
at Hancock. They had fought together, before, in
Mexico. The Second Corps bore their brunt of the
battle with all their wonted steadiness. The General
was at every post where his presence was needed,
cheering on his men, standing, at times, like a private in the ranks, and aiding to hurl back the surging columns of the foe thrown so furiously against
him. Every inch of the desperate assault was contested along the whole line, and, by a wise combi-
nation of forces, the order of battle was maintained,
and the enemy repulsed, with great slaughter.

The part taken by the Corps of Hancock is well
attested by the number of its slain and wounded, in
officers and men. Among the former were General
Hays, commander of the Second Brigade, Third
Division, who fell mortally wounded on that bloody
field of glory; and Getty, Gregg, Owen, Bartlett, and
Carroll, were wounded. While in the act of rallying
his men, in the front of the battle, Hancock was
again wounded, but maintained his position on the
field. The enemy rushed upon him in solid masses,
line sweeping on behind line. Some portions of the

ground on his front were fought over four or five times in succession.

The arrival of reinforcements, under Burnside, with the Ninth Corps, was most opportune. His appearance was loudly cheered by the brave men who had so nobly met and overcome the enemy. His colored troops rendered effective service in guarding exposed points, while the great body of his men participated with signal success in the severe battle of Friday.

Our cavalry, under Custer, Gregg, Merritt, Davis, and others equally deserving of mention if their names were at command, pursued the retreating columns of Lee. The battle became general toward the close of Saturday, in which we held our own against considerable odds, and, at certain points, continued to drive the enemy.

Hancock pushed forward his advance. On the ensuing Sunday he reached Alsop's farm, where a severe engagement ensued. In the evening, as the result of this battle, Grant advanced his entire lines — Hancock on the right. The forward movement brought us into a position for the employment of our guns, and on Monday ensued that sharp artillery conflict in which the brave and accomplished Sedgwick fell in his ramparts, while personally engaged in the location of his cannon.

The ensuing Tuesday, May **10th,** witnessed a ter-rific battle. Our troops were still advancing, driving the enemy before them, turning their flanks at every point, and convincing them, if they needed any con-victions on that subject, that one patriot was at least equal to one traitor. The old and idle boast that the South could whip us, at the rate of one man to our four, faded away in those sanguinary fields of Vir-ginia, like the dissolving views of an illusory pic-ture. Never was a man more taken by surprise than Lee. He found to his severe cost that

> " The best laid schemes o' mice and men
> Gang aft a-gley."

He schemed for the massing of his legions on our weak points; hoping, with his infuriate charges, to break our lines, and sweep everything before him. But he found Grant fully prepared for him, on all hands. That brave General and consummate strate gist was ready to meet mass with mass, strategy with straiegy, battle with battle, until, outflanked and out-generalled, the wily Lee was forced sullenly to retreat.

Hancock, on the extreme right wing, was in exactly the position to guard against every cunning device

20*

of the enemy; and, by his coolness, watchfulness, and courage, to prevent every attack on the flank that Lee might attempt. This was one of the favorite movements of the vigorous Southern strategist, and one upon which he often relied to compensate for any deficiency of numbers in his own ranks; but he here met his match, for Hancock checked him in several hard-fought battles at these points, and, in every instance, had the pleasure to join with his compatriots, Warren and Burnside, in compelling the daring soldier to fall back still further to the rear.

On Thursday, the 12th of May, he made that splendid dash, which resulted in the capture of an entire division of the enemy, four thousand strong, two Major-Generals, a large number of colors, and thirty cannon.

It was on this occasion that a personal interview took place between HANCOCK and the captive Major-Generals George H. Stuart and Ed. Johnson, in the tent of the conqueror. The gentlemen had known each other in former years. They had been cadets together at West Point, and fellow officers in the Army of the United States.

As both the prisoner-Generals entered the tent of Hancock, the following dialogue ensued:

Hancock.—"Ah! Johnson! Is it you? Let us shake hands."

Johnson.—"Hancock! this is dreadful." Accepting the hand so courteously proffered him, he burst into tears, and added:

"I should have much preferred death to captivity."

Hancock.—"I sympathize with you, Johnson; but such, you know, is sometimes the fortune of war. You have fought well, and have no reason to feel personally disgraced. It might have been my lot to be your prisoner."

Johnson.—"I know that; but to be taken in such a wholesale manner is hard to bear. It is rough."

Hancock.—"You know you will be treated like a gentleman, Johnson; and held under the laws of war, with which you are familiar."

During this conversation Stuart was moving nervously around, his countenance the picture of dejection and chagrin.

Hancock, who had sought to speak with him before, now approached him, with his hand extended.

Hancock.—"How are *you*, Stuart?"

Stuart.—"I am *General* Stuart, sir! of the Army of the Confederate States."

Hancock.—"I am well aware of that, General; but

I think I can venture to address you as an acquaintance of other days."

Stuart.—"Under present circumstances, sir, I decline to take your hand."

Hancock.—O! very well, sir! you can suit yourself in that matter; and, as my prisoner, you will certainly suit me.

Under any other circumstances, sir, I should not have offered you my hand!"

The chop-fallen look of Stuart at this instant can be better imagined than described. Whatever his feelings may have been under the courteous rebuke, all who witnessed it felt that Hancock was as cutting with the edge of his satire as he is with that of his victorious sword. He had beaten his prisoner with valor in the field, and he now conquered him again with gentlemanly bearing.

It was with an increased relish for his patriotic duties in the field that, after this interview, Hancock resumed his position in the ensuing fight. All day Thursday, and from sundown until near daylight of Friday morning, he was in action. He shared in the contest for a long line of rebel rifle-pits, in front, which he had the satisfaction of seeing wrested from the hands of the enemy.

The signal victories won in the Wilderness are

largely attributable to the cavalry arm of the service. Although an infantry officer by position, Hancock had repeatedly tested, in the vigorous practice at West Point, and in several of the fields of action in which he had engaged, the efficiency of this arm, especially in great strategic movements. He was much indebted to it for his commanding positions at the front. By their rapid evolutions in the face of the enemy, by dashing along by-paths and through forests and jungles, not accessible to infantry or artillery, they prepared the way for those steady advances and vigorous assaults that have rendered the Union armies so famous in the annals of American military history.

Nor this alone. Our cavalry have not only contributed largely to every success, by concerted action, but they have made numerous independent movements—especially in the vicinity of Richmond, and in the brilliant campaign in the Valley of the Shenandoah, in 1864 under that splendid cavalry officer, General PHILIP SHERIDAN—that have won them imperishable honor.

Cheers for the Union cavalry!

CHAPTER XXVI

*General Hancock in the Advanced Front in Spottsylvania—Another
Glorious Charge and Another Brilliant Victory to add to his Noble
Record.*

ON the 18th of May, 1864, the order came from
the Lieutenant-General, through his efficient
associate in command, General MEADE, for the entire
line of battle to be advanced to Spottsylvania Court
House, Virginia.

At this important strategic point the enemy had
thrown up strong entrenchments. Here Lee waited
in grim determination a direct attack on his front.
We shall see, as we progress, that he was doomed to
meet now one of the first of the series of those bitter
disappointments that mark his last luckless campaign
in the Old Dominion His hidden purpose was so to
entrench himself in the path he supposed we would
inevitably take, so to lie in ambush behind embankments that could not be enfiladed, that, when our men

were thrown against his impregnable works, **we** should be so decimated before his secreted and protected cannon and rifles, that we should be driven back, defeated, from exhaustion of strength. Vain and impotent conclusion! He had not calculated on the stern valor, on the persistent energy, on the skilful and well-practiced strategy now in the field for that glorious Union of States he was so daringly aiming to destroy. He had forgotten, apparently, what, of all other men, he, from his long practice, should **have** remembered, that powerful flank movements constitute **a** game of **war, at** which at least two accomplished commanders **can** play.

Grant immediately determined, as he approached Spottsylvania, to turn the right of Lee, attack him in the rear, and thus force his further retreat upon his final base, Richmond.

The fighting on Thursday and Friday of this week was very severe. The lines of Hancock, being then far in the front, were repeatedly attacked by the enemy, and as often repulsed. The division of his Corps commanded by General Seymour was exposed to a heavy fire, and suffered considerably. But the enemy were handled with still greater severity, and again compelled to retreat, leaving their dead and wounded in our hands. The iron old Second Corps nobly stood its ground, at every point, under the immediate lead of HANCOCK, who was vigilant and active, as usual, in all parts of the field. He was again wounded in this action, but kept his position at the post of duty.

On Saturday the Second Corps again advanced beyond the Wilderness Tavern, and formed line of battle against the enemy at Spottsylvania Court House. At daylight he passed through this strategic point, and found the enemy entrenched a short distance beyond. Heavy skirmishing was immediately commenced, and by Sunday morning the whole army of Grant was in vigorous pursuit of Lee. The proof that we held the field was shown in the fact that we now occupied Fredericksburg as a depot for our wounded, and a base of supplies. Our headquarters at the noon of Sunday were twenty miles south of the previous battle-field.

The stand made by Lee in the vicinity of Spottsylvania was a strong one. But he was not permitted to hold it long. SEDGWICK, WADSWORTH, and other brave soldiers, had fallen; but our army of kindred heroes pushed gallantly on, compelling Lee to retreat to the banks of the North Anna river.

At this point another severe battle was fought. The right of the enemy was crushed. Three brigades

and four guns were captured. Hancock crossed the
River Po, under a tremendous enfilading fire, driving the enemy before him, and establishing himself
on the south bank. The possession of Spottsylvania,
after a hotly contested fight, carried us out of the
Wilderness; although, in retreating, in consequence
of their greater familiarity with the broken and wild
country, the enemy had the advantage of us. By
the necessities of the position, we could not drive on
as fast as the foe could be driven. Hancock, holding
the extreme right of our line, took possession of the
Block-House road, and thus prepared the way for the
continued advance of the main army. Breastworks
were thrown up by his men, and every disposition
made for any attack the enemy might make. But
they prudently abstained from all assaults at this
point. One after another their wild yells died away;
and it soon became evident that sullenness and des-
pondency reigned among them. Hancock had added
another line to his entrenchments in the open ground
contiguous to Todd's Tavern, a portion of his heavy
artillery working all night to accomplish the feat.
The sight of these brave cannoniers thus at work for
their country is described by one who witnessed it
as extremely picturesque. The lanterns of the armed
workmen hung in festoons from the wild cherry trees,

21 Q

flashing their lights among the May blossoms of the branches. The batteries were harnessed up among the patriot diggers, who laid aside their pickaxes and spades occasionally to look to their guns and bayonets. Thus passed the watchful night of war. As the sun rose scouts reported the enemy still in front, but in small force; and at noon Hancock had again advanced and taken possession of his new field.

A light-horse battery of the enemy, on the approach of our troops at a brisk charge, quickly limbered up, and posted off in hot haste. It was well for them that they did. A lively engagement ensued, during which the enemy made the best use in their power of a secreted position they held in an adjacent wood. They dared not meet us there in the open field. Some of them who ventured out were taken prisoners, and in other parts of the battle ground considerable supplies and munitions of war were captured.

The marching of HANCOCK to form a junction with Sedgwick and Warren had been well done. He moved in line of battle by the left flank to mass, fighting every foot of the way against an entrenched enemy, who was determined, at all hazards, to prevent the strategic movement of our General. Every position that he took he obstinately held, completely foiling the enemy, and effecting his junction at the desired time and designated place. The great **object** was attained by the exertion of his utmost skill and vigor. The part he had to perform was realized by him, and all, to be a severe one; but ably, bravely, successfully he performed it. He took the whole line of rifle pits at a most critical moment, and five stands of colors. It is admitted that his heroism and skill in these preliminary engagements did much toward saving our army.

By his passage of **the Po** HANCOCK secured a coigne of vantage over the enemy. He enfiladed the **entire** position, commanding their roads, on which their trains were passing. It was a bold move, but like the dashing character he had so nobly won. His two divisions thrown over the river connected with the right of WARREN. By this junction the enemy were driven from their coverts in the woods, where we had been exposed to some damage from their shells. A general attack followed along the entire line, continuing for several hours. The enemy could not withstand our charge, but fell back in confusion, leaving a large number of killed, wounded, and prisoners, on the field.

Early in the morning of the 12th of May, fighting was resumed by HANCOCK. In one of his brilliant

charges, for which he has become so justly famous,
he dashed on the division of Hill, planted in its entrenchments, five miles below Spottsylvania Court
House.   At the head of his gallant Corps, fired with
the energy peculiar to him, he charged on the foe at
the double quick.   His appearance on this occasion
is described as the impersonation of the heroism of
war.   Cheering his men as he placed himself at their
head, receiving ·their cheers in return with the waving of his sword, he gave the word "Charge!" with
a, shout that rang along the lines like the clangor
of a trumpet.   The steady columns swept onward at
that familiar word, and followed their great commander into the very centre of the breaking lines of
the enemy.   They wavered, staggered, fell back, step
by step; then broke into a confused mass, and fled
in all directions.   Colors struck the ground, horses
tumbled headlong in the wreck, shattered cannon
ploughed the reeking earth, bayonets crossed in wild,
discordant clatter, heaps of confused bodies strewed
the crimson grass on every side · while over all,
louder than the roar of guns, amid the advancing
standards of the Union, all unfurled and flapping in
the smoky air, rose on high the shout — " Victory!"
" Victory!"

As our columns dashed over the field, HANCOCK

still at their head, the prisoners and trophies of war were gathered around him. They numbered three thousand men,—among whom were one Major General, two Brigadier Generals, fifty officers, and twelve pieces of artillery.

The result of the battle was a flag of truce from Lee, and the capture of despatches, in which he confessed that he was short of supplies. It was evident that he must fall back on Richmond, as his final base.

The valor of HANCOCK in this splendid engagement has been well characterised as sublime. He placed himself at the head of his entire Corps; every division, every brigade, every regiment, being under his eagle eye. His orders were his own, from first to last. Every movement was his, from the beginning to the close of the fight. His presence was seen, heard, and felt, in all parts of the field; until the enthusiasm of his men, as they rushed eagerly on the enemies of their land, knew no bounds. His associates in command rallied around him with a readiness that never wavered, a skill that never failed, a courage that never faltered. The whole mass moved together, like a terrific engine of war in the grasp of one strong hand, and controlled by the will of one gifted mind. What wonder that he achieved so glorious a victory?

21*

CHAPTER XXVII.

THE pursuit of the retreating army of Lee was made with as much rapidity as an unfavorable change in the roads would permit. HANCOCK, still again in the advance, had accomplished the feat, described in another chapter, which resulted in the capture of Major Generals Edward Johnson and George H. Stuart, and a large portion of their commands.

The fatigue of our army was great, and the line of march was much impeded by a fall of rain of thirty-six hours' duration. The glorious success of HANCOCK had inspired all hearts, and the resolution to achieve new victories over the galled and retreating rebels was instantly formed. As the rain ceased and the sun broke forth on the day that witnessed the close. of the last splendid achievements of the Wilderness, the order to advance again was obeyed with alacrity. Our men were in high spirits, and impatient to meet the foe in any field he might choose.

The characteristic despatch of HANCOCK to Lieutenant General GRANT, includes, in a few words, the progress thus far made:

"HEADQUARTERS SECOND CORPS, May 12th, '64.

"GENERAL: I have captured from thirty to forty guns. I have finished up Johnson, and am now going into Early.

W. S. HANCOCK."

Thirteen of the captured guns were brought to General GRANT's headquarters. The remainder were placed at different points in our rear.

At daylight of the morning of this attack the brigade of General BARLOW, of HANCOCK's Corps, appeared like a war apparition before the enemy. They had advanced and steadily driven the enemy; and, before they were aware of it, had reached their entrenchments, directly in front. With a dash they charged on the works, swept over them, and, before their foes had time to fire a gun, captured the whole command. The enemy were compelled to surrender by the butts of the muskets in the hands of our brave men.

By another advance of HANCOCK, on the 15th of May, the fact was developed that Lee had fallen back four miles. The charge of General BIRNEY'S division, of the Second Corps, which aided materially to produce this auspicious result, was one of the most splendid of any made during the war. Every regiment in his command covered itself with honor. Rebels were surprised in their strongholds in the woods, and several stands of colors captured from them.

The two armies were now on the main road leading from Fredericksburg to Richmond, but the condition of travelling rendered it impossible to make any movement to advantage. Reinforcements continued to arrive, and the most confident expectations of final success were felt and expressed on the Union side The position of Lee was still strong, and the state of the weather was much in his favor. But the indomitable GRANT was determined to pursue him. Rest and recruiting were needed by our troops.

Our advance, under HANCOCK, possessed one of the strongest keys of the whole hostile position, and the most desperate efforts were made by them to regain it; but all in vain. He proved himself as tenacious in holding his point as he was dashing in winning it. No language can describe the desperate energy with which his troops had carried the day. BARLOW, BIRNEY, GIBBON, MOTT, and others, had won the highest distinction on this field; and the men they commanded were entitled to bear with them their imperishable laurels. The breastworks captured in this advance were very strong; the ditches in front were deep and wide; and the enemy defended their position as if they held it to be impregnable. It was reserved for HANCOCK to undeceive them.

Several important reconnoissances followed, and preparations were made for another general advance.

On the 18th of May the roads had considerably improved, and active operations were immediately resumed. Large reinforcements had reached the Union army, and the spirits of the men continued elastic. Skirmishing began by BIRNEY's division, of HANCOCK's Corps, shell being thrown in the contiguous woods to feel the position of the enemy.

Early in the morning of this day HANCOCK made another of his brilliant charges, with the most beneficial results. His attack was begun from our right wing, and was prosecuted with such vigor that the enemy were forced back a considerable distance. He carried their line of entrenchments, and all attempts to dislodge him proved utterly futile. Our lines continued steadily to advance. Lee was again taken entirely by surprise. He had not anticipated and was evidently not prepared for these repeated and powerful assaults on his flanks. While our feints in front with artillery completely deceived him, he found us more than a match for him in the strategy of flanking, and was again compelled to withdraw. HANCOCK had advanced successfully upon him, turned his left flank, driven his sharp-shooters out of their rifle-pits, captured fifteen guns, and a large body of prisoners.

Not long after this successful assault, the enemy attempted to turn our right. But they were promptly met by the Heavy Artillery, under that brave and energetic officer, General TYLER, who was ably supported by the division of General BIRNEY, of the Second Corps, and handsomely repulsed. Although these troops of TYLER were just arrived on the field, from garrison duty at Washington, and had never been under fire before, they conducted themselves with so much steadiness, managed their guns with such skill, and were handled in so admirable a manner by their General, that they kept the enemy at bay until the reinforcements of BIRNEY and CRAWFORD arrived, and joined with them to drive the enemy from the field.

At half-past eleven o'clock in the night of Friday,

May 20th, HANCOCK again rapidly advanced, in pursuit of a portion of the enemy in command of Longstreet, one of his former fellow lieutenants in the Army of the United States. His pursuit was as rapid as the condition of the roads would permit, and soon developed the fact that the enemy had retreated beyond the North Anna river. HANCOCK, on the extreme left, had driven them from the entrenchments they occupied previous to this advance. The Second Corps, under cover of night, had bivouacked within the breastworks from which they had previously captured their prisoners. The veterans had used their bayonets with such effect that the field of their march was like a review. They were again in the vanguard, with HANCOCK at their head. Marching on the road parallel with the river Ny, the troops continued to advance southward, still pursuing the retreating foe. By daylight of the 21st they reached Guinea's Station, on the Fredericksburg and Richmond railroad; from thence pushing onward, until by nightfall the head of the column had reached Bowling Green.

The effect of this movement was to turn the right flank of Lee, and compel him to retreat still again, to find his hiding places on the banks of the South Anna.

At the position attacked by HANCOCK the enemy had thrown up strong entrenchments. They were in considerable force at the point where he had crossed, and made a determined resistance. But his pertinacious courage and skill overcame them, and they were compelled to flee. Before dark of the day of his attack he had forced them out of their works, and driven them across the stream.

WARREN and BURNSIDE were on the same line with HANCOCK, and their two Corps, the Fifth and Ninth, won equal distinctions with the Second, on that gallant onward march into the heart of the enemy's country.

The divisions of BARLOW, BIRNEY and GIBBON, in the Second Corps, were close on the heels of the fleeing enemy at the North Anna. Skirmishing began on the front of BIRNEY's division, and soon became general along the entire line. At this point HANCOCK ordered BIRNEY to charge the enemy. It was done, in most splendid style. The works were carried, the bridge taken, the enemy driven in confusion, and our guns placed so as to command the position.

The gallant conduct of that division on this occasion drew forth warm praises from General HANCOCK. He complimented it on the field in the most cordial manner, and was himself received with enthusiastic cheers by the troops.

Over a thousand prisoners were captured by this combined advance.

The position now assumed by Lee was one of the strongest he could obtain. He had not yet crossed the South Anna, but was entrenched between that and the North Anna. But he soon found the difference between his stand here, in these comparatively low and open lands of Virginia, and that he had made on the heights of Fredericksburg. He could no longer hide himself to advantage, but was compelled to the onset of a fair field.

At this point he concentrated all his available force, and was evidently prepared for a stubborn defence.

GRANT, on the other hand, was by no means idle. It is well known that it is not his nature to be, on all such occasions. He gathered his army more closely in hand, adding to his regular force the independent command of General BURNSIDE, known as the Ninth Corps. As the Lieutenant General, in supreme command of the field, he had made his dispositions with SHERMAN, BUTLER, CANBY, HUNTER, SHERIDAN, and others, and was now prepared for such an advance as would be sure to intercept the retreat of Lee.

22

From their base in the vicinity of the Rapidan, the enemy had been driven a distance of over fifty miles. Through all this long march of pursuit the Union army had fought its way in triumph. At every point the commanders had vied with each other in the meritorious discharge of their nigh duties. Our province is to speak, especially, of HANCOCK; but in depicting his valiant deeds we are not to be understood as undervaluing those of other equally brave men. We should be happy to describe them, too, did the limits of our volume allow us.

It is the position of HANCOCK at the front, in this memorable and triumphant march, and the signal manner in which he discharged the high responsibilities laid upon him, that demand the narration of his heroic deeds; that make the task of recording them so agreeable, and that cause the lesson taught by this part of his life to be so instructive.

The advance of the Second Corps, under HANCOCK, was one of the signals of the retreat of that part of the enemy immediately on his front. Ewell and Longstreet, who were in that position, had heard from him before, at Gettysburg. When he moved, therefore, both these distinguished Confederates withdrew.

At the passage of the North Anna, while the Corps

of WARREN crossed with but little opposition, that of HANCOCK encountered a severe fight. He met the enemy at Chesterfield bridge, where strong works had been thrown up, in a commanding position. These had all to be carried, and then the obstacle of an intervening creek overcome, ere he could plant his colors on the opposite bank. Gorges and ditches were immediately on his front; rifle pits and frowning embankments beyond.

For the conquest of these difficult points the division of General BIRNEY was detailed; and nobly did he perform the task assigned him. With GIB-BON on his left, BARLOW on his right, and supported in the rear by TYLER's splendid Heavy Artillery, he marched to the attack. The open space in front was swept over by his men at double quick, under a terrific fire of infantry and artillery; they reached the redans without a pause, and drove out the enemy at the point of the bayonet.

The enemy were thunderstruck at this unexpected and rapid movement, and large bodies of them fled headlong in dismay. The whole Corps of HANCOCK immediately massed, and held the head of the bridge until the time came for a still further advance, and preparations were completed for the capture of the rifle-pits and entrenchments in front.

GRANT immediately executed another flank move
ment.   The position of Lee was such that to attack
his front, at a disadvantage, would cause an unnecessary loss of life, while, by flanking him, he could
compel his further retreat.   The movement by flank
was executed with such skill, secrecy, and rapidity,
that it was all accomplished before Lee was aware
that GRANT had thought of it.   The South Anna,
with all its grim array of embankments, its rifle pits,
its hidden ambuscades, was left to frown in its solitary neglect, while the victorious army of the Union
marched steadily on.   By Sunday, the 29th of May,
it had swung around its base, and on the morning
of Monday, the 30th, occupied a new field, in the
region of the Pamunkey river.

This was a most disagreeable surprise to Lee. · He
had calculated on our throwing ourselves, over broken
plains, and through miry morasses, on his strong
earthworks, which he had taken the trouble to build
directly in the way he desired us to take.   How
could the Lieutenant General, the stubborn GRANT,
be so very disobliging?   How dare he take the
liberty thus to move his army about at will, over the
sacred soil of Virginia?   Why did he not consent
to be led, as a sheep to the slaughter, in the commodious pens he had been so kind as to construct on

the convenient banks of the South Anna? Was it chivalrous in him to flank off from his proud and valiant foe in this secret manner? Clearly not. Th whole thing was wrong. The movement was all disgraceful, cowardly, mean. It was not according to Hoyle.

Be all this as it may, GRANT did it; and most nobly did his great and gallant army sustain him in doing it.

On the morning of the 27th of May, at the early hour of four o'clock, the whole command had been set in motion, the glorious old Second Corps still in the advance. The march was made with a celerity on the part of the men that showed their hearts were in the work before them. Lee was outgeneralled on his own chosen ground. Our troops struck off in a new direction, passing through a region not before trodden by the feet of contending armies, during this war for the Union, in which they found the most abundant supplies of provisions, cattle, and horses.

By the evening of May 30th, the whole army was afely across the Pamunkey, the head of the column oeing within four hours of the Confederate capital. The movement was the most astonishing to Lee of any GRANT had yet made. On the first of June we occupied a front of three miles on the South bank

22 * R

of the river, having had several cavalry engagements with the enemy in that vicinity, in all of which
we drove them.

Fighting was resumed on the Mechanicsville road,
south of Totopatamoy creek, and between that
stream and Hawes's Shop. The bridges over the
Little River and the South Anna were destroyed by
our cavalry, under WILSON, and the Union headquarters established in the place long before selected
by the Lieutenant General.

General HANCOCK made his attack on the lines of
the enemy the moment he received the order. It was
toward evening of the 30th of May, and the darkness
soon set in. But he pressed on to the front, assailed
the new works the enemy had thrown up, and carried
them by assault. When the morning broke over the
field, the Union colors were seen floating from the
conquered ramparts. This was a strongly entrenched
skirmish line of the enemy, and held by HANCOCK
in the face of a deadly fire. The distance from that
point to Richmond was but fourteen miles.

On the night of the 31st of May, a desperate assault was made on the lines of HANCOCK. The sud-
denness of the movement which brought him to the
banks of the Pamunkey, would not allow him to entrench as much as was desirable. But he was pre-

pared for the furious onslaught, though it came on him suddenly and in darkness.

His brave hosts were rallied with a celerity and skill that proved the soldierly qualities of the General, and the enemy everywhere repulsed. They made not the slightest trifle by their midnight motion. On the contrary, it put our men more completely on the alert, led to reinforcements at all weak points, and made us more than ever masters of the field.

The fight was sharp; but so signal a victory to us that it not only drove off the enemy discomfited, but left several hundred prisoners in our hands. He continued to hold the rifle-pits from which he had driven the enemy the previous evening, and was prepared to defend his position at all points. Our whole line was immediately advanced along his front, and by daylight the army was so massed at that position as to resist successfully every attack.

CHAPTER XXVIII.

*On the Banks of the Famous Chickahominy — Capture of the Ford
at Taylor's Bridge — Cold Harbor, Bottom's Bridge, and the
James River — "On to Richmond."*

LEE was now on the north bank of the historic
Chickahominy. This little stream, which occu-
pies so prominent a place in American military annals, is located in the south-eastern part of Virginia.
It rises in the county of Hanover, and falls into the
York river, about eight miles above Jamestown —
one of the oldest English settlements in America.
It divides Henrico and Charles City counties on the
right, from Hanover, New Kent and James City
counties on the left. It has to be approached and
crossed by armies reaching Richmond from the direction taken by the army of GRANT. It is capable of
being strongly defended, and is remarkable for the
several sanguinary engagements that took place in

(260)

its vicinity between the Union and rebel armies during the years 1861, '62 and '64.

Our line of battle had now been formed on a radius within a few miles of Richmond. Lee, without waiting for our renewed attacks, had stealthily retreated before our advancing legions. The capture of the ford at Taylor's Bridge by HANCOCK had enabled us to stretch our columns above and beyond the strategic point at Sexton's Junction. In moving on the Virginia Central railroad, he had been furiously attacked by Lee, and severely repulsed him. The conduct of the Fifth Corps, under WARREN, at this place, had been complimented by General MEADE, and that of the division of BIRNEY had received similar encomiums from HANCOCK. The arrival of BURNSIDE and WRIGHT — the latter now commanding the Corps of noble old SEDGWICK — had brought large reinforcements, and the ground taken from the enemy was firmly held. By repeated assaults the enemy attempted to retake the bridge from HANCOCK, but they were foiled and driven back on every occasion. Constant fighting and skirmishing had been continued by the Second and Ninth Corps, the headquarters being located at Jericho Mills.

From these points began another of those high strategic movements for which the Lieutenant General is so deservedly famous. Swiftly and silently he withdraws, under the feint of an attack on the Virginia Central, from before the strong entrenchments of Lee, and moves directly in a contrary manner from what the enemy expected. The Confederate commander was again utterly deceived. Our troops rapidly crossed the Pamunkey, swept on through Hanovertown, at a distance of only fifteen miles from Richmond, and very soon reached the strong strategic point and convenient base of supplies, at White House.

The fights on Totopatomoy creek had all resulted in our favor. The enemy were forced back at every point, and our whole army was soon in its chosen position.

Lee was again on the Chickahominy. It had become, once more, his line of battle. He hoped, in maintaining it, to drive and keep our whole force in the unhealthy swamps beyond, where all our military movements would have to be made under the greatest disadvantages. But the strategy of GRANT was fully equal to the emergency. By his rapid flankings he had moved just where he wanted to go, avoiding all battles which he would have fought at a disadvantage, saving the lives of his men, keeping up their spirits by continued advances, and outgeneraling and mystifying the enemy.

The battles of Cold Harbor and Bottom's Bridge, which preceded our victorious approach to the James River, had been sanguinary in their character; but they were short and successful.

The attack at Cold Harbor was made at five o'clock in the afternoon of the 1st of June. The Second Corps, under HANCOCK, was in position to resist any sudden assault that might be made on our rear. The gallant Sixth Corps led the van, assisted by SMITH, WARREN, BURNSIDE and HANCOCK. It was in all respects a brilliant affair. The battle continued until after dark, and resulted in our carrying the enemy's works at all points. Repeated attempts were made by bold strokes to retake them, but in vain. In every instance they were repulsed, with heavy loss on their side. Several hundred of them were captured during the night, and other injuries inflicted on Lee that were evidently severely felt.

We were now approaching the centre stronghold more closely than ever, and the resistance of the enemy was every hour becoming more fierce and more determined. The hostile front was formed on our line only five miles distant from Richmond. The thunder of the guns could now be heard, as they never had been heard before, in the ears of the Confederated troops. Gaines' Mills, Mechanicsville, Fair Oaks, and other spots near

Richmond, made memorable in history by the conflicts there of the Union forces with their foes, clustered around, and by their battle memories aroused anew the enthusiasm of our ranks. All the enemies' works constructed at various intersecting points had been rendered useless by the strategy of GRANT, and the approaches of Lee to Richmond were seriously endangered.

The Southern commander was still strong, still wily still courageous; but his forces had been fearfully decimated, even when assailed by us behind his entrenchments, and his communications with other parts of the Confederate lines were daily and hourly growing

"Small, by degrees, and beautifully less."

The enemy vainly and boastfully asserted that GRANT had declined the gage of battle. But he had done nothing of the kind. He was always ready for battle, and always delivered it, when he thought proper. He did not, however, deem it wise to fight on the ground chosen by the enemy, when he could fight so much better on ground chosen by himself. The truth is, his strategy, skill, and generalship were too much for General Lee, however reluctant sympathizing publicists in every section were then, and for long after, to admit it.

GRANT started from Washington to reach the

James River, in his own way. He had marked out his line of battle to suit himself, not the enemy and, as he naively expressed it in his famous dispatch to the Secretary of War, he was determined to "fight it out on this line, if it should take all summer."

The enemy had expended a prodigious amount of labor—the most of it performed by the unpaid hands of their slaves — in erecting strong fortifications, renewing the ambuscades of old Manassas, Bull Run, and Ball's Bluff, all along the line which they were extremely desirous to have GRANT adopt and pursue. But he, obstinate man! deliberately insisted in flanking these formidable works, passing by and beyond them, and leaving them as useless lumber on the deserted field. It was a very inconvenient, disagreeable and damaging operation for the enemy. But alas! for them. There was no way in which they could prevent it.

The water-base of the Union army being opened at White House, near the James, the hostile embankments outflanked and rendered harmless, a long and unhealthy campaign on the Chickahominy being avoided, the conquest of Richmond now became an object of pursuit from another point of strategy. We shall see how successfully that conquest is finally accomplished.

23

On Monday, the 31st of May, our line extended from the Pamunkey, immediately in front of Hanover Court House, to beyond Totopatomoy creek. A strong assault was made by the enemy in the evening of this day, in which HANCOCK was called into action. He commenced by a diversion upon the foe with a heavy cannonade, that lasted for a number of hours, the position of the enemy being assailed by several batteries, and six Cohorn mortars. HANCOCK's Corps occupied the right centre, WRIGHT, the worthy successor of SEDGWICK, holding the extreme right, WARREN the left centre, and BURNSIDE the extreme .eft. In this position the attack was made by BIRNEY, under HANCOCK, and well sustained. BIRNEY advanced on the right, BARLOW on the centre. The first line of the enemy was carried by a brilliant charge, in which a considerable number of prisoners were captured from the command of Breckinridge.

Thus the Union forces fought their way to the banks of the James, and the contiguous region. Richmond was to be approached through its outposts. Whether it was to be conquered by a direct assault, or reduced by a continued siege, was yet to be determined.

A severe assault was made on our lines on the evening of Friday, the 3d of June. The troops first attacked were those of SMITH's brigade, GIBBON's division, HANCOCK's Corps. It was a sharp attack, and began with the customary horrid yells. The battle raged with great fury for some time; but the enemy were gallantly repulsed, and prevented for that day from trying their assault again. They were driven back still further, their entrenchments occupied, and lost over three hundred prisoners, beside many killed and wounded.

The Heavy Artillery of HANCOCK, under TYLER, rendered signal service on this occasion. The latter General was severely wounded.

CHAPTER XXIX.

Hancock's Siege-Lines Closing in on the Confederate Capital — Hancock Carries Bottom's Bridge at the Point of the Bayonet — The Mississippi Valley Sanitary Fair Presents a Sword to General Hancock.

IN reviewing the battles leading from the Potomac to the James, from Washington to Richmond, in which General HANCOCK took so active a part, we continue to find much to admire in his character as a soldier. These battles constitute a series of engagements, among the most sanguinary of any on record. The purpose to advance on the part of the patriot army was fixed and unyielding. The purpose to resist was the same on the part of the enemy. Nothing carried the day for us and secured our steady progress toward our noble object, the suppression of armed rebellion, but the courage and endurance of the Union armies under GRANT, co-operated with at other points by the distinguished Generals SHERMAN, in Georgia, SHERIDAN, in the Valley of the Shenandoah

(208)

and the equally distinguished Admiral FARRAGUT, on the Atlantic coast.

Our space will not allow us to review in detail all the battles in which HANCOCK occupied so prominent a position. We can only follow him as he advances with the main army, and incidentally describe such scenes in which he was an actor, as come under view in our limited pages.

One of the features of his career in this campaign that cannot fail to attract attention, is the promptness with which he always moved. When he received an order, for instance, to move on a given line at thirty minutes past four o'clock in the morning, at thirty-one minutes past that hour he was in motion. There was no delay — not even that of a moment. His attacks and conquests were of a similar character. Sometimes in thirty minutes from the time he moved, he had fought and won the field. His men were so accustomed to his rapid movements that lines of battle six miles in length responded to his calls, as if formed immediately around him. Here is the secret of his power as a great General. His lines were always well in hand. His power was never scattered. In all this promptness of energy, he was perfectly responded to by every one of his commanders, who richly deserve to share with him the gratitude and

23*

praise of a ransomed country. Special mention is due here to Colonel TOMPKINS, Chief of Artillery in the Second Corps, as well as to the cavalry, for their invaluable services in securing our continued advance. It is not too much to say that the artillery practice of the United States army is among the best in the world.

On the 7th of June the advancing siege lines of HANCOCK had materially increased the uneasiness of the enemy. They could not understand what he meant by continuing to approach so near to their front line of battle. It was not necessary to his purpose that they should. Every attempt they made to feel our lines met only with repulse and capture. Under cover of the thick fog peculiar to that part of the country, they had advanced to within pistol-shot range of our works, intending to make a dash and surprise us. But our pickets were on the alert. A sheet of flame from the entire line of the division of the Second Corps commanded by GIBBON drove back the invaders in confusion. The fire from our ranks enfiladed their progress, and they fell back in confusion, leaving many of their number dead and wounded on the field.

The exposure of General HANCOCK at this point was so imminent, that Lieutenant McCUNE, of his staff, had his leg shot off, while standing near the General's headquarters. But he held his ground on the extreme left of our line, stretching along the road leading to Dispatch Station, while the cavalry pickets of the dashing SHERIDAN guarded the banks of the Chickahominy.

It was evidently the firm purpose of the enemy to turn the position of HANCOCK. They opened their most furious fire on his lines, keeping up the rattle of musketry and roar of artillery with a steadiness and perseverance rarely equalled. The attempt was clearly made to break the brigade of Smith, in the Second Corps, in the hope of penetrating to the main army. Delusive hope! It was doomed to share the fate of those that had gone before it. Through all the darkness of those hours of the thunder of battle, the noble old Second stood to their guns; and, when the morning broke, their gallant lines were intact as of yore

A change of base was effected for strategic purposes, from the White House, near the junction of the York and Pamunkey rivers, on the 10th of June, to Harrison's Landing and other suitable points on the James. This object of GRANT had thus been accomplished. Up to this moment both armies had continued to occupy their relative positions.

During the night of Saturday, HANCOCK had made a successful attack on the enemy at Bottom's Bridge. The cannonading was heavy, and the result auspicious to our arms. The Chickahominy was crossed at this point, at a distance of only about twelve miles from Richmond, seven miles northeast of Four-Mile creek, on the James river. HANCOCK, after a desperate fight, had succeeded in dislodging the enemy, carrying the bridge at the point of the bayonet. It was securely held by his Corps, and the whole army safely crossed the stream at that point and at other bridges. The Second Corps marched at once to a selected station on the James.

The whole movement was executed with consummate skill; and reflects the highest credit not only on the Lieutenant General, but on all concerned. Like other strategic plans of this memorable campaign, it took the Southerners completely by surprise, and was all the more effective on that account. The bridges generally occupied were those of our own pontoons. The rapidity of their preparation, and the speed with which so large an army crossed such a river in perfect safety, show to advantage the military skill which prevails in the American army.

By this masterly movement our army was now on the banks of the James, on which Richmond is situ-

ated, and occupying a strong position at the south of
that doomed Southern capital. Little or no opposition had been made to our crossing. Our cavalry
had several skirmishes, the result of reconnoissances,
to feel the positions of the enemy. If they were
aware of our proceeding they did not attempt to
interrupt it. Perhaps it was best for them that they
did not.

The post of duty assigned to HANCOCK was that
the farthest up the river — the nearest toward the
Southern capital. At this point he threw out his advanced pickets, and proceeded to entrench. All
around him were signs of the ravages of war; but
there were portions of the country still clothed in
green, and smiling in the sunny rays of June. Some
fields of grain had not been trodden by the march
of armed men, horses and trains of artillery, and the
forests towered up in the distance in all their primeval
beauty. Nearly all the adult population had been
ruthlessly conscripted into the insurgent armies, leaving the houses to be occupied by the old people and
children; while the neglected fields told too plainly
a sad tale of the havoc and neglect that the terrible
plague of war had poured over them, like a desolat-
ing tide of fire.

While thus patriotically occupied in the field of
S

duty, Hancock was not forgotten by his friends at home. It is pleasant to turn away from the scenes of carnage and suffering that accompany the movements of armies, and contemplate the grateful proceedings of his fellow-citizens in the peaceful walks of life.

At the time he was thus bravely fighting for his country, the public Fairs of the United States Sanitary Commission were being held, in different parts of the country. This Commission is composed of volunteer citizens of the Republic, who formed themselves into an association for the purpose of aiding the government in caring for our brave soldiers in the fields and hospitals, and our equally brave seamen in the navy. They had held several festivals and other appropriate gatherings, at which large sums of money were raised by the free-will offerings of the people, and abundant supplies procured for the necessities of our sick and wounded heroes. To further this good object, several expedients had been resorted to, especially at the instigation of patriotic ladies, to swell the funds of this most commendable purpose. Among these the managers of the Mississippi Valley Sanitary Fair adopted the plan of presenting a sword to General HANCOCK. The amount necessary to procure this elegant gift was all obtained from among volunteer donors, while the act of de ciding the sword to be his, elicited a competition that largely swelled the gross receipts for the noble object in view.

The following is the correspondence on this sub- ject:

"SAINT LOUIS, MISSOURI, JUNE 18th, 1864.

Major General W. S. HANCOCK;

SIR :—

It is with great pleasure I announce to you that the handsome sword donated to the Mississippi Valley Sanitary Fair, to be voted for by those who make donations in voting, has been awarded to you; there having been a large plurality of votes in your favor.

It is highly gratifying to the people of Saint Louis, who regard you as more than half a citizen, that the sword has been awarded to you, as an humble but respectful appreciation of your gallant and distinguished services in the field.

That success may continue to attend your noble efforts to crush out the rebellion against our country, is my earnest and heart- felt prayer.

You will please indicate the disposition you wish made of the sword, which awaits your order.

Very respectfully and truly yours,

JAMES E. YEATMAN,

Chairman Executive Committee, Mississippi Valley Sanitary Fair."

REPLY OF GENERAL HANCOCK

"HEADQUARTERS SECOND ARMY CORPS, JUNE 27, 1864.

MY DEAR SIR :—

Your favor of the 18th instant, informing me that the handsome sword donated to the Mississippi Valley Sanitary Fair has been awarded to me, is received.

Such a mark of consideration, from the citizens of Saint Louis, is truly gratifying. Having married in that city, and residing there for many years, I regard it as a home.

Only the soldier can fully appreciate the benefit of your noble efforts in behalf of the Sanitary Commission. The effects of its kind offices in ameliorating our wants and sufferings are felt, with a grateful remembrance, through every part of our vast army.

I am, sir, very respectfully,

Your obedient servant,

W. S. Hancock,

Major General United States Volunteers.

To James E. Yeatman, Esq., Chairman of the Executive Committee, Western Sanitary Commission, Saint Louis, Missouri.

P. S. Please send the sword to Mrs. W. S. Hancock, Carondelet, Missouri.

W. S. H."

At the great Central Sanitary Fair, held with such marked success in the city of Philadelphia, during the current month of June, 1864, the citizens of the States especially represented, Pennsylvania, New Jersey, and Delaware, manifested their deep interest in General Hancock, and their high appreciation of his services for the country, by the presentation of a splendid full set of horse equipments, valued at five hundred dollars, manufactured for the occasion, by Messrs. Mage, of Philadelphia.

The correspondence on the subject has not yet appeared. It is known that the General has expressed his grateful appreciation of the handsome gift, especially on account of the application of the money derived from it in the Fair, to the relief of our suffering troops and sailors.

Several other gentlemen, actuated by similar motives of patriotism and personal good will, took measures to present him a commodious dwelling in Philadelphia, the particulars of which reflect much credit on the parties concerned. From considerations of delicacy we abstain from inserting all the names of parties in this place, with regard to this honorable and generous proceeding.

The Coal Exchange of Philadelphia, through the personal exertions of JOHN R. BLACKISTON, Esq., DAVIS PEARSON, Esq., and other gentlemen, gave a practical proof of their good will by placing at the disposal of General HANCOCK the handsome sum of fifteen thousand dollars, to be used by him at his discretion, in the work of procuring recruits for his Corps.

Mr. PEARSON followed his proofs of attachment to the General by raising, in connection with his own liberal subscription, the sum of twenty-four hundred dollars, with a view to presenting him another elegant sword and accoutrements. But, in consequence of his having received a similar present from Saint Louis, this

24

testimonial was deferred. The subscription was therefore retained until, at a later date, the contributions of his Philadelphia friends should make it possible to present him with a durable gift, which could be treasured by his family.

It was perfectly natural and proper that the citizens of Saint Louis should feel a peculiar interest in General HANCOCK. Beside their high appreciation of his character as an officer, they had known him among them as a resident. As a General, they regarded his brilliant military achievements as fully equal to the best of those of the most distinguished commanders of NAPOLEON—MURAT, DESSAIX, JUNOT, and DUROC. They felt that the nation owed him a debt of gratitude, which would be well repaid; but their attachment to his person was originated and cemented by still other causes.

He had come among them from his campaigns in Mexico, and by his modest bearing, his gentlemanly courtesies, his skillful attention to his duties, had won all their hearts. It was nearly seventeen years since he first came to Missouri—a young Lieutenant and Aid to General CLARK, then in command of Jefferson Barracks. Here he had married the only daughter of the late Mr. SAMUEL RUSSELL, one of the oldest and most highly esteemed merchants of

Saint Louis. The name of this gentleman is never mentioned but with respect among all who knew him. His house, on Fourth street, in that city, was for years the seat of generous and elegant hospitality; while his career as a merchant exerted a wide-spread influence in the prosecution of Western trade. Here General HANCOCK had resided, for several years; here his children were born; here his character as a soldier and a gentleman had been regarded with pride. Nothing of the kind, therefore, could be more becoming, than that St. Louis should honor herself by honoring him with an elegant and costly sword.

CHAPTER XXX.

The Second Army Corps Advancing on Petersburg—General Meade Congratulates General Hancock—Closing in upon Richmond—A Magnificent Ruse and a Midnight Surprise.

WE are now to take our stand with HANCOCK, in front of Petersburg, Virginia. The intermediate steps by which he reached this important point are passing into the current history of the country. His Corps moved, in conjunction with that of WARREN, across the intervening region, until they arrived at the position of most strategic value. He was in the advance of the extreme left, on the fifteenth of June, and immediately opened on the enemy. The outer works assailed were pronounced by competent judges to be more difficult to capture than those taken from the enemy at Missionary Ridge and Chattanooga.

It seemed natural that the old Second Corps should be among the first to make the attack on these new and powerful strongholds of the enemy. It was still meet and fitting that they should be in the advance. Their well-tried guns were among the earliest to wake the echoes of Petersburg.

Up to this time the leaders at Richmond had no correct idea of our movements. They were not at all aware of our having crossed the James. It was their expectation—their fond hope—that we should take the old route, by way of Malvern Hills, where they were prepared to greet us with secret embankments, ambuscades, and surprises; if possible to drive us back, and keep us through the summer in the pestilential swamps of the Chickahominy, and contiguous streams. They did not dream that by a bold movement GRANT would again change his whole base, dash across the James river in darkness and silence, and plant himself opposite their intrenchments in front of Petersburg, and south of Richmond. They awoke to the discovery of the fact that the arduous and gallant deed was done—and they knew it not! Their defences at a strong strategic point were not only now to be assailed, but both Petersburg and Richmond were to be virtually besieged,

24*

and the long lines of communications with other parts of the Confederation seriously endangered.

Large rebel reinforcements were now sent rapidly forward to confront us. By placing a strong force across the Appomattox river, in the immediate vicinity of Petersburg, the enemy prevented us from the speedy capture of that place, except at a greater sacrifice of life, on both sides, than the Lieutenant General felt warranted in making.

The next strategy of GRANT was the possession of the contiguous railroads. By shutting up considerable bodies of hostile troops in Richmond and Petersburg, he prevented Lee from employing them against us at other points, and prepared the way for those movements in certain directions which he knew would greatly weaken the military power of the South. Saving his men from severe losses by direct attacks and defences, he could enclose the enemy within their entrenchments; and then, by gradually cutting off their supplies, either compel an evacuation or surrender. He had already inflicted considerable damage on some of their lines of communication; but the facilities for repairing then enjoyed by the enemy, in consequence of the secret assistance they derived from their sympathizers abroad, enabled them to keep the most active of them in occasional use. The lines of our army were gradually and steadily being drawn over all this net-work of railroads; but they were not yet sufficiently strong and compact to be completely effective in holding them.

The Second Corps had been advanced toward Petersburg, resting its right wing on the Jerusalem plank road, running across from the railroad to Norfolk and Weldon. In the absence of HANCOCK, who was kept from the field by the breaking out, in consequence of his severe duties, of his Gettysburg wound, there was a gap allowed to occur between his Corps and the Sixth. Taking advantage of this fact, revealed to them by spies, the enemy made a dash on his lines, and inflicted some damage. It is due to General BIRNEY, who was in temporary command of the Second Corps, at the time, that he should be exonerated from all blame for this reverse. It was not owing to any lack of vigilance or courage on his part, but to the occurrence of fortuitous circumstances not in the power of man to prevent.

The twentieth Massachusetts regiment of volunteers, attached to the Second Corps, rallied at the call of danger, and rendered great service on this occasion. It was in command, at the time, of Captain PATTEN, to whom much credit is due for the manner in which he came to the rescue, and whose coolness and daring prepared the way for the gradual rescue of the Corps from its sudden exposure.

HANCOCK was in his tent, suffering extreme pain. As the cry came to him —

"The Second Corps is attacked!" he rushed from his couch, in his night dress, and, calling an ambulance, rode directly to the front.

"What is the matter with the Second Corps?" he asked, in tones that betokened the deepest feeling.

"We are assailed by a superior force, in mass; cut off from support on the left flank!" replied one of his Aids, who had galloped ahead of him, to the scene of danger.

In a moment more HANCOCK, wrapped in his army overcoat, sword in hand, was mounted and rushing to the field. But by the time he reached the centre of the fight, and had begun to rally his men, the enemy had been driven back, and the danger was passed. Some losses were experienced, but they were soon repaired, and plans were instantly laid for preventing any such occurrence in the future.

The brave old Corps could still sing:

> "Though some may sleep 'neath Virginia's sod,
> We still bear the flag of the free, my boys;
> And those who are true to our land and God,
> Will meet at the last reveille, my boys."

It is a strong proof of the confidence reposed in HANCOCK by GRANT that in the attacks first made on Petersburg his command was materially enlarged. In addition to his own Corps, detachments from the forces under SMITH and BURNSIDE were placed at his immediate disposal. His main attacks were begun by the Division of BIRNEY, who conducted himself with his usual gallantry. The enemy were repeatedly driven from strong positions, with severe losses in men and guns. BIRNEY's troops behaved in the most splendid manner in their assaults, winning the highest admiration from all their fellow-soldiers. His division advanced, under a heavy fire, to within a few hundred yards of the enemy's works, and his guns commanded the city.

Lee now rapidly crossed the James, reinforced Beauregard, in command of Petersburg, and postponed, though he could not prevent its ultimate capture. Severe fighting ensued; but every attempt to drive us from our siege position was a signal failure. Our lines continued to extend; our works gradually grew more numerous, extensive, and powerful; and it was soon evident that our grasp, at this vital point of the enemy, could not and would not be loosened, until victory ensued.

The health of HANCOCK speedily improved, and

he immediately resumed his more active duties in the field. He had placed his artillery in the most commanding positions, and was doing his work with his usual vigor.

The distinguished honor of making the first direct assault on Petersburg was assigned to the Second Corps, in conjunction with the troops from Bermuda Hundred, under SMITH. HANCOCK was ready with his men, and eager for the brave attempt; but a delay in furnishing him supplies caused a detention of several hours, which prevented the success of the measure. It was soon after found that the arrival of reinforcements had much strengthened the enemy; and the peculiar location of the city would defer its capture by any other method than a regular siege. On this basis GRANT now laid his plans; and, with his usual reticence and coolness, proceeded to carry them into effect.

A much needed opportunity for rest was afforded our great army. Entrenching, bombarding, mining, was now the order of the day and night. The latter process was conducted in a manner that must always attract the attention of military historians. The ground was dug in such an angle as to form a subterranean gallery, and the miners were pushed forward by their pickaxes and spades under the solid earth, the exca-

vations being made without the use of coffer works,
or frames of any kind. Dangerous as this process
was, it prevented the enemy from hearing our progress under their works and beneath their feet. Silently, steadily, in a darkness illumined by only a
few army lights, our brave men dug their way; no
sound of hammers being heard in their under-ground
march, the opening to their mine being adroitly hidden from view; and occasional fusilades of musketry
and salutes of artillery deluding the watchful enemy
from our secret purpose.

As a still further foil to the enemy, the Second
Corps was ordered over the Appomattox, aided by
other troops, who together formed a junction at Point
of Rocks. This so attracted the attention of the
rebels, that they were completely divested of all idea
as to where and how any mining operations might
be going on. At the same time a detachment of
cavalry, under SHERIDAN, crossed the James, at Jones'
Neck, whose open movements, followed by a line of
four hundred empty army wagons, so completely
deceived Lee that he at once detached a special force
to intercept us.

The Second Corps, and its allies, performed their
part with skill. The enemy were drawn on after

them, in a bootless pursuit, leaving the entrenchments at Petersburg still more exposed.

At this moment, while the attention of the enemy
is completely diverted, and while many of our own
men are wondering what is to come from the unexpected movement, the mine is sprung. The explosion is tremendous. Immense masses of earthworks
and of the adjacent enclosure are thrown high in the
air, and a wide breach is made in the enemy's defences. The attacking parties rush forward with
determined valor; but, for want of adequate support,
at this most critical juncture, they are too much exposed to achieve all the results that such an explosion
had warranted us to expect. The enemy recover
from the shock just in time to bring their heaviest
and best posted guns to bear on our exposed columns,
and the advantages we had hoped to gain by this
great strategic movement are suddenly wrested from
us. But the experience gained by this explosion
was invaluable, and we shall see that it was successfully employed on several future occasions.

It was a gratifying coincidence that soon after the
occurrence in the advance, in which, during the absence of HANCOCK, the Second Corps met with some
losses, he should have the honor in person to repay
them. Immediately on resuming his active command

he commenced forward demonstrations. He issued an earnest address to his troops, in which he adjured them to haste to wipe out any reproach that might be supposed to rest on their long-honored colors. He called upon them to follow him again in repulsing the misguided enemies of their country, and to win back their guns. Nobly, enthusiastically his brave men responded. In a few hours only after he entered the field again an attack was made on the rebels, in which the Corps captured four guns of heavier calibre than those they had lost. The deed was done. Their honored name was re-established.

Immediately on receiving the announcement of this gallant capture, General MEADE dispatched this congratulatory note to General HANCOCK:

"HEADQUARTERS ARMY OF the POTOMAC, }
9 A. M., July 27, 1864. }

GENERAL HANCOCK:

Your dispatch of twenty minutes past seven is just received.

I congratulate you and your gallant Corps on your success, and trust it will be continued.

GEO. G. MEADE,
Major General.

For some weeks previous to this characteristic occurrence, the troops of HANCOCK had been among the most active of any engaged in the siege. The divisions of BIRNEY, BARLOW and GIBBON were frequently in motion, inflicting severe blows on the enemy, at every assailable point. In consequence of the character of the hostile entrenchments, it was discovered that general advances along our whole line were inexpedient. The gains were not commensurate with the losses of men and time. BARLOW's division, in conjunction with a detachment of sharpshooters, was sent out on important reconnoissances, and steps were continually taken to possess ourselves of the contiguous railroads, for the purpose of more effectually cutting off the supplies of the enemy. The enemy were frequently encountered in considerable force, and in every case driven back. By combining on our rear and massing on our flanks the wily Lee succeeded in inflicting losses upon us, occasionally, especially at points where the Corps had not been able, owing to the nature of the country, to complete their junctions; but they were soon repaired, and the lines of entrenchment were drawn closer and closer around the walls of Petersburg.

The activity of our cavalry, under WILSON, continued to be felt at all points. He succeeded in reaching several parts of the enemy's railroad communications, and in cutting them asunder. Their rations were growing less and less reliable, smaller and smaller in quantity. Large bodies of hostile raiders were sent into comparatively new regions, to procure those indispensable supplies, the want of which was now so much felt by Lee in his camps, and by the schemers in Richmond and other besieged places.

General HANCOCK had resumed the active command of his Corps on the evening of the 27th of June. General BIRNEY, who had so well conducted himself at its head for the past few weeks, now resumed his position in the Third Division.

Demonstrations were soon began to be made for the complete possession of the Weldon railroad. The occupation of this important means of communication would leave the besieged enemy only one permanent railroad — the Danville — and such outside roads as the country afforded. Many and difficult preparatory steps were essential to secure this important result.

At daylight of Saturday, July 30, the Union forces opened on the enemy with a battery of one hundred guns. HANCOCK had recrossed the James, and was prepared to take part in the contemplated assault. He had been operating to advantage for two days on the north bank of the river, and now joined his forces with those of SHERIDAN and KAUTZ, on the south side of the Appomattox. He had come to the rescue at the most critical moment. His rapid movements in the direction of Malvern Hill had resulted in the capture of several guns and a considerable body of prisoners.

The position of the campaign after the explosion and assault was as formidable as ever. Our lines were still advancing; the coils of war were being drawn more and more closely around the enemies of the Republic.

It was now the 30th of July. Gratifying intelligence came pouring in of the operations of SHERMAN at Atlanta, and of FARRAGUT, at Mobile Bay. The spirits of our men, in spite of the intense heats and droughts they were called to encounter, and their losses by repulses at the open jaws of death in the explosion of our mine, were still exultant, and every movement was onward.

The great aim of GRANT was the complete and final possession of the Weldon railroad. All his strategy now tended to this important point.

On the 9th of August came the glorious news that Admiral FARRAGUT had passed the forts in Mobile Bay, which the over-confident Confederates had boldly and loudly predicted he could not pass. Stationed at the mast-head of his gallant flag-ship, the *Hartford*, with his speaking-trumpet placed, by means of tubes, on the deck, he had swept into the waters of the enemy, attacking them at every assailable point, sinking and capturing their ships, taking possession of their forts, and planting the national flag on the ramparts from which, with so much of treasonable infamy, it had been hauled down. The nation was electrified at the welcome intelligence, and shouts of joy ran along the Union lines in front of Petersburg. New successes were granted us in the variable Valley of the Shenandoah, and the movements of Sherman, in Georgia, were highly encouraging.

The continued and skillful strategy of GRANT completely deceived the enemy. They were being paid off in their own coin. Greater familiarity with their location and wily stratagems had prepared the way for those strategic movements which surprised and annoyed them to a degree they had never experienced before. But greater and more signal defeats awaited them. Instead of ending his campaign before Petersburg, the enemy found, to their deep grief and ill-dissembled chagrin, that he had but just begun it. Gradually, but surely, one after another, their avowed contempt for the Lieutenant-General died away; and they were reluctantly forced to confess that Lee had, at last, met a foeman worthy of his steel. We thought he was more than worthy.

25 *

On Saturday, August 13th, the Corps of HANCOCK was thrown across the James, at Deep Bottom. This was the same point at which he had made a successful feint movement, on a previous occasion. It had been sent to City Point, on special service, and embarked on transports. Conjecture as to its ultimate destination had been busy, as usual; but all doubt was dispelled by its passing up the river, and landing at Dutch Gap. A little after sunrise, on Sunday morning, BIRNEY advanced, with FOSTER's division, and drove the enemy a considerable distance. The lines of the enemy were broken, and a capture made of nearly a hundred prisoners.

The cavalry, under GREGG, had now cleared the road for HANCOCK, and he steadily advanced. He posted his Corps on the Newmarket road, which leads directly from Malvern Hill to Richmond—distant, at that point, only about ten miles.

BIRNEY, now promoted, and most deservedly, too, to the command of the Tenth Corps, made a gallant assault on the front of the enemy, carrying their works, which guarded the approaches to Richmond in that direction, capturing six pieces of cannon and two mortars.

The position of the enemy was a strong one, and they parted with it very reluctantly. But the skilful manœuvring of HANCOCK had enabled him to reach their front in a way they were not all prepared for; and there was no resort left them but to withdraw. Our troops held the position.

But little hard fighting took place, as the strategy of HANCOCK rendered it unnecessary. The enemy were taken by surprise, and our loss was small.

The whole movement was a perfect blind to the enemy. Our troops, which they saw moving down the river, on transports, during the day, turned back again at night, and, surprising the enemy in their entrenchments, captured them with ease.

As the Second started on this imaginary voyage, their bands struck up gaily, and gave to the winds several martial and playful airs to be wafted to rebel ears. They thought we were bound to Charleston, perhaps to Washington, it might be to Mobile, peradventure to Atlanta. But when we returned that same night, up the still waters of that same river, in silence and in darkness, they woke to their sad mistake, as our men charged with a victorious shout on their works, and carried everything before them. By daylight of the next morning the splendid artillery of the Second Corps could be heard along the hostile lines, its thunders waking from their fitful slumbers the guilty dreamers of Richmond.

CHAPTER XXXI.

THE Union forces operating on the north bank of the James, in the middle of August, remained for a time in boding silence. Their position was one of great strategic importance. It was a mystery to the enemy. They dared not attempt to dislodge it, for they knew not how large a support might be awaiting them in its rear; and yet it did not seem to them of sufficient magnitude to warrant its long continued advance.

This habit of mystifying the enemy by his movements had become a fixed one with GRANT. It was like a second nature with him. Heretofore, in nearly every instance, the enemy could read our plans of battle, discern and predict our campaigns, before we

(296)

nad begun to develop or enter upon them. Now, however, the case was widely different. If Lee was wily, GRANT was equally so. If Lee was good at strategy, GRANT was better. If Lee was great at manœuvring, GRANT was greater. The history of the war will abundantly prove all this to be true.

There was a period, during this diversion of HAN-COCK and BIRNEY, when the advance front of our lines was within six miles of the Secesh capital. The object of the reconnoissance was soon attained. It was to protect our men, working, at Dutch Gap, on the canal, being constructed there to aid our approaches to the city. The cavalry of GREGG was posted on the Charles City Road, protecting our right wing, the left flank of which extended to the banks of the James. Lee was prevented, by this means, from interfering with our workmen, and taught that we knew, as well as he, that there was more than one way of advancing on his base. By this extension of our forces we could assail both Richmond and Petersburg at the same moment; and the better watch the immediate movements of the enemy. If it were true, as the Confederates and their sympathizers so blatantly asserted, that 'Richmond could not be taken,' GRANT, his Generals, and his army, could not see it in that point of light.

Our continued progress had further developed the position of the enemy. In a spirited engagement we had captured four hundred more prisoners, and killed two general officers — Chamblin and Gherrard — their bodies being left in our hands. All our plans and combinations were proved to be effective; the signs of its coming doom were concentrating more and more closely around the focus of the rebellion. It was evident to all reflecting minds that there must be more severe fighting, and that Richmond and vicinity were yet to contain many other sanguinary fields, ere the war could be brought to an honorable and permanent close.

It was now past the middle of August. Many attacks were made on our lines, but they were invariably repulsed. Obstacles to the progress of the Union arms that had been potential in former campaigns, failed to retard us now. The siege of Richmond was a fixed fact. Nothing seemed to relax our hold on the central power of the enemy. Every thing transpired to prove that the final victory over the army of Lee would terminate the struggle in the complete restoration of the Union.

On the morning of the 18th of August, our troops made a most important movement. They crossed from their seemingly quiet position, and, by rapid advances, captured and held certain strong points on the Weldon railroad. Severe fighting ensued; but we held all that we had gained, capturing a considerable number of prisoners from Heth's, Mahone's, and Hoke's divisions — some of the best of the Southern forces.

Meanwhile the continued efforts of the enemy to dislodge us from the north bank of the James, were all futile. We remained in our positions, and entrenched.

There was a surprise of our lines on the Weldon road during the night of the 20th of August, in which we lost some guns and prisoners. But it was soon recovered from them; and, while our entrenchments were increased and materially strengthened, other measures were promptly adopted to prevent a similar occurrence in the future.

The tenacity of GRANT exceeded any thing previously displayed by him, in any of his movements. At each attempt of the enemy to move him from his hold, he grasped it all the more firmly. He was furiously attacked during several successive days; and each engagement gave him a new victory. We more than regained the number of prisoners we had lost in the previous surprise. At the last of these onsets four active Generals were killed and wounded.

It was perfectly evident that the enemy could not dislodge us from the coveted strategic points. By the 25th of August it became apparent that they had desisted, at least for the present, from all attempts to repossess them.

Comparatively quiet possession of the road now being obtained, our forces proceeded thoroughly to destroy all those portions of it under their immediate control. The work was quickly and effectually done. Our men divided their forces to the best advantage. A part worked night and day in completing fortifications; the soldier of one hour was the digger of the next; the musket and the spade interchanged with each other in the ramparts, at regular intervals; while the silent cannon, glistening in the sun, or glimmering in the light of army lanterns, pushed out their open mouths over the heads of the men, as their grim defenders, ready to plead for the continuance of their industry, at a moment's warning.

The Weldon railroad was ours.

Richmond papers, coming within our now protected lines, acknowledged, with ill-concealed shame, their loss of this important position. They taunted us with endeavoring to starve them out of their stronghold; as if they had not attempted the same thing with us, every time they had the opportunity.

The first division of the Second Corps were among the most active of all our troops in destroying this necessary means of army communication. They were accustomed to labor; and these fighting work-men were not ashamed to work hard here, in so good a cause. They completely destroyed the road; tearing up and burning it, from the first point of conquest to Reams's station, and for a distance of three miles beyond. The whole line held by our forces at that place was nearly eight miles.

Another desperate attempt was made by the enemy to regain possession of the road toward evening of the 27th of August. The attack was made on HAN-COCK, who was stationed at an exposed point, isolated from the main line—as was so often his position, far in the advance.

The attack began south of Reams's station, and was made with great desperation. But he met it with all his unflinching valor, and gave it a severe repulse. It was a combined assault on his centre and left. Support was out of the question. He took up the gage of battle single-handed, and fought it out on that line. The fight was one of the fiercest of any field, of any campaign. But he met the enemy at every point, and drove them, routed, from

26

the field. Their dead and wounded, which were numerous, were left in our hands.

This attack was evidently intended to be simultaneous against HANCOCK, by Wilcox on his centre, and Heth on his left. They had expected to find him scattered, busy at the work of railroad destruction, and, comparatively, unprepared. They were mistaken. He was ready for them. Exposed as his position was, he defended it with such vigor and skill that they were completely foiled.

Forming in the adjacent woods, placing their artillery so as to be ambushed, and, at the same time, to enfilade our lines, the enemy flattered themselves with a sudden scare on the part of HANCOCK, and an easy conquest on theirs. He very soon undeceived them. Their cannonading was heavy, lasting a considerable time. They then massed under cover, and charged on our unprotected columns. But our men dropped their work instantly, seized their rifles with a rush, swept into line like a wave of the sea rolling on the even beach, and met the shock of arms without a waver. Bayonet clashed with bayonet, sword with sword, in rapid succession. Hand to hand, foot to foot, shoulder to shoulder, face to face, our men held every inch of their ground, taking not a step backward from the foe, but hurling him in defiance along the earth, in every instance, where there was any-thing like an equality of forces. In one or two cases, where the numbers of the enemy were overpowering, and a slight foothold was gained by them, our men rushed from one weak point to another, strengthen-ing each other's hands, cheering one another to the onset, until the union was secured, the enemy were driven back, and our original position regained and held. Our troops rushed from right to left, in aid of the assailed columns, beating back the repeated assaults from the weaker points, and massing into stronger lines of defence.

General GIBBON displayed great courage and presence of mind on this occasion. He checked the advancing foes in the midst of one of their most furious onsets, and hurled them back in confusion. General GREGG, with his dismounted cavalry, render-ed important service. His improvised infantry were handled in the most handsome manner; meeting the enemy in a way for which they were not prepared. The command of MILES, which was the first assailed, won high distinction, notwithstanding its scattered condition. The General and his staff officers behaved with great gallantry, and received the commendation of HANCOCK, on the field.

This severe fight was continued through the afternoon, until dark; the enemy being held in check by artillery, dismounted cavalry, and skirmishers. General HANCOCK speaks of it as acknowledged to have been one of the most determined and desperate conflicts of the war; resembling Spottsylvania in its character. Had there been more troops at his com mand, at the moment, the victory would have been still more decisive.

A considerable number of prisoners were sent forward from the divisions of Wilcox and Heth.

The enemy disappeared from the hard-fought field, evidently much discomfited, leaving his dead and wounded in our hands. Their losses were admitted by prisoners to have been greater, in proportion, than any they had experienced during the war.

The object of HANCOCK in the temporary occupation of his portion of the road was attained, and our onward movements continued to progress. The Southern press acknowledged severe losses in this fierce action with HANCOCK, four of their general officers being among the number. The destruction of the road contiguous to Reams's Station by the Second Corps had been so thorough that the enemy were compelled to transport all their stores from that point by means of army wagons, over difficult byways. They would have had but little even of these with which to supply their increasing wants, had it not been for the support afforded them by their foreign allies, who managed to evade our blockade at Wilmington. The best of their arms and munitions of war had come to their diminished camps from this alien source; their dependence for them on other parts of the seceding States being now materially lessened by the capture of more Southern positions. The strong point of Atlanta, Georgia, was rendered comparatively useless to the rebellion, by the consummate strategy and invincible courage of SHERMAN, in co-operation with the indomitable FARRAGUT, at Mobile, Alabama, and the gallant SHERIDAN, in the Valley of Virginia. The glorious news soon came that Atlanta was ours. The able General Hood, on whom so much dependence had been placed by the Confederate authorities, was compelled to evacuate that south-western stronghold, leaving in our possession all its defences, a large number of prisoners, and an immense supply of munitions of war.

Repeated attempts continued to be made by Lee to regain possession of the much needed Weldon road. But they all failed. Every attack was gallantly repulsed, and we held on. The spirits of the army remained as exultant as ever. There was no such word as fail in all our increasing ranks. President LIN-

26*   U

COLN issued a special Order, as Commander in Chief
of the Army and Navy, recapitulating the victories
won by General SHERMAN and Admiral FARRAGUT,
returning thanks to the soldiers and seamen concerned, for their glorious achievements, and calling
on the people of the United States to assemble in
their respective places of public worship, to render
thanks to ALMIGHTY GOD for these signal proofs of
the Divine favor on the Union arms. A salute of
one hundred shotted guns was ordered by General
GRANT, in honor of these great victories.

Meanwhile, as the summer closed, and the month
of September came upon us, our advance toward
Richmond steadily continued. It was as rapid as
such siege approaches could be made, consistent with
a due regard to the lives of our men, and our bases
of operations. Every day of the months devoted to
the conquest of Richmond city had been profitably
employed. Not an hour, not a moment, had been
lost in idle inactivity or supine indifference. The
army and the navy efficiently co-operated with each
other, and the prospect of ultimate victory over the
secession was as cheering as ever. The capture of
Richmond, now undertaken in downright earnest,
was prosecuted with vigor, although the plans contemplated and put in operation by the Lieutenant-

General, could not, with propriety, be made known
to the American people, quietly pursuing their avo-
cations at home.   Delays, which they could neither
understand nor appreciate, were necessary to the successful termination of the closing scenes of the great
struggle.

Vigorous measures were constantly in progress.
By the middle of September large masses of Union
troops were stationed at different points on the railroads, a few miles South of Petersburg.   Our left
line, in strong force, was pushed across the Weldon
road, to a mile beyond it, on the west.   The movement was a cause of some excitement among the
enemy, who watched its progress with the deepest
interest.   General GRANT does not appear to have
taken the trouble to inform them what it all meant.
Probably he was of the opinion that they would find
it out themselves, in due time.   At all events, they
took the hint sufficiently to strengthen their entrenchments in that immediate neighborhood.

In order to render our operations more effective, a
railroad was constructed by our able engineer corps
from City Point, on the James, only a few miles south
of Richmond, to a convenient terminus on the Weldon road.   This means of communication was soon
opened to great advantage, the arrival of the first

trains of cars, suitably loaded, being received with cheering all along our lines. It was another stretch of the conquering chain of war that was environing Richmond — a chain that the Confederates had with their own hands forged, and from the coils of which they were soon to find there was no escape.

Large reinforcements continued to swell the **Union** army under GRANT, who quickly massed them on his left, immediately confronting the rebel right. Where they came from, and what the hero of Vicksburg was going to do with them, seemed to pass the foe's comprehension. His movements, on all hands, continued to be to them a profound mystery. This was exactly what he intended. When the time should come — and he, of all men, knew when that time would come—he was prepared to encircle Petersburg, as he had Vicksburg, with a grasp that would either compel its evacuation or destruction. For reasons creditable to his noble soldierly qualities, he much preferred the former to the latter alternative.

Matters remained in this favorable condition, when, after a short visit to the headquarters of General SHERIDAN by the Lieutenant General, the Army of the Shenandoah suddenly moved on the enemy, and won the splendid victory before Winchester, Virginia, which occurred on the 19th of September. By a series of rapid engagements, commencing, very properly, at Bunker Hill, Sheridan drove the enemy from all their positions, killing large numbers, capturing several thousand prisoners, a large supply of provisions and many munitions of war. The rout of the enemy was complete, continuing through a series of battles, at different points, to Staunton, Virginia, when the town was possessed, with all the adjacent region, and much of the Confederate property destroyed. Every position was temporarily held for strategic purposes, and a blow inflicted on the secession in that quarter of the country from which it never could recover.

The effect of this brilliant victory on the army before Richmond can be well conceived. It cheered every loyal heart. It strengthened every patriotic arm. It had been won in accordance with plans previously laid down by GRANT, and was designed to aid him in his immediate movements on the enemy's capital and its surroundings.

On the 30th of September another onward movement began. The Tenth Corps, under BIRNEY, co-operating with other selected bodies of veteran troops, moved on the strong entrenchments of the enemy, at Chapin's Farm, the nearest point to Richmond yet reached, and carried them by storm. The hostile line was found to be thin, and the embankments,

which were among the strongest thrown up around
the rebel capital, were defended by only a small force.
The subsequent attempts made by the enemy to retake these commanding approaches to Richmond
were so easily repulsed that the impression began to
prevail in certain quarters that Lee would evacuate
his capital and thus surrender his base of operations.
But GRANT, and those who better comprehended the
strategy of the Confederate leader, knew better than
this.   He and they were perfectly assured that there
must be much more severe fighting at this point,
before the rebellion would be subdued.

On the 2d of October, HANCOCK advanced a portion of his Corps to a point considerably nearer the
enemy.   He took possession of the Boynton road,
over which the enemy had been carrying their supplies, in wagons, to Petersburg.   Two lines of works
were found unoccupied.   A skirmish line opposed
our advance, but gradually fell back before the continued attacks of our troops.

CHAPTER XXXII.

The Battle of Gettysburg described by General Hancock — Full Details of the Fight that Saved Philadelphia — The Order that Placed General Hancock over General Howard — The Second and Third Divisions of the Second Corps Bear the Brunt of Battle.

PAUSING for a brief space in our record of General HANCOCK's war career, now rapidly drawing to a close so far as active service at the front is concerned, it will be interesting here to retrace our steps over the fields of carnage, to introduce, in our hero's own words, a description of the ever-memorable three days' struggle around the Heights of Gettysburg; that fierce and bloody conflict between the desperate and determined invaders of the Keystone State and the equally resolute defenders of her sacred soil; that bitter battle upon which hung the fate of Philadelphia. We quote, therefore, from General HANCOCK's evidence given on March 22, 1864, before the Committee on the Conduct of the War, then in session at Washington. He commences by alluding to the receipt of Major-General BUTTERFIELD's order, which we here insert.

HEADQUARTERS ARMY OF THE POTOMAC,

July 1, 1863, 1.10 P. M.

COMMANDING OFFICER, SECOND CORPS (GENERAL HANCOCK):

The Major-General commanding has just been informed that General REYNOLDS has been killed or badly wounded. He directs that you turn over the command of your Corps to General GIBBON: that you proceed to the front, and by virtue of this order, in case of the truth of General REYNOLDS's death, you assume command of the corps there assembled, viz., the 11th, 1st and 3d, at Emmetts- burg. If you think the ground and position there a better one to fight a battle under existing circumstances, you will so advise the General, and he will order all the troops up. You know the Gen- eral's views, and General WARREN, who is fully aware of them, has gone out to see General REYNOLDS.

LATER, 1.15 P. M.—REYNOLDS has possession of Gettysburg, and the enemy are reported as falling back from in front of Gettys- burg. Hold your column ready to move.

Very respectfully, your obedient servant,

D. BUTTERFIELD,

Major-General and Chief of Staff.

After referring to this order, the General said: "I started a little before half-past one, turning over the command of my corps to General GIBBON, under General MEADE's directions. General GIBBON was not the next in rank in that corps; but he was the one General MEADE directed should assume the com- mand, as he considered him the most suitable person for it.

"Several such instances occurred during that battle. General MEADE, prior to the battle, showed me or told me of a letter he had received from the Secretary of War on this subject. The Government recognizing the difficulty of the situation, believing that a battle was imminent, and might occur in one, two, or three days, and not knowing the views of General MEADE in relation to his commanders, the Secretary of War wrote him a note, authorizing him to make any changes in his army that he pleased, and that he would be sustained by the President and himself. That did not make it legal, because it was contrary to the law to place a junior officer over a senior. At the same time it was one of those emergencies in which General MEADE was authorized, as before stated, to exercise that power. I was not the senior of either General HOWARD, of the Eleventh Corps, or General SICKLES, of the Third Corps. My commission bore date on the same day with theirs; by my prior commission they both ranked me. Of course, it was not a very agreeable office for me to fill, to go and take command of my seniors. However, I did not feel much embarrassment about it, because I was an older soldier than either of them. But I knew that legally it was not proper, and that, if they chose to resist it, it might become a very troublesome matter to me for the time-being

27

Whether or not General MEADE, when he gave me the order, knew about this relative rank, I do not know. I say this because I have since understood that he did not. When I spoke to him about it before departing, however, he remarked in substance that he was obliged to use such persons as he felt disposed to use; that in this case he sent me because he had explained his views to me, and had not explained them to the others; that I knew his plans and ideas, and could better accord with him in my operations than anybody else. I went to Gettysburg, arriving on the ground not later than half-past three o'clock. I found that, practically, the fight was then over. The rear of our column, with the enemy in pursuit, was then coming through the town of Gettysburg. General HOWARD was on Cemetery Hill, and there had evidently been an attempt on his part to stop and form some of his troops there; what troops he had formed there, I do not know. I understood afterwards, and accepted it as the fact, that he had formed one division there prior to this time. I told General HOWARD I had orders to take command in the front. I did not show him the orders, because he did not demand it. He acquiesced.

"I exercised the command until evening, when General SLOCUM arrived, about six or seven o'clock.

His troops were in the neighborhood, for they apparently had been summoned up before I arrived, by General HOWARD possibly, as well as the Third Corps. When General SLOCUM arrived, he being my senior, and not included in this order to me, I turned the command over to him. In fact, I was instructed verbally by General BUTTERFIELD, Chief of Staff, before I left for the front, that I was to do so.

"When I arrived and took command, I extended the lines. I sent General WADSWORTH to the right to take possession of Culp's Hill with his division. I directed General GEARY, whose division belonged to the Twelfth Corps (its commander, General SLOCUM, not then having arrived), to take possession of the high ground towards Round Top. I made such disposition as I thought wise and proper. The enemy, evidently believing that we were reinforced, or that our whole army was there, discontinued their great efforts, and the battle for that day was virtually over. There was firing of artillery and skirmishing all along the front, but that was the end of that day's battle. By verbal instructions, and in the order which I had received from General MEADE, I was directed to report, after having arrived on the ground, whether it would be necessary or wise to continue to fight the battle at Gettysburg, or whether it was

possible for the fight to be had on the ground General MEADE had selected. About four o'clock, P.M.,
I sent word by Major MITCHELL, aide-de-camp to
General MEADE, that I would hold the ground until
dark, meaning to allow him time to decide the matter for himself. As soon as I had gotten matters
arranged to my satisfaction, and saw that the troops
were being formed again, and I felt secure, I wrote
a note to General MEADE, and informed him of my
views of the ground at Gettysburg. I told him that
the only disadvantage which I thought it had was
that it could be readily turned by way of Emmetts-
burg, and that the roads were clear for any movement he might make. I had ordered all the trains
back, as I came up, to clear the roads.

"General MEADE had directed my corps, the Second Corps, to march up towards Gettysburg, under the
command of General GIBBON. When I found that
the enemy had ceased their operations, I directed
General GIBBON to halt his corps two or three miles
behind Gettysburg, in order to protect our rear from
any flank movement of the enemy. Then my operations in the front being closed, I turned the command over to General SLOCUM, and immediately
started to report to General MEADE in detail what I
had done, in order to express my views clearly to

him, and to see what he was disposed to do. I rode back, and found General MEADE about nine o'clock. He told me he had received my messages and note, and had decided, upon the representations I had made, and the existence of known facts of the case, to fight at Gettysburg, and had ordered all the corps to the front. That was the end of operations for that day.

"On the third day, in the morning, the enemy and General SLOCUM were a good deal engaged. About one or two o'clock in the afternoon, the enemy commenced a terrific cannonade, from probably one hundred and twenty pieces of artillery, on the front of the line connecting Cemetery Hill with Round Top, the left centre commanded by me. That line consisted of the 1st, 2d, and 3d Corps, of which I had the general command. *I commanded that whole front.* General GIBBON commanded the Second Corps in my absence, General NEWTON the First Corps, and General BIRNEY the Third. That cannonade continued for probably an hour and a half. The enemy then made an assault at the end of that time. It was a very formidable assault, and made, I should judge, with about 18,000 infantry. When the columns of the enemy appeared, it looked as if they were going to attack the centre of our line, but, after marching

27 *

straight out a little distance, they seemed to incline a little to their left, as if their object was to march through my command. and seize Cemetery Hill, which, I have no doubt, was their intention. They attacked with wonderful spirit; nothing could have been more spirited. The shock of the assault fell upon the 2d and 3d Divisions of the Second Corps, assisted by a small brigade of Vermont troops, together with the artillery of our line, which fired from Round Top to Cemetery Hill at the enemy all the way as they advanced, whenever they had the opportunity. Those were the troops that really met the assault. No doubt there were other troops that fired a little, but those were the troops that really withstood the shock of the assault and repulsed it. The attack of the enemy was met by about six small brigades of our troops, and was finally repulsed after a terrific contest at very close quarters, in which our troops took about thirty or forty colors and some 4000 to 5000 prisoners, with great loss to the enemy in killed and wounded. The repulse was a most signal one, and that decided the battle, and was practically the end of the fight.' I was wounded at the close of the assault, and that ended my operations with the army for that campaign. I did not follow it in its future movements.

" *This practically ended* **the** *fighting of the battle of* *Gettysburg.* There was **no** serious fighting there after that, save on the left, in an advance by a small command of the Pennsylvania Reserves, made very soon afterwards, and based upon our success. I may say one thing here: I think it was probably an unfortunate thing that I was wounded at the time I was, and equally unfortunate that General GIBBON was also wounded; because the absence of a prominent commander, who knew the circumstances thoroughly at such a moment as that, was a great disadvantage. I think that our lines should have advanced immediately, and I believe we should have won a great victory. I was very confident that the advance would be made. General MEADE told me before the fight that if the enemy attacked me, he intended to put the Fifth and Sixth Corps on the enemy's flank; therefore, when I was wounded and lying down in my ambulance, and about leaving the field, I dictated a note to General MEADE, and told him if he would put in the Fifth and Sixth Corps, I believed he would win a great victory. I asked him afterwards, when I returned to the army, what he had done in the premises. He said he had ordered the movement, but the troops were slow in collecting, and moved so slowly that nothing was done before night, except that some of the Pennsylvania Reserves went out and met Hood's division, it was understood, of the enemy, and actually overthrew it, assisted, no doubt, in some measure, by their knowledge of their failure in the assault. There were only two divisions of the enemy on our extreme left, opposite Round Top, and there was a gap in their line of one mile that their assault had left, and I believe if our whole line had advanced with spirit, it is not unlikely that we would have taken all their artillery at that point. I think that was a fault; that we should have pushed the enemy there, for we do not often catch them in that position; and the rule is, and it is natural, that when you repulse or defeat an enemy, you should pursue him; and I believe it is a rare thing that one party beats another and does not pursue him; and I think that on that occasion it only required an order and prompt execution.

"I have no doubt the enemy regarded the success of their assault as certain, so much so that they were willing to expend all their ammunition. They did not suppose that any troops could live under that cannonade; but they met troops that had been so accustomed to artillery fire that it did not have the effect on them that they expected. It was a most terrific and appalling cannonade,—one possibly hardly ever paralleled.

" *Question.* — Was there ever, in any battle of which you have read, more artillery brought into action than in that battle?

" *Answer.* — I doubt whether there has ever been more concentrated upon an equal space and opening at one time. I think there has been more artillery engaged in many battles, but do not believe there has been more upon both sides concentrated on an equal space.

" *Question.* — You did not follow the army from there?

" *Answer.* — No, sir; I left the field the moment the fight was over.

" *Question.* — When did you join the army again?

" *Answer.*— I did not join it again until some time in December, when active operations had ceased. I was then ordered by the Secretary of War into the States from whence the regiments of my corps came to fill them up by recruitment, and I am now on my return to the army.

" *Question.* — But, with equal numbers, you would not hesitate to attack the enemy anywhere under equal circumstances?

" *Answer.* — No, sir; I would not. In fact, there

V

is no finer army, if as fine, in existence in the world than the Army of the Potomac. The troops will do anything if they are only ordered. If they have not made this or that attack, it is because their commanders did not order them to make it."

In this statement we have a complete epitome of General HANCOCK's character, since it demonstrates his prompt and unquestioning obedience to orders, his fearless bravery, his keen and rapid appreciation of military positions, and not less his innate courtesy, his delicate appreciation of the feelings of others, and that modest self-abnegation which has ever been one of his marked characteristics. One sentence embodies this: "I think it was probably an unfortunate thing that I was wounded at the time I was." Not a word as to the fearful peril in which he had been placed; not a sigh of anguish, as his severe wound was even then, probably, administering sharp reminders, but merely the regret of the soldier that he was prevented from completing the work in hand, and thus reaping for his country the fruits of the great victory which his valor had practically placed within grasp. Lying wounded in his ambulance, he suggested a movement which, if it had been carried out, would doubtless have saved many months of hard fighting afterwards.

CHAPTER XXXIII.

Brigadier-General Hancock — **Battles of** *Tolopatomoy* **Creek, North
Anna, Cold Harbor,** *the Sanguinary* **Chickahominy, Deep Bottom,
Reams's Station, and** *Boydton Plank-Road* — **The End of** *his Fight-
ing Career* — **An Important Mission Conferred upon him.**

RESUMING our narrative, we may mention here
that the **rank** of Brigadier-General **was** conferred upon General HANCOCK for the brilliant action
of May 12th. The **next** engagement **of** any note
was at Tolopatomoy Creek, on May 30th, HAN-
COCK having led the advance of the left flank and
pushed on to Bowling Green, thence to Milford
bridge, where he crossed the Mattapony, still seek-
ing the enemy and thirsting for battle, on Saturday,
May 21st. During that **day and** Sunday the army
advanced along the line of the Fredericksburg Railroad, its **right** at Guinney's Station, its centre at
Bowling Green, and its left at Milford Station. The
enemy's cavalry were met and repulsed in small detachments. By nightfall on Monday, General HAN-
COCK, with the Second and Fifth Corps, reached the
North Anna River in the neighborhood of Jericho

bridge. These two corps were in the advance of the main body, the Fifth being on the right of the Second. The enemy, having carefully removed all his stores along the route, was here found formed in very strong position, and evidently bent on holding his ground. With characteristic impetuosity, HAN-COCK rapidly formed his plans, and, leading his men in a desperate charge, forced the enemy's works and carried the position, with the loss of about three hundred men. The Fifth Corps crossed the river higher up, and were at once attacked, but repulsed the enemy and inflicted considerable damage. General GRANT, in writing of these engagements, said he had never heard more rapid or massive firing either of artillery or musketry. At night the Second and Fifth Corps were on the south side of the North Anna, and by Wednesday the whole army had crossed, after some severe fighting at Chesterfield bridge and Jericho bridge and ford.

Pushing onward, the infantry got possession of Hanovertown and the crossing of the Pamunkey, GREGG's cavalry, with SHERIDAN's corps co-operating, moving southward. Near Tolopatomoy Creek, an affluent of the Pamunkey, GREGG's cavalry encountered Hampton's and Fitzhugh Lee's cavalry, and a sharp engagement ensued. GREGG was greatly outnumbered, and must have fallen back, but for the timely aid of CUSTER's brigade of TORBERT's division, armed with the Spencer repeating-rifle, the deadly fire of which forced the enemy back, and he retreated in great disorder, leaving his dead and wounded in the hands of the Union troops.

On Monday, May 30th, the enemy drove in the Union skirmishers on the road leading from Cold Harbor to Old Church Tavern, and attempted a raid on the rear of the Union army. They were beaten back, but returning in force towards evening, one division of Ewell's corps and two cavalry brigades attacked CRAWFORD's division with such determination that it was forced back from its position near Shady Grove Church, and almost endangered the turning of WARREN's flank. General MEADE ordered an attack along the whole line, but only the Second Corps received the order before dark. General HANCOCK, without a moment's delay, dashed upon the enemy's skirmish-line, captured the rifle-pits, and held them all night.

Several sharp but brief engagements occurred during Monday and Tuesday, the enemy obstinately holding the roads running parallel to the Chickahominy, as well as the river bank from near Atlee's Station to Bottom's Bridge.

28

On Wednesday, there was desperate fighting at
Cold Harbor, which, by the way, was but a single
building, the Cold Harbor Tavern; but the position
was important, as being the junction of the roads
leading to White House on the east, Dispatch Station and Bottom's Bridge on the south, Richmond,
by way of Gaines's Mill, on the west, and Hanover-
town and New Castle on the north. After a fierce
conflict and several brilliant charges, the Union
troops held Cold Harbor, but could not turn the
enemy's position. They were able, however, to repulse his every attempt to recover his lost ground,
but at a heavy cost, the Union loss being near upon
two thousand. The enemy fighting behind breastworks did not suffer so severely, but still their killed
and wounded were considerable, and six hundred
prisoners were taken. On Wednesday night, General
GRANT decided to follow up the occupation of Cold
Harbor, and attempt to push the enemy across the
Chickahominy, so as to establish a fording-place for
his own troops. Therefore HANCOCK, with his Second Corps, was drawn off the right, and marched
across the lines to the extreme left, reaching that
point by noon on Thursday. It had been intended
to make the attack that evening, but a heavy thun-
der-storm, with torrents of rain, checked the move-

ment, and the enemy took advantage of the respite to strengthen his works.

At dawn on the 3d of June, the attack was commenced. The assault of HANCOCK's Second Corps on the enemy's lines, on this eventful morning, the bloody battle of the Chickahominy, was never surpassed for daring, lofty courage, and stubborn persistence, even by the gallant action of the same corps at the battle of Spottsylvania. In their daring sweep over the enemy's works, the troops of Breckinridge were driven from the summit, and for a few minutes they were masters of the position; but their eagerness had carried them beyond their supporting columns, and the enemy noting this, as well as knowing the importance of the position, launched A. P. Hill's Corps upon them, while an enfilading fire played havoc with their decimated columns. They were compelled to fall back, but did so in good order, carrying with them three hundred prisoners and a captured color. In spite of a deadly fire, they merely crossed the brow of the nearest ridge, where they reformed and entrenched, remaining all day within fifty yards of the enemy's breastworks. By nightfall the whole of the Union lines was advanced to the same position and intrenched. For the next nine days, only fifty yards apart, there were no more pitched battles, but

occasional dashes were made on either side, only to
be met by heavy artillery and musketry fire. So
close were the two armies that they could look each
other in the face, except that every officer or soldier
who exposed his head was certain to be a target for
a sharpshooter's bullet. The carnage of the four
weeks had been terrible on both sides. On the
Union side two hundred and seventy officers, and
three thousand seven hundred and thirty-one enlisted
men had been killed; seven hundred and forty-seven
officers, and seventeen thousand three hundred and
eighty-one men wounded, and eighty-five officers, and
twenty-nine hundred and twenty-seven men were
missing, mostly prisoners; making a total of twenty-
five thousand one hundred and forty-one killed,
wounded, and missing. The enemy's losses must have
been nearly if not quite as heavy, though fighting
behind breastworks their killed and wounded had
been less; still they lost a far larger proportion of
prisoners.

In all the battles of this campaign, General HAN-
COCK, among the many brave officers of the army,
was conspicuous for daring, enthusiasm, and steady
valor. Wherever there was the most difficult work
to be done, and it was necessary that an attack
should be made promptly, earnestly, and unflinch

ingly, there HANCOCK and his gallant Second Corps
were sure to be, ready to do and dare anything that
human courage and skill could undertake. If there
was one post of greater danger than another, or re-
quiring those shrewd acts of gallantry which men
will only attempt under the eye and stimulated by
the approbation of a beloved and honored commander, there HANCOCK was certain to be found,
encouraging his men to higher exertion and the
accomplishment of seeming impossibilities. And
all this time that terrible wound in his thigh—the
bitter memento of his Gettysburg bravery—was rack-
ing him, and was soon to force him, for a brief interval, away from that field in which all his energies,
all his ideas, were concentrated; but human nature
must yield sometimes, and the actual reopening of
his wound forced the brave soldier to retire on the
19th of June. Before this, however, at midnight of
June 12th, he led the advance to Long Bridge, thence
to and across the James River, doing some desperate
fighting, as the enemy had strongly-fortified positions. During the 15th, 16th, and 17th, HANCOCK
participated in the assaults on Petersburg. On the
latter day, however, his iron constitution gave way,
and he was compelled, though with great reluctance,
to turn over his command to General BIRNEY and

28 *

cease active work. He did not, however, leave **the
field.** During the greater part of the campaign,
indeed, he had suffered the most intense pain, being
compelled to occupy an ambulance during the march,
and only mounting his horse when his troops came
in contact with the enemy. The wound was in the
upper part of the thigh. It had fractured and splin-
tered the upper part of the femur, and at one time it
was thought that his life could not be saved. A
splendid constitution, however, and the best surgical
skill, had brought him through the worst, and his
entire recovery would have followed, had not his
impatience to be with his command in the field
prevailed over his judgment. The penalty for this
he now had to pay by a brief retirement from the
command of the corps.

On the 27th of June, however, General HANCOCK
again took command, and participated in the operations before Petersburg until July 26th, when he
crossed to the north side of James River with his
corps and a division of cavalry, and assaulted the
enemy's line at Deep Bottom, capturing the outer
works, two hundred prisoners, several stands of
colors, and four pieces of artillery. On the 12th of
August, he was made Brigadier-General in the Regular Army. On the same day, in command of his

own, the Second Corps, the Tenth Corps, and a division of cavalry, he again assaulted the enemy's lines
at Deep Bottom. The fighting was severe. A part
of the enemy's works was carried; three hundred
prisoners, three stands of colors, and four howitzers
being taken. On the 25th of August, he fought the
battle of Reams's Station, with two divisions of his
own corps and a division of cavalry, against a greatly
superior force of the enemy. Another horse was
shot under him here.

In this battle the Union forces were heavily outnumbered, and the enemy determined and vigorous.
MILES's division of the Second Corps had been occupied throughout Monday in breaking up the Weldon
Railroad as far as Reams's Station, and was joined at
night by GIBBON's division of the same corps, who
finished the work to a point two miles beyond
Reams's Station, in all a distance of about eleven
miles. GREGG's cavalry had, meanwhile, covered
and protected the infantry, and had sharp skirmishes
with the enemy. On Thursday morning, June 25th,
GIBBON's division of HANCOCK's corps moved down
from Reams's to continue the work of destruction,
but encountered the enemy's skirmishers, and soon
afterwards the main body. There was considerable
skirmishing, but the enemy did not appear to want

battle; and HANCOCK promptly realized that this was merely a demonstration on the part of General A. P. Hill to conceal his attack on MILES's division (formerly BARLOW's), which was still at Reams's Station. This proved correct, and in the meantime HANCOCK had ordered GIBBON to fall back and form a junction with MILES's left, to protect that flank. The cavalry followed and covered the left flank and rear. At two P. M., the enemy's skirmish line swept forward with the usual horrid yells, but, being met by a heavy fire of artillery and musketry, fell back in confusion. The enemy, having got his batteries into position, opened a terrible concentric fire on the Union troops, pouring in shell and solid shot without a moment's cessation. After maintaining this for nearly half an hour, the recurrence of the demoniac yells announced a fourth assault, and the enemy's solidly massed column, in overwhelming numbers, rushed forward with fierce impetuosity. A galling fire of artillery and musketry met them point-blank; but they pressed on, and, after a bloody hand-to-hand conflict, gained the breastworks and broke the Union lines. The centre was gone, but some of the regiments continued to fight with marvellous valor. During this last attack against MILES, part of GIBBON's division was hurried across the circle, under a heavy fire, nearly a mile, to his support. At this moment the enemy broke in on the Union left, weakened by GIBBON's withdrawal, and GIBBON's troops were again hurried back across the fatal open space, and hurled upon the enemy. The sheer weight of the enemy, however, bore back the gallant left, except some regiments, which were actually cut to pieces on the ground they occupied. GREGG's dismounted cavalry prevented the enemy's further progress, and soon after dark HANCOCK withdrew, leaving Reams's Station in the hands of the enemy. The Weldon road, however, had been hopelessly destroyed for a long distance, and a considerable portion of it was still held by our forces. We must now pass on rapidly to the battle of Boydton Plank-road, which virtually ended General HANCOCK's active operations at the immediate front.

On the 1st of October, Generals TERRY and KAUNTZ made a reconnoissance towards Richmond, and with two brigades of infantry and a few cavalry actually penetrated within two miles of the city. This so irritated the enemy that a vigorous effort was made to turn the right flank of the Army of the James. In the meantime General GRANT deemed the time had come for another blow on Lee's right, accompanying it with a demonstration upon his left. The troops north of the James were to make a demonstration, while those south were to undertake a combined movement upon Hatcher's Run, a small tributary of Rowanty Creek, an affluent of the Nottaway River. Along this run and the Boydton Plank-road, and other roads partly parallel and partly crossing it, the enemy's lines of defence ran, protecting his communication with Wilmington, Danville, Lynchburg, and other sources of supply. GRANT'S view was, if he could obtain possession of that road, he could compel the evacuation of Petersburg and Richmond within forty-eight hours. The demonstration was not a success, as the enemy laid an ambush trap for the Union forces, and although stubborn resistance was offered, the troops were compelled to retreat with considerable loss. The attack on the position was assigned to HANCOCK'S Corps, aided by GREGG'S cavalry. This force was to march round the enemy's right flank, turn it, and seize the line of defences on Hatcher's Run, at the same time that the Fifth and Ninth Corps approached and attacked the works in front. General HANCOCK, therefore, drew out of camp on Wednesday evening, October 26th, and marched across Church Road; at 3.30 A. M., on Thursday, he reached the Vaughan Road, and moved along it to Hatcher's Run, coming to the crossing of that stream at 7.30 A. M. Here a small force attempted to dispute his passage, but were speedily repulsed and driven off, the corps proceeding to Boydton Plank-road, which it reached by 11.15 A.M. GREGG'S cavalry joined them here on the left, and Generals GRANT and MEADE came on the field at about the same time. EGAN'S division deployed on the right of the Plank-road, facing towards the bridge over Hatcher's Run; MOTT'S division took the left of the road; DE TROBRIAND'S brigade connected with GREGG'S cavalry, which held the extreme left. RUGG'S brigade, the advance of EGAN'S division, rushed forward, seized the bridge at Hatcher's Run, and crossed the creek.

The next point was to carry the enemy's works beyond, and for this purpose EGAN'S division, with BECK'S battery and WALLISTON'S brigade of MOTT'S division supporting, pressed onward. At this juncture the firing of the Fifth Corps was heard on the right, and it was expected that they would sweep round and form a junction with the Second Corps, but the perplexing nature of the roads — a perfect maze — prevented this, and the enemy were not slow to take advantage of the opportunity. About four P. M., Mahone's division of Hill's corps broke in upon HANCOCK's right flank, and, dashing through with irresistible fury, swept off one section of BECK's battery, then crossing the Boydton Plank-road, bore down on EGAN's division. EGAN promptly changed front with his own and McALLISTER's brigades, and, with the aid of BECK's, RODER's, and HESPER's batteries, repulsed the enemy, after a desperate conflict. HANCOCK, in the meantime, by prompt and skilful handling, had restored his line, and, with EGAN, then fell on Mahone's flank and drove him back, compelling him to abandon the guns he had captured, and leave behind him also three flags and five or six hundred prisoners. In this engagement the Second Corps and the cavalry lost about nine hundred killed and wounded and four hundred prisoners. The rain was falling in torrents and ammunition and rations were growing short, though orders for a four days' supply had been given. The Second Corps and the cavalry, therefore, retraced their way to camp. In the meanwhile the Fifth and Ninth Corps had not fared much better, except that they had inflicted a loss of about a thousand on the enemy and lost themselves about four hundred. Altogether, it was estimated that the movements on both sides of the James, which had promised so fairly, had cost the Union army some three thousand men, and had really effected nothing, in spite of brilliant daring and dauntless valor. From this time forward, for three months, there were but petty skirmishes and occasional conflicts along the lines of the Army of the Potomac and the Army of the James. In the meantime, the President saw other work for General HANCOCK, and detaching him, on November 26th, from the Army of the Potomac, he ordered him to Washington, where his ability and peculiar qualities could best serve his country in the particular needs of the hour, by re-cruiting the veterans of the war.

29   W

CHAPTER XXXIV.

In Washington — The Organization of the First Army Veteran Corps — Hancock a Major-General — In Charge of the Middle Military Division — He has Charge of Washington after the Assassination of President Lincoln — The Surratt Matter.

AT this period, November, 1864, a vast number of the veteran soldiers had served their enlistment term, and it was deemed by President LINCOLN and his advisers that this valuable element might be again induced to take the field; but they could not be expected to re-enter the service in regiments recruited since their own enlistment. After anxious deliberation, it was considered that a corps consisting of veterans alone could be raised if a veteran General, having the esteem and confidence of the men, should be placed at the head of it. President LINCOLN at once fixed upon HANCOCK, who was made Brigadier-General, U. S. A., to date from August 12, 1864. He was, therefore, summoned, as we have previously mentioned, to Washington on November 27, and from that time until February 27, 1865, was actively engaged in raising a new First Army Corps.

(338)

The anticipations of the President proved correct, and the old soldiers flocked to his standard with alacrity, the corps being raised to 50,000 strong. The selection of HANCOCK for this task was a happy inspiration, based upon the length and severity of his service, and the high estimation of the rank and file, to whom he was at once an example and an object of adoration. This work completed, General HANCOCK was again ordered to the front in command of the Middle Military Division, making his head-quarters at Winchester, the division embracing the Departments of West Virginia, Pennsylvania, and Washington, and the force under his command, including the Army of the Shenandoah, amounting to about 100,000 men of all arms. With such a force of veterans and under such a military genius, it was expected that at a decisive moment a blow could be struck in either direction; and HANCOCK was, therefore, under orders to be ready to move at short notice either on Lynchburg, to co-operate with the Army of the Potomac, or to take transports for the Southern coast, to co-operate with General SHERMAN. On March 13, 1865, he was breveted Major-General, U. S. A., "for gallant and meritorious services at the battle of Spottsylvania, Va."

The events of the war had, meanwhile, taken

gigantic strides, and the sudden breaking of Lee's line at Petersburg, followed by the surrender of that General at Appomattox Court-House, on April 9, 1865, rendered neither of these movements necessary. General HANCOCK remained in the Valley of the Shenandoah until the assassination of President LINCOLN, on April 14, 1865, threw the whole country into a state of dread and terror. He was immediately summoned to Washington, and placed in command of the Federal troops there. His presence at once calmed the apprehensions of the public, for it was felt that there was a man at the helm who could be relied upon to be cool, resolute, and brave in any emergency. His position here placed upon him the painful duty of directing the carrying out of the death-sentence upon Mrs. Surratt and others convicted of participation in the plot for the assassination of President LINCOLN. Upon this point a most unworthy attempt has been made to throw odium upon General HANCOCK, but common sense and common justice alike forbid such malicious scandals any weight with thinking people. He was military commander, having but President JOHNSON and the Secretary of War as his superiors. With the details of the guarding and care of the prisoners he had nothing whatever to do. They were confined in the arsenal, and the commander there was General HARTRANFT, who took the position by order of the Secretary of War. A military commission, ordered by the President, tried the prisoners, found them guilty, condemned some of them to death, and the findings of the military court were approved by the President. It was, unquestionably, to be lamented that they should have been thus tried. The conviction of the guilty could, in all probability, have been effected by a jury; but the nation was in a bloody struggle for existence, and martial law prevailed. It was particularly to be lamented that one of the condemned persons was a woman, and the regret is the deeper when, in calmer times, people who considered the case carefully are convinced that, so far as the crime of assassination was concerned, she was guiltless. The execution had been ordered for the 8th day of July. On the 6th, Messrs. Aiken and Clampitt, the counsel of Mrs. Surratt, went before United States Justice Wylie and procured a writ of *habeas corpus*. This was served by the marshal of the district on General HANCOCK, as the military head of the division. As was his duty, he forwarded it to his superior, the President of the United States and the Commander-in-Chief. Presi-

29 *

dent JOHNSON at once issued the following proclamation:

EXECUTIVE OFFICE, July 7th, 1865. — *To Major-
General Hancock, Commander, etc.* I, Andrew Johnson, President of the United States, do hereby declare
that the writ of *habeas corpus* has been heretofore
suspended in such cases as this; and I do hereby
especially suspend this writ, and direct that you proceed and execute the order heretofore given you
upon the judgment of the Military Commission, and
you will give this order in return to this writ.

This was indorsed on the writ, and, accompanied
by United States Attorney-General Speed, General
HANCOCK presented himself before Justice Wylie,
and made return to the writ. The execution took
place the following day. General HANCOCK saw that
the only hope for Mrs. Surratt lay in the power of
her daughter to move the President's heart; and he
so informed the daughter, and gave her every facility
in his power to gain access to the President. So
great was his anxiety in regard to the looked-for
pardon or reprieve, that he placed a line of mounted
sentinels from the White House to the place of execution, that the words of grace, if spoken at the last

minute, should go surely and swiftly. But no such words were spoken, and, to the now almost universal regret of the people, Mrs. Surratt died.

It is barely necessary to add anything to the simple statement that throughout the whole of this unhappy business General HANCOCK did nothing that the strict letter of his duty did not demand, and an avoidance of which would have contradicted the whole tenor of his career; in so far as the man could suppress the soldier in obedience to the dictates of humanity, he yielded to that impulse, even at a time when by so doing his own fealty might have been questioned in the then heated state of public feeling. An interview, however, since the Cincinnati nomination, which a correspondent of the New York *Herald* had with the Right Reverend Bishop Keane, elicited evidence which removes even a shadow of doubt as to the opinions entertained by those who are best qualified to speak on the subject. The correspondent, after ascertaining the Bishop's views, which were that the charges against General HANCOCK had been disproved as preposterous and false, was asked as to a letter which Father Walter, of St. Patrick's Church, Washington, who had attended Mrs. Surratt through all her affliction till the last moment, was alleged to have written entirely exculpating General HANCOCK from all responsibility in the matter. He replied: "I happened to be in Washington about the time, a few months ago, when these charges were reiterated by the press against General HANCOCK. I was there for the purpose of delivering a lecture. Father Walter then had a consultation with me regarding those charges, and asked my advice as to what he should do in the premises. He stated in the most emphatic language that there was no truth whatever in the charges. Father Walter was the spiritual adviser and confessor of Mrs. Surratt. I told him that it was his duty to truth and to history, as well to General HANCOCK, that he should write the letter which he did in reference to the matter."

"Of course," the Bishop again remarked, "the charges were preposterously false, and devoid of even a shadow of truth."

Upon this subject we may have more to say at a further stage of our history; but it was necessary here to allude to it in its order. We must now return to his active career.

CHAPTER XXXV.

Sketches and Anecdotes —" Jineing the Pint" — Hancock as a Cadet, as a Junior Officer, and as a Commander —" I always Know where to find Hancock." (Gen. Grant.) — The Magic Influence of his Presence on the Field.

BEFORE following our hero into other phases of his eventful career, and taking up his record as a statesman and an ardent supporter of Constitutional law, it may be interesting to take a retrospective glance — to incorporate just here some anecdotes and sketches illustrative of his ability, his goodness of heart, and his military genius. We commence with "The Lawyer's Son"

AS A CADET.

There was nothing remarkable in his cadetship. He is remembered by those who knew him at West Point as a quiet, unassuming Pennsylvanian youth, for whom no special credit was claimed. He was strict in conforming to the rules, quick in acquiring learning, ambitious to excel in drill and discipline, fluent in expressing what he learned, amiable in his

(345)

deportment, adding some graceful accomplishments
to his list of studies as a draughtsman, and excelling
as a sketcher of scenery and characters, as is shown
by his drawing in another part of this volume. The
whole of that sketch, to which the reader is referred,
was drawn by General HANCOCK while a cadet at
West Point. It is designed to hit off a class of persons who were in the habit of boring the cadets, by
applying to be received into the Academy. The
scene is a literal one, as true as it is graphic.

A greenhorn approaches a drummer, who is gazing
at him with astonishment, and asks:

"How d'ye do, boy? Where's your capting? I
want ter jine the Pint!"

The looks of the parties around, the marching of
the other applicants, who, in the distance are seen to
be put through the motions by the cadet officer of
the day; the groupings of the scene, the dresses and
expressions, are all precisely as executed by Cadet
HANCOCK, and preserved in his Album.

He graduated with credit as a cadet, enjoying the
confidence and esteem of all his classmates. It is
due to West Point Academy to say that he owes all
that he is as a military man to the superior culture
and discipline of that institution.

AS A JUNIOR OFFICER.

It is not by any means pretended that there was anything very remarkable in young Lieutenant HAN-COCK, when he took his place in the line of the Sixth United States Regular Infantry. His fellow officers around him had equal positions in the military school they had just left. Some of them had graduated with higher honors. He was fighting under the same flag with them when he drew his sword, for the first time, in battle, on the shores of Mexico. All that need be said of him as a junior officer is this — he did his duty.

AS A COMMANDER.

In this position he was ever found at his post, discharging his duty faithfully. He was severely tried, and found equal, as a patriot commander, to the great cause in which he had enlisted with all his heart.

It is not the slightest disparagement to his compatriots in this noble struggle, to quote the appropriate testimony of Lieutenant-General GRANT:

"I always know where to find HANCOCK."

When he returned to his corps, in the spring of 1864, and was preparing to lead the advance, his officers and men gathered around him, and tendered him a voluntary salute of welcome, with music and banners. A song of congratulation on his return was composed for the occasion, and sung with loud acclaim by the strong voices of his thousands of gallant soldiers. The following is the closing verse of this heart-felt, soldierly welcome:

> " Welcome **back, Oh!** General, brave,
>   Welcome **to your corps** again!
> **Trumpets sound and** banners wave,
>   Shouts ascend from gallant men.
> Many a hard-contested field
>   **Proved you a** true-hearted man:
> **Ay!** many a field saw foemen yield,
>   Where HANCOCK **lead the van!**"

At the terrible conflicts of the Wilderness, when the men of the Second Corps were falling by thousands, their patriotic devotion to him and their cause was poured out with their life's blood.

In one of the field hospitals we met a group of these noble fellows, **just brought in,** wounded, bleeding, dying.

"How goes the battle, boys?" asked one of these gallant sufferers of a wounded comrade, borne from the front.

"All right!" replied the bleeding hero. "We're driving them!"

"They've broke in upon us pretty rough!" said a true Yankee, as he limped along, with a dismal wound, to his stretcher.

"Ar-r-ah! but they'll niver git thrrough the ould Sicond Cowrps! You may bit ye're life o' that, my boy!" cried a brave Irishman, at the top of a voice half stifled with the flow of blood in his throat.

"Lie still, Maurice," quietly and soothingly said one of the surgeons. "You must lose your arm, my good fellow!"

"Lose my arrm, is it?" returned the enthusiastic Hibernian, more excited than ever. "Will! I'm ready to do that for HANCOCK, any day; and, if need be, I'll lose both my arms for the Union. Hur-r-ah for the Stars and Stripes, my boys! and the Sicond Cowrps foriver!"

A break had occurred on a road in our lines, through which the enemy pressed with all the combined power within their reach. They anticipated a certain victory as they swooped down on our unprotected columns, and planted their colors defiantly on our front. At this perilous moment HANCOCK dashed forward, with the greatest promptness and energy, determined on a rescue of his troops.

Hat in hand, he raised himself in his stirrups, and, spurring forward, with his staff around him, shouted, at the top of his voice:

"We must hold this road to the last extremity! Stand your ground, men! Stand your ground!"

30 '

"They are enfilading our breastworks!" exclaimed one of his command.

"Then we must meet them behind the breastworks, and drive them out!" continued HANCOCK, with tremendous emphasis.

Turning to a body of troops who seemed disposed to waver, he thundered:

"No flinching there! What can the country hope from cowards?"

No better proof of the valor with which he fought his command, and of the brave alacrity with which they followed his lead, can be found than the well-established fact that the Second Corps lost not less than *thirty* **thousand** *men* from the opening of the campaign with GRANT to the front of Petersburg. *Twenty-five thousand* of these gallant fellows had followed him to victory and **death before** he had crossed the James River.

When, on another occasion, already alluded to, before Petersburg, in which his corps was overpowered on a portion of its lines, he left his sick couch, and placed himself at their head, the effect of his presence, though scarcely able to sit on his horse, was magical.

"HANCOCK! HANCOCK is here!" rang along the front.

"HANCOCK is sick!" was the response.

"Sick or well, he's with us! Don't you hear his voice?"

At that moment his clarion notes sounded out as strong and clear as ever:

"Rally, men! rally! By the left flank — march! Steady! — steady! to the front!"

His orders being rapidly obeyed, quickly came another:

"Charge!"

It was done instantly; the enemy fled, and the lost ground was triumphantly retaken.

During one of the fiercest battles of the Wilderness, late in the evening, Colonel CARROLL, commanding a brigade in his corps, was seriously wounded. A previous commander of this brigade, the gallant General ALEXANDER HAYS, had just been killed, his body placed in an ambulance, and carried from the field.

"You are wounded, Colonel CARROLL," said HANCOCK, riding up to his side.

"Yes, General," replied the Colonel; "but I shall not leave the front."

"Who will command your brigade, Colonel?"

"I'll command it myself, sir!" promptly added the Colonel, rising and giving the salute.

It should be remembered that through all the vigorous campaign of HANCOCK with GRANT, he was himself a wounded man. He did not complain, or allow his duties to be in any way neglected; but his wound was still serious, and would have caused many other men to have retired from the fight. When laid aside in his tent, he still maintained his hold on his command of the Second Corps. Nothing of importance was allowed to transpire without his notice. A rest of a few days brought him again into the saddle, and to the front of battle. A piece of bone was taken from his wound, where it had been chafing his flesh constantly, and depriving him, at times, of the sleep so much needed by a man in such a responsible position. But he would not, and did not, yield his post in the fights until completely prostrated by disease.

The soldiers who served under others always united to bear testimony to his worth.

"Did you ever serve under General HANCOCK?" we inquired of an old war-worn veteran just from Louisiana.

"No, sir," he answered us; "I will not tell a lie. I never served under General HANCOCK; but, sir, he's a noble man."

Such uniform testimony as this from the men of other corps is peculiarly valuable.

The rapidity of the movements of HANCOCK as a commander is shown most strikingly in his position in support of WARREN, in the battle fought early in May, 1864, near Parker's store. The moment the order for support came, his whole corps was in motion. By two o'clock of that day he had marched the whole distance from his position on the Brock road, and precisely at the time designated he was in line of battle, fronting the enemy. As the command marched, often at the double quick, the sound of the enemy's guns in the distance, responding to those of WARREN, quickened the pace of the corps. They rushed on, with shouts that made the welkin ring, the music pouring forth its loudest strains, and the colors flapping proudly in the rushing air. It was just like HANCOCK and his gallant men. He had command, at that moment, of troops from nearly every corps in the whole army, and handled them with most consummate skill.

During the height of this engagement HANCOCK's line was the grand centre of attraction. All his movements were watched with the keenest interest by Lieutenant-General GRANT and General MEADE. His caution in every movement was equal to his

80 *

X

valor. He was very careful not to extend his lines too far, especially on his left, as he was wisely apprehensive — as it proved afterwards correctly so — that Longstreet might make a sudden attack in that direction. By holding his strong position, and keeping his men well in hand, he beat back the enemy until sufficient reinforcements arrived to secure a final victory.

His conduct on this tremendous field is described by those who saw it as magnificent. Prompt in arriving, ready, in a moment after, for fight, he dashed at once on the wily foe. His labors in massing his men had been herculean. With a quickness of perception, a grasp of thought, peculiar to his character, he had divined the whole purpose of the enemy, and was instantly prepared to meet it, at every point. Nothing of the kind could be more exciting than the whole scene. His entire combined command was to be hurled in solid columns on the enemy How vast the importance that his every movement should be directed right! A single mistake, in such a crisis, might derange his whole plan, and lose the day for his country.

As quickly as he had moved his gallant troops, so quickly he formed them in line of battle; and just as quickly he issued his orders. It was the thunderbolt of war launched with the electric flash from the wire in his hand. It was the crash of the avalanche of battle that his skill had poised on the towering cliff of his noble purpose. It was the roll of a wave of valor poured forth from his sea of thought, that was to bear down all before it; the swoop of an eagle from a mountain eyrie of vision, where his eye had grasped all the field, and was sure of his prey. No wonder that he conquered.

But, with all this brilliancy of execution, the caution of HANCOCK was fully equal to his dashing courage. Not a point was neglected. Not a line was left uncovered. Not a defence was allowed to remain unavailable. His heroism, that knew no fear, shone side by side with his modesty and grace, on that terrific area of carnage. There was impetuosity; but it was sobered by calmness. There was invincibility; but it was graced by modesty. There was enthusiasm, rising to its utmost height; but it was controlled by a wise caution. There was the transport of action, the shout of command, in the midst of the roar and clangor of conflict; but it was chastened by a prudence that valued human life, and that would not needlessly waste or even put it in peril.

CHAPTER XXXVI.

Hancock a Major-General — His Military Command in the South — The Celebrated "General Orders No. 40" — His Support of Civil Authority — Military Rule Subservient to Constitutional Law — The Civilian Soldier Demonstrating his Statesmanship.

GENERAL HANCOCK was placed in the so-called Middle Department, with headquarters at Baltimore, July 18, 1865, and on August 10, 1866, was transferred to the Department of the Missouri, with headquarters at St. Louis. On May 30, 1866, the thanks of Congress were tendered to Major-General HANCOCK "for his gallant, meritorious, and conspicuous share in the great and decisive victory of Gettysburg," and on July 26, 1866, he was made a full Major-General, United States Army. He served on the Board for retiring disabled officers at Philadelphia, 1865–66, and on the Board to make recommendations in regard to ordnance from January to June, 1866. In 1867 he was engaged upon expeditions against hostile Indians on the plains of Kansas, Colorado, and the Indian Territory. With the as-

sumption of this command his purely military career
was closed, and opportunity began to be afforded for
his appearance in another character — that of a skilled
administrator and far-seeing statesman.

In the general shuffle of military commands which
was effected by President JOHNSON in November, 1867,
General HANCOCK was commissioned as Commander
of the Fifth Military District and the Department of
the Gulf, with headquarters at New Orleans. The
powers of a military commander in the South at that
chaotic epoch of reconstruction were large and in-
definite. It is one of General HANCOCK'S principal
titles to civic renown that he took a statesmanlike
view of his powers and responsibilities. His reputation was that of a somewhat stern disciplinarian,
but at New Orleans he showed himself superior to
the passion for discipline. The wisdom and policy
of the legislation under which the South was par-
celled out, under the rule of several irresponsible
military dictators, will not now be seriously maintained, but at that time the passions of the Northern
States were too violently excited by the contest between President JOHNSON and Congress to admit of
impartial reasoning upon the proper line of demar-
cation between military and civic powers. The constitutions of ten Southern States had been nullified

by Congress, and personal liberty was everywhere in jeopardy.

Under these circumstances, the advent of General Hancock at New Orleans was marked by the promulgation of a document which rang through the South like a new Declaration of Independence, and was greeted with delirious enthusiasm as the dawn of a happier day. On taking command at New Orleans, General Hancock issued his famous "General Orders No. 40," the text of which is as follows: —

"Headquarters Fifth Military District,
New Orleans, La., Nov. 29, 1867.

"I. In accordance with General Orders No. 81, Headquarters of the Army, Adjutant-General's Office, Washington, D. C., August 27, 1867, Major-General W. S. Hancock hereby assumes command of the Fifth Military District and of the Department composed of the States of Louisiana and Texas.

"II. The General commanding is gratified to learn that peace and quiet reign in this department. It will be his purpose to preserve this condition of things. As a means to this great end he regards the maintenance of the civil authorities in the faithful execution of the laws as the most efficient under existing circumstances.

"In war it is indispensable to repel force by force and overthrow and destroy opposition to lawful authority. But when insurrectionary force has been overthrown and peace established, and the civil authorities are ready and willing to perform their duties, the military power should cease to lead, and the civil administration resume its natural and rightful dominion. Solemnly impressed with these views, the General announces that the great principles of American liberty still are the lawful inheritance of this people, and ever should be. The right of trial by jury, the habeas corpus, the liberty of the press, the freedom of speech and the natural rights of persons and the rights of property, must be preserved.

"Free institutions, while they are essential to the prosperity and happiness of the people, always furnish the strongest inducements to peace and order. Crimes and offences committed in this District must be referred to the consideration and judgment of the regular civil tribunals, and those tribunals will be supported in their lawful jurisdiction.

"Should there be violations of existing laws which are not inquired into by the civil magistrates, or should failures in the administration of justice by the courts be complained of, the cases will be reported to these headquarters, when such orders will be made as may be deemed necessary.

"While the General thus indicates his purpose to respect the liberties of the people, he wishes all to understand that armed insurrections or forcible resistance to the law will be instantly suppressed by arms.

"By command of Major-General W. S. HANCOCK.

"W. G. MITCHELL,

"Brevet Lieutenant-Colonel, Acting Assistant Adjutant-General."

This order, so distinctly declaring the subordination of the military to the civil power, was followed by others equally emphatic. An order dated December 5th contains the following clauses:

"The Commanding General has been officially in-

formed that the administration of justice, and especially of criminal justice, in the courts, is clogged, if
not entirely frustrated, by the enforcement of paragraph No. 2 of the military order numbered special
orders 125, current series, from these headquarters,
issued on the 24th of August, A. D. 1867, relative to
the qualification of persons to be placed on the jury
lists of the State of Louisiana. To determine who
shall and who shall not be jurors appertains to the
legislative power, and until the laws in existence
regulating this subject shall be amended or changed
by that department of the civil government which
the constitutions of all the States under our republican system vest with that power, it is deemed best
to carry out the will of the people as expressed in the
last legislative act on this subject. The qualification
of a juror under the law is a proper subject for the
decision of the courts. The Commanding General,
in the discharge of the trust reposed in him, will
maintain the just power of the judiciary, and is unwilling to permit the civil authorities and laws to be
embarrassed by military interference. It is ordered
that said paragraph, which relates to the qualifica-
tions of persons to be placed on the jury lists of the
State of Louisiana, be and the same is hereby re
voked."

An election for delegates to a Constitutional Convention was ordered in Texas at this time, and among other provisions was this:

"Military interference with elections, 'unless it shall be necessary to keep the peace at the polls,' is prohibited by law, and no soldiers will be allowed to appear at any polling-place, unless as citizens of the State they are registered as voters, and then only for the purpose of voting; but the commanders of posts will be prepared to act promptly if the civil authorities fail to preserve the peace."

Another order has reference to the applications made at headquarters, "implying the existence of an arbitrary authority in the Commanding General touching purely civil controversies:"

"The rights of litigants do not depend on the views of the General. They are to be judged and settled according to the laws. Arbitrary power, such as he has been urged to assume, has no existence here. It is not found in the laws of Louisiana or Texas. It cannot be derived from any act or acts of Congress. It is restrained by a constitution and prohibited from action in many particulars. The Major-General commanding takes occasion to repeat that, while disclaiming judicial functions in civil cases, he can suffer no

31

forcible resistance to the execution of processes of the courts."

On the 9th of March, 1868, these emphatic declarations were supplemented by the letter to Governor E. M. Pease, of Texas, given in the following chapter, a document at once able, forcible, cool, and logical. It surpassed all he had previously written, and deserves to go on record as one of the most statesmanlike papers ever issued at a time of ferment, when prejudice had usurped the functions of reason, and passion had warped judgment to a perilous extent

CHAPTER XXXVII.

The Celebrated Letter to Governor Pease, of Texas—General Hancock's Careful Exposition of the Relation between the Military and the Civil Administration—A Valuable and Remarkable Document.

THE following letter, which deserves a chapter to itself, will bear careful study. It exhibits General HANCOCK in the light of a thorough statesman, and proves him as capable to handle the destinies of a people in time of peace as he had before proved himself able to defend their liberties and their honor in time of war.

GENERAL HANCOCK'S LETTER.

"HEADQUARTERS FIFTH MILITARY DISTRICT,
NEW ORLEANS, LA., March 9, 1868.

"To His Excellency, E. M. PEASE, Governor of Texas:

"*Sir*—Your communication of the 17th January last was received in due course of mail (the 27th January), but not until it had been widely circulated by the newspaper press. To such a letter—written and published for manifest purposes—it has been my

(363)

intention to reply as soon as leisure from more im
portant business would permit.

"Your statement that the act of Congress 'to pro-
vide for the more efficient government of the rebel
States' declares that whatever government existed
in Texas was provisional; that peace and order
should be enforced; that Texas should be part of
the Fifth Military District, and subject to military
power; that the President should appoint an officer
to command in said district, and detail a force to
protect the rights of person and property, suppress
insurrection and violence, and punish offenders, either
by military commission or through the action of
local civil tribunals, as in his judgment might seem
best, will not be disputed. One need only read the
act to perceive it contains such provisions. But
how all this is supposed to have made it my duty to
order the military commission you requested, you
have entirely failed to show. The power to do a
thing, if shown, and the propriety of doing it, are
often very different matters. You observe you are
at a loss to understand how a government, without
representation in Congress or a militia force, and
subject to military power, can be said to be in the
full exercise of all its proper powers. You do not
reflect that this government, created or permitted

by Congress, has all the powers which the act in-
tends, and may fully exercise them accordingly. If
you think it ought to have more powers; should be
allowed to send members to Congress; wield a militia
force; and possess yet other powers, your complaint
is not to be preferred against me, but against Congress, who made it what it is.

"As respects the issue between us, any question as
to what Congress ought to have done has no perti-
nence. You admit the act of Congress authorizes me
to try an offender by military commission, or allow
the local civil tribunals to try, as I shall deem best;
and you cannot deny the act expressly recognizes
such local civil tribunals as legal authorities for the
purpose specified. When you contend there are no
legal local tribunals for any purpose in Texas, you
must either deny the plain reading of the act of Congress or the power of Congress to pass the act.

"You next remark that you dissent from my declaration, 'that the country (Texas) is in a state of profound peace,' and proceed to state the grounds of
your dissent. They appear to me not a little ex-
traordinary I quote your words: 'It is true there
no longer exists here (Texas) any organized resistance
to the authority of the United States.' 'But a large
majority of the white population who participated in
31 *

the late rebellion are embittered against the Government, and yield to it an unwilling obedience.' Nevertheless, you concede they do yield it obedience. You proceed:

" ' None of this class have any affection for the Government, and very few any respect for it. They regard the legislation of Congress on the subject of reconstruction as unconstitutional and hostile to their interests, and consider the government now existing here under authority of the United States, as an usurpation on their rights. They look on the emancipation of their late slaves, and the disfranchisement of a portion of their own class, as an act of insult and oppression.'

" And this is all you have to present for proof that war and not peace prevails in Texas; and hence it becomes my duty — so you suppose — to set aside the local civil tribunals, and enforce the penal code against citizens by means of military commissions.

" My dear sir, I am not a lawyer, nor has it been my business, as it may have been yours, to study the philosophy of state-craft and politics. But I may lay claim, after an experience of more than half a lifetime, to some poor knowledge of men, and some appreciation of what is necessary to social order and happiness. And for the future of our common country, I could devoutly wish that no great number of our people have yet fallen in with the views you appear to entertain. Woe be to us whenever it shall come to pass that the power of the magistrate — civil or military — is permitted to deal with the mere opinions or feelings of the people.

"I have been accustomed to believe that sentiments of respect or disrespect, and feelings of affection, love, or hatred, so long as not developed into acts in violation of law, were matters wholly beyond the punitory power of human tribunals.

"I will maintain that the entire freedom of thought and speech, however acrimoniously indulged, is consistent with the noblest aspirations of man, and the happiest condition of his race.

"When a boy, I remember to have read a speech of Lord Chatham, delivered in Parliament. It was during our Revolutionary War, and related to the policy of employing the savages on the side of Britain. You may be more familiar with the speech than I am. If I am not greatly mistaken, his lordship denounced the British Government — his government — in terms of unmeasured bitterness. He characterized its policy as revolting to every sentiment of humanity and religion, proclaimed it covered with disgrace, and vented his eternal abhorrence of it and its measures. It may, I think, be safely asserted·that a majority of the British nation concurred in the views of Lord Chatham. But whoever supposed that profound peace was not existing in that kingdom, or that government had any authority to question the absolute right of the opposition to express their objections to the propriety of the king's measures in any words or to any extent they pleased? It would be difficult to show that the opponents of the Government in the days of the elder Adams, or Jefferson, or Jackson, exhibited for it either 'affection' or 'respect.' You are conversant with the history of our past parties and political struggles touching legislation on alienage, sedition, the embargo, national banks, our wars with England and Mexico, and cannot be ignorant of the fact that for one party to assert that a law or system of legislation is unconstitutional, oppressive, and usurpative is not a new thing in the United States. That the people of Texas consider acts of Congress unconstitutional, oppressive, or insulting to them is of no consequence to the matter in hand. The President of the United States has announced his opinion that these acts of Congress are unconstitutional. The Supreme Court, as·you are aware, not long ago decided unanimously that a certain military commission was unconstitutional. Our people everywhere, in every State, without reference to the side they took during the rebellion, differ as to the constitutionality of these acts of Congress. How the matter really is, neither you nor I may dogmatically affirm.

"If you deem them constitutional laws, and beneficial to the country, you not only have the right to publish your opinions, but it might be your bounden duty as a citizen to do so. Not less is it the privilege and duty of any and every citizen, wherever residing, to publish his opinion freely and fearlessly on this and every question which he thinks concerns his interest. This is merely in accordance with the principles of our free government; and neither you nor I would wish to live under any other. It is time now, at the end of almost two years from the close of the war, we should begin to recollect what manner of people we are; to tolerate again free, popular discussion, and extend some forbearance and consideration to opposing views. The maxims that in all intellectual contests truth is mighty, and must prevail, and that error is harmless, when reason is left free to combat it, are not only sound, but salutary. It is a poor compliment to the merits of such a cause, that its advocates would silence opposition by force; and generally those only who are in the wrong will

resort to this ungenerous means. I am confident you
will not commit your serious judgment to the proposition that any amount of discussion, or any sort of
opinions, however unwise in your judgment; or any
assertion or feeling, however resentful or bitter, not
resulting in a breach of law, can furnish justification
for your denial, that profound peace exists in Texas.
You might as well deny that profound peace exists
in New York, Pennsylvania, Maryland, California,
Ohio, and Kentucky, where a majority of the people
differ with a minority on these questions; or that
profound peace exists in the House of Representatives, or the Senate, at Washington, or in the Supreme Court, where all these questions have been
repeatedly discussed, and parties respectfully and
patiently heard. You next complain that in parts
of the State (Texas) it is difficult to enforce the
criminal laws; that sheriffs fail to arrest; that grand
jurors will not always indict; that in some cases the
military acting in aid of the civil authorities have
not been able to execute the process of the courts;
that petit jurors have acquitted persons adjudged
guilty by you; and that other persons charged with
offences have broke jail and fled from prosecution.

"I know not how these things are; but admitting
your representations literally true, if for such reasons

I should set aside the local civil tribunals and order
a military commission, there is no place in the United
States where it might not be done with equal propriety. There is not a State in the Union — North
or South — where the like facts are not continually
happening. Perfection is not to be predicated of man
or his works. No one can reasonably expect certain
and absolute justice in human transactions; and if
military power is to be set in motion, on the principles for which you would seem to contend, I fear that
a civil government, regulated by laws, could have no
abiding place beneath the circuit of the sun. It is
rather more than hinted in your letter, that there is
no local State Government in Texas, and no local
laws outside of the acts of Congress, which I ought
to respect; and that I should undertake to protect
the rights of persons and property in *my own way*
and in an *arbitrary manner.* If such be your meaning, I am compelled to differ with you. After the
abolition of slavery (an event which I hope no one
now regrets), the laws of Louisiana and Texas existing prior to the rebellion, and not in conflict with
the acts of Congress, comprised a vast system of
jurisprudence, both civil and criminal. It required
not volumes only, but libraries to contain them.
They laid down principles and precedents for ascer-

taining the rights and adjusting the controversies of men in every conceivable case. They were the creations of great and good and learned men, who had labored, in their day, for their kind, and gone down to the grave long before our recent troubles, leaving their works an inestimable legacy to the human race. These laws, as I am informed, connected the civilization of past and present ages, and testified of the justice, wisdom, humanity, and patriotism of more than one nation, through whose records they descended to the present people of these States. I am satisfied, from representations of persons competent to judge, they are as perfect a system of laws as may be found elsewhere, and better suited than any other to the condition of this people, for by them they have long been governed. Why should it be supposed Congress has abolished these laws? Why should any one wish to abolish them? They have committed no treason, nor are hostile to the United States, nor countenance crime, nor favor injustice. On them, as on a foundation of rock, reposes almost the entire superstructure of social order in these two States. Annul this code of local laws, and there would be no longer any rights either of person or property here. Abolish the local civil tribunals made to execute them, and you would virtually annul the laws, except in reference to the very few cases cognizable in the Federal courts. Let us for a moment suppose the whole local civil code annulled, and that I am left, as commander of the Fifth Military District, the sole fountain of law and justice. This is the position in which you would place me.

"I am now to protect all rights and redress all wrongs. How is it possible for me to do it? Innumerable questions arise, of which I am not only ignorant, but for the solution of which a military court is entirely unfitted. One would establish a will, another a deed; or the question is one of succession, or partnership, or descent, or trust; a suit of ejectment or claim to chattels; or the application may relate to robbery, theft, arson, or murder. How am I to take the first step in any such matter? If I turn to the acts of Congress, I find nothing on the subject. I dare not open the authors on the local code, for it has ceased to exist.

"And you tell me that in this perplexing condition I am to furnish, by dint of my own hasty and crude judgment, the legislation demanded by the vast and manifold interests of the people! I repeat, Sir! that you, and not Congress, are responsible for the monstrous suggestion that there are no local laws or institutions here to be respected by me, outside the acts of Congress. I say, unhesitatingly, if it were possible that Congress should pass an act abolishing the local codes for Louisiana and Texas,—which I do not believe,—and it should fall to my lot to supply their places with something of my own, I do not see how I could do better than follow the laws in force here prior to the rebellion, excepting whatever therein shall relate to slavery. Power may destroy the forms, but not the principles, of justice; these will live in spite even of the sword. History tells us that the Roman pandects were lost for a long period among the rubbish that war and revolution had heaped upon them, but at length were dug out of the ruins, again to be regarded as a precious treasure.

"You are pleased to state that 'since the publication of (my) General Orders No. 40, there has been a perceptible increase of crime and manifestations of hostile feeling towards the Government and its supporters,' and add that it is 'an unpleasant duty to give such a recital of the condition of the country.'

"You will permit me to say that I deem it impossible the first of these statements can be true, and that I do very greatly doubt the correctness of the second. General Orders No. 40 was issued at New Orleans, November 29, 1867, and your letter

was dated January 17, 1863. Allowing time for
Order No. 40 to reach Texas and become generally
known, some additional time must have elapsed before its effect would be manifested, and yet a further
time must transpire before you would be able to col-
lect the evidence of what you term 'the condition
of the country;' and yet, after all this, you would
have to make the necessary investigations to ascer-
tain if Order No. 40, or something else, was the cause.
The time, therefore, remaining to enable you, before
the 17th of January, 1868, to reach a satisfactory
conclusion on so delicate and nice a question must
have been very short. How you proceeded, whether
you investigated yourself or through third persons,
and if so, who they were, what their competency and
fairness, on what evidence you rested your conclusion,
or whether you ascertained any facts at all, are points
upon which your letter so discreetly omits all mention, that I may well be excused for not relying im-
plicitly upon it; nor is my difficulty diminished by
the fact that in another part of your letter you state
that ever since the close of the war a very large
portion of the people have had no affection for the
Government, but bitterness of feeling only. Had the
duty of publishing and circulating through the
country, long before it reached me, your statement

that the action of the district commander was increasing crime and hostile feeling against the Government, been less painful to your sensibilities, it might
possibly have occurred to you to furnish something
on the subject in addition to your bare assertion.

"But what was Order No. 40, and how could it
have the effect you attribute to it? It sets forth
that 'the great principles of American liberty are
still the inheritance of this people, and ever should
be; that the right of trial by jury, the habeas corpus,
the liberty of the press, the freedom of speech, and
the natural rights of persons and property must be
preserved.' Will you question the truth of these
declarations? Which one of these great principles
of liberty are you ready to deny and repudiate?
Whoever does so, avows himself the enemy of human
liberty and the advocate of despotism. Was there
any intimation in General Orders No. 40 that any
crimes or breaches of law would be countenanced?
You know that there was not. On the contrary,
you know perfectly well that, while 'the consideration of crime and offences committed in the Fifth
Military District was referred to the judgment of
the regular civil tribunals,' a pledge was given in
Order No. 40, which all understood, that tribunals
would be supported in their lawful jurisdiction, and

that 'forcible resistance to law would be instantly suppressed by arms.' You will not affirm that this pledge has ever been forfeited. There has not been a moment since I have been in command of the Fifth District when the whole military force in my hands has not been ready to support the civil authorities of Texas in the execution of the laws. And I am unwilling to believe they would refuse to call for aid if they needed it.

"There are some considerations which, it seems to me, should cause you to hesitate before indulging in wholesale censures against the civil authorities of Texas. You are yourself the chief of these authorities, not elected by the people, but created by the military. Not long after you had thus come into office, all the judges of the Supreme Court of Texas — five in number — were removed from office, and new appointments made; twelve of the seventeen district judges were removed, and others appointed. County officers, more or less, in seventy-five out of one hundred and twenty-eight counties, were removed, and others appointed in their places. It is fair to conclude that the executive and judicial civil functionaries in Texas are the persons whom you desired to fill the offices. It is proper to mention, also, that none but registered citizens, and only those

32 *

who could take the test-oath, have been allowed to
serve as jurors during your administration. Now,
it is against this local government, created by military power prior to my coming here, and so composed of your personal and political friends, that
you have preferred the most grievous complaints.
It is of them that you have asserted they will not
do their duty; they will not maintain justice, will
not arrest offenders, will not punish crimes, and that
out of one hundred homicides committed in the last
twelve months, not over ten arrests have been made;
and by means of such gross disregard of duty, you
declare that neither property nor life is safe in
Texas.

"Certainly you could have said nothing more to
the discredit of the officials who are now in office.
If the facts be as you allege, a mystery is presented
for which I can imagine no explanation. Why is it
that your political friends, backed up and sustained
by the whole military power of the United States in
this district, should be unwilling to enforce the laws
against that part of the population lately in rebellion,
and whom you represent as the offenders? In all the
history of these troubles, I have never seen or heard
before of such a fact. I repeat, if the fact be so, it is
a profound mystery, utterly surpassing my compre-

hension. I am constrained to declare that I believe
you are in very great error as to facts. On careful
examination at the proper source, I find that at the
date of your letter four cases only of homicides had
been reported to these headquarters as having occurred since November 29, 1867, the date of Order 40,
and these cases were ordered to be tried or investigated as soon as the reports were received. However, the fact of the one hundred homicides may still
be correct, as stated by you. The Freedman's Bu-
reau, in Texas, reported one hundred and sixty;
how many of these were by Indians and Mexicans,
and how the remainder were classified, is not known;
nor is it known whether these data are accurate.

"The report of the commanding officer of the District of Texas shows that since I assumed command
no applications have been made to him, by you, for
the arrest of criminals in the State of Texas.

"To this date eighteen cases of homicides have
been reported to me as having occurred since November 29, 1867; although special instructions had
been given to report such cases as they occur.
Of these, five were committed by Indians, one by a
Mexican, one by an insane man, three by colored
men, two of women by their husbands, and of the
remainder, some by parties unknown — all of which

could scarcely be attributable to Order No. 40. If
the reports received since the issuing of Order No.
40 are correct, they exhibit no increase of homicides
in my time, if you are correct that one hundred had
occurred in the past twelve months.

"That there has not been a perfect administration
of justice in Texas, I am not prepared to deny.

"That there has been no such wanton disregard
of duty on the part of officials as you allege, I am
well satisfied. A very little while ago you regarded
the present officials in Texas the only ones who
could be safely trusted with power. Now you pro-
nounce them worthless, and would cast them aside.

"I have found little else in your letter but indica-
tions of temper, lashed into excitement by causes
which I deem mostly imaginary; a great confidence
in the accuracy of your own opinions, and an intoler-
ance of the opinions of others; a desire to punish the
thoughts and feelings of those who differ from you,
and an impatience which magnifies the shortcomings
of officials who are perhaps as earnest and conscientious in the discharge of their duties as yourself, and
a most unsound conclusion that while any persons
are to be found wanting in affection or respect for
government, or yielding it obedience from motives
which you do not approve, war, and not peace, is the

status, and all such persons are the proper subjects for military penal jurisdiction.

"If I have written anything to disabuse your mind of so grave an error, I shall be gratified.

"I am, sir, very respectfully, your obedient servant,

"W. S. HANCOCK,
Major-General Commanding."

CHAPTER XXXVIII.

THE policy of reconstruction thus boldly laid down by General HANCOCK, based upon his high sense of honor, his humanitarian principles, his respect for the rights of the people, and his Constitutional belief in the subordination of the military to the civil authority, when the clangor of war had ceased and the sulphurous smoke of battle had rolled sullenly away, could not but be objectionable to those who desired to hold the sword of Damocles perpetually suspended over the heads of the defeated; who proposed to carry the camp-fire into the Cabinet; who relied upon the drum-head courts-martial to supersede trial by a jury of peers; who essayed to turn loose upon the South the vultures of the carnage-fields and the carpet-bag camp followers, whose instincts were those of plunder and oppression only. Consequently, the dominant party in Congress aimed

hostile legislation at him with the intent to make his
position too irksome and embarrassing to be endured.
General GRANT was brought into this unworthy fight
by playing on his predilections for his favorite, General SHERIDAN, whose course was represented as being
openly impugned by the change of policy. General
HANCOCK speedily had occasion to notice this change,
and the revocation of some of his orders by General
GRANT was felt as a rebuke, an undeserved one, and
resented accordingly. He was not, however, to be
turned from his course while in authority, and he
wrote to a friend, "*nothing can intimidate me from
doing what I believe to be honest and right.*" Still, the
idea of such a conflict to a disciplinarian was un-
endurable, and on February 27, 1868, he applied to
be relieved. This request was complied with, March
16, 1868, and he was assigned to the command of the
Military Division of the Atlantic. Subsequently, he
was transferred to the Department of Dakota, where
although it was virtually a position of exile, his constant care, his courteous treatment, and strict integrity
rendered his services of inestimable value in that
Territory. Here he remained three years, until the
death of General MEADE, November 16, 1872. He
then resumed command of the Military Division of
the Atlantic, with headquarters on Governor's Island,

New York, where he has since resided, and to which place was telegraphed on June 24, 1880, the news of his enthusiastic nomination as Presidential Candidate, by the Democratic Convention at Cincinnati.

The ill-feeling subsisting, on the part of General GRANT towards General HANCOCK found expression at the time of the death of General GEORGE HENRY THOMAS, at San Francisco, March 28, 1870, for this event left four major-generals in the service. HALLECK had served out a term of duty and MEADE preferred to remain in Philadelphia, so that the succession to the command of the Department of the Pacific was between HANCOCK, the senior, and SCHOFIELD, the junior major-general. According to precedent, GRANT should have sent HANCOCK to the Pacific, but, remembering the Louisiana episode, he preferred SCHOFIELD. General HANCOCK always regarded this act as a degradation of rank, caused by spite. In April, 1870, General SHERMAN wrote to HANCOCK:

"The President authorizes me to say to you that it belongs to his office to select the commanding generals of divisions and departments, and that the relations you choose to assume towards him officially and privately absolve him from regarding your personal preferences."

In reply, General HANCOCK wrote:

"The rule that would place a junior major-general in a higher grade of command than a senior major general, in time of peace, or which gave all the major-generals save one (and he not a junior) divisions, and that senior major-general a department with brigadier-generals and colonels, and not allow him a choice of a department in his own division, is certainly a violation of the principle upon which rank is established, as well as the customs of military service in all countries governed by law, and would equally sanction that the lieutenant-general, who now commands a division, might be placed in command of a department, while some one or all of the major-generals had divisions. As the President leads me to believe that, because I have not his personal sympathy, my preferences for command will not be regarded, notwithstanding my rank, I shall not again open this subject."

As military commander of the Atlantic Division, the services of Major-General HANCOCK, (he is now senior major-general of the United States Army,) though always actively performed, have not been of a nature to call for public notice or description, but he has always occupied a prominent position in military and in social circles. He is president of the Military Order of the Loyal Legion and of several other military organizations. The last occasion on which he came before the notice of the public in an active military capacity, was when he again saved his native State from rapine and desolation, this time springing from internal sources. This was in July, 1877, when he came to Philadelphia to take command of the troops ordered here for the suppression of the riots, and to his promptness, energy, and moderation may justly be ascribed the speedy termination of that threatening movement. Thus again did he earn the lasting gratitude of the citizens of the Keystone State and of the city of Brotherly Love.

To turn to the political record of General HAN-COCK, we must revert to his "General Orders No. 40," and his equally-celebrated letter to Governor Pease, which were accepted by the Democracy in 1868 as his platform, and one which met with their entire approval. Consequently, but not by his own choice, he came before the Democratic National Convention which met in New York in July, 1868, soon after his service in Louisiana, Maine — which State voted solidly for him recently at Cincinnati — presenting his name, Pennsylvania's candidate at that time being Asa Packer. Hancock started with 33½ votes, and ran up and down, with no considerable changes, till the fifteenth ballot, when he received 79½, and, with lively gains, received 144½ on the eighteenth ballot, when the Convention adjourned to the following day. The chances at this time were that HANCOCK would be the choice of the Convention. On the nineteenth ballot, taken on the next morning, HANCOCK had 135½; he reached 142½ on the next, and on the twenty-first was back again to 135½. Pennsylvania was voting as a unit for her soldier at this time, and had been doing so from the fifteenth ballot. On the twenty-second ballot Ohio broke for Seymour and effected his nomination, although Pennsylvania stood by HANCOCK to the last, and was to the last supported by South Carolina. The Democratic nomination for Governor of Pennsylvania was tendered him in 1869, but declined He was again a prominent candidate for the presidential nomination at Baltimore, in 1872. In the Convention of 1876, at St. Louis, Hiester Clymer, on behalf of the Pennsylvania delegation, again presented General HANCOCK for the nomination. On the first ballot he had 75 votes—58 from Pennsylvania, 2 each from Alabama, Iowa, and Texas, 5 each from Louisiana and North Carolina, and 1 from Georgia. On the second ballot, when most of the States went for

Tilden, Pennsylvania remained by HANCOCK with her 58 votes.

That for twelve years he has retained the esteem, the confidence, and the affection of the great Democratic party is an honor of which he might well be proud, for during the whole of that time, wherever the name of HANCOCK was heard in Democratic gatherings, it was the signal for a burst of enthusiasm or a quietly-uttered warm eulogium, which found its vent in the recent Convention and carried all by storm, as he was wont to do the works of an enemy, with a steady, resistless sweep as "superb" as the hero himself.

Here we must again turn aside and ask the reader to visit Cincinnati with us; take a seat in its Music Hall, and listen to the surging swell of applause as the name of "HANCOCK" is made the unanimous choice of the Democratic National Convention.

CHAPTER XXXIX.

The Cincinnati Convention, which Nominated Major-General Winfield Scott Hancock, U. S. A., for President of the United States, June 24, 1880.

PURSUANT to call, the National Democratic Convention, to nominate candidates for President and Vice-President, met in the Music Hall, Cincinnati, Ohio, on the morning of Tuesday, June 22, 1880. The Music Hall began to fill soon after eleven o'clock, the seating capacity being perhaps about one-half that of the building used at Chicago. The platform was at the west end of the hall, and there were galleries on the north and south sides. These were filled with spectators, quite a number of whom were ladies. The positions for the delegates in the body of the hall were indicated by blue silk bannerets, edged with gold, and bearing the names of the different States. A profusion of bunting decorated the sides and windows, and a blue canvas, bearing the words "Ohio greets the nation," hung from the centre of the ceiling. The large organ at the back of the platform and a military band afforded

33 *

plenty of music. Among the decorations brought by the delegates were some handsome banners — one of dark velvet, with a medallion-portrait of Samuel J. Randall; another with an embroidered owl, indicating the Americus Club; and yet another, with the like-ness of Hendricks and the words "Indiana — For President, Thomas A. Hendricks."

Ex-Senator Barnum, of Connecticut, called the Convention to order at 12.45 P. M., after which Rev. Charles W. Wendte, of the Unitarian Church, de-livered the opening prayer, in which he spoke of the young Democracy of America as the refuge and asylum for the distressed and downtrodden through-out the world, the light and hope of the nations, and prayed that with an unfaltering hand every unjust law on the statute-book might be erased, and our political life purged from every evil that keeps back the people from the highest measure of virtue and happiness. He continued:

"Above all, let there be an end of all sectional divisions and strifes. Let every root of bitterness, every occasion of estrangement, be removed, and let our whole people, forgetting the things that are behind, and pressing forward to the things that are before, be united heart and hand in the bonds of mutual confidence and good-will. Help this Convention to choose for leaders, in the approaching and honorable struggle, men of large wisdom and experience; of lofty character and irreproachable life; men true and fearless in the hour of trial, yet ardent lovers of justice and peace. Enable the members of this Convention to rise above all self-seeking, and personal preferences, and indiscreet party zeal, into the larger sentiment of public good of American nationality and human brotherhood. Let them remember that he serves his party best who serves God. We ask that our action to-day may be well pleasing in the sight of God."

Under the instructions of the National Committee, Mr. Barnum presented the name of Hon. George Hoadley, of Ohio, for temporary chairman, which was agreed to. Judge Hoadley, on taking his seat, made an address, in which, after thanking the Convention for the confidence reposed in him, he pledged himself to the exercise of the strictest impartiality in exercising the authority with which he had been invested. He alluded to the Convention at St. Louis four years ago, and claimed that its nominees, Samuel J. Tilden and Thomas A. Hendricks, had been as fairly elected as George Washington or James Monroe, and that, in consequence of their not having been inaugurated, "government by the people" in the executive department has been in abeyance since March 4, 1877. He closed with the hope that vigilance would ensure victory to the Democratic principles and the Democratic candidates; that the "melancholy days of November" shall be radiant with joy, and on the wings of the strong winds of March shall be wafted blessings.

The following were nominated and accepted as the remaining temporary officers:

Mr. F. O. Prince, Massachusetts, temporary secretary.

ASSISTANT SECRETARIES. — George W. Guthrie, Pennsylvania; Charles Ridley, Tennessee; C. S. Dodd, Ohio; O. M. Hall, Minnesota; Major A. Orendorff, Illinois; William H. Gill, New Jersey; and A. C. Parkinson, Wisconsin.

READING CLERKS.—Neal S. Brown, Jr., Reading Clerk of the United States House of Representatives; Mark A. Hardin, Georgia; T. O. Walker, Iowa; Thomas S. Pettit, of the House of Representatives; Nicholas M. Bell, Missouri; James E. Morrison, New York; and H. L. Bryan, Delaware.

SERGEANT-AT-ARMS.—Isaac L. Miller, Ohio.

OFFICIAL STENOGRAPHER.—Edward B. Dickinson, New York.

On motion of Mr. Beebe, New York, the rules of

the last National Convention were adopted. Mr. Martin, Delaware, offered a resolution for a call of the roll by States for Committees on Permanent Organization, Credentials, and Resolutions, which was adopted, though Mr. Weed (New York) desired a roll-call for the presentation of credentials. The roll-call was then proceeded with until New York was called on the Credentials Committee, when John Kelly, who was in the rear of the delegation, rose and claimed the attention of the Chair This produced, for a time, considerable confusion, which, however, was promptly checked by the presiding officer, who declined to allow the roll-call to be interrupted.

The Committees on Permanent Organization, Resolutions, and Credentials were then appointed.

Mr. Avery, of Massachusetts, moved that when the Convention adjourn it be to ten o'clock next morning.

Mr. Martin, of Delaware, moved an amendment to make the hour of reconvening six o'clock that evening.

Mr. Martin subsequently withdrew his amendment, and Mr. Avery's motion was adopted.

After some unimportant discussion about Press tickets, Mr. Watterson, of Kentucky, presented an application, on behalf of the delegates from the Territories, asking recognition in the Convention, which was referred without discussion to the Committee on Permanent Organization.

David A. Wells, of Connecticut, offered the usual resolution referring to the Committee on Resolutions, without debate, all resolutions regarding the platform. Adopted.

The Convention then adjourned for the day.

After the adjournment of the Convention, the Committee on Permanent Organization organized by electing Mr. Martin, of Delaware, chairman, and Mr. Dawson, of South Carolina, secretary. The Committee by a unanimous vote determined to report to the Convention the name of J. W. Stevenson, of Kentucky, for permanent president, and the following list of vice-presidents and secretaries:

States.	Vice-Presidents.	Secretaries.
Alabama	C. C. Langdon	J. S. Ferguson.
Arkansas	O. A. Gault	J. P. Coffin.
California	W. C. Hendricks	J. B. Metcalf.
Colorado	Alva Adams	John Stone.
Connecticut	Curtis Bacon	Samuel Simpson.
Delaware	James Williams	A. P. Robinson.
Florida	Wm. Judge	J. B. Marshall.
Georgia	J. R. Alexander	Mark A. Hardin.
Illinois	H. M. Vanderen	W. A. Day.
Indiana	J. R. Slack	Rufus Magee.
Iowa	S. B. Evans	J. J. Snouffer.
Kansas	W. V. Bennett	J. B. Chapman.

States.	Vice-Presidents.	Secretaries.
Kentucky . . .	Henry Burnett . . .	T. G. Stuart.
Louisiana . . .	J. D. Jefferies . . .	Martin McNamara.
Maine	Darius Alden . . .	John R. Redman.
Maryland . . .	Philip F. Thomas . .	Morris A. Thomas.
Massachusetts .	Jonas H. French . .	John M. Thayer.
Michigan . . .	Charles H. Richmond .	A. J. Shakspeare.
Minnesota . . .	L. L. Baxter	L. A. Evans.
Mississippi . .	W. S. Featherstone .	R. C. Patty.
Missouri · . . .	B. F. Dillon	N. C. Dryden.
Nebraska . . .	R. S. Maloney . . .	James North.
Nevada. . . .	Not named.	
New Hampshire .	Frank Jones	Charles A. Busiel.
New Jersey . .	Hezekiah B. Smith .	James S. Coleman.
New York . .	Not named.	
North Carolina .	W. T. Dortch . . .	R. M. Furman.
Ohio	J. L. McSweeny . .	C. T. Lewis.
Oregon	J. W. Winson . . .	A. Noltner.
Pennsylvania . .	D. E. Ermentrout.	
Rhode Island . .	Thomas W. Segar . .	John Waters.
South Carolina .	M. C. Butler	J. R. Abney.
Tennessee . . .	J. W. Childress . . .	C. L. Ridley.
Texas	Joel W. Robinson . .	B. P. Paddock
Vermont . . .	Nathan P. Bowman .	H. W. McGettrick.
Virginia . . .	J. W. Daniel	R. W. Hunter.
West Virginia .	C. P. Snyder . . .	H. C. Simms.
Wisconsin . . .	J. C. Gregory . . .	J. M. Smith.

The committee then recommended that the secretaries, reading clerks, and sergeant-at-arms of the temporary organization be retained. · The report concluded as follows:

"The committee further report that they have duly considered the memorial in relation to the representation of the District of Columbia and of the Territories, and have heard the arguments of the memorialists, and respectfully commend the following resolution:

"*Resolved*, That two delegates from the District of Columbia, and two delegates from each of the Territories, be admitted to the Convention, and have the right to participate in debate, and every other right and privilege enjoyed by delegates from the States, excepting only the right to vote."

The Committee on Credentials met immediately after the adjournment, and was organized by the election of P. M. B. Young, of Georgia, chairman, and A. Woltner, of Oregon, secretary. The Tammany men met with the committee, but were requested to withdraw. A delegate from Arkansas objected to Smith M. Weed, of New York, sitting as a member of the Credentials Committee, inasmuch as his own seat was contested. The Chairman ruled the objection out of order, as there was no notice of the contest before the committee. A long time was spent in fixing the length of time for argument. It was finally resolved to give each side an hour and a half to present its case. The committee then adjourned to meet at seven o'clock. The question of admitting Tammany led to a long discussion, and at eleven o'clock the committee went into secret session, and at 12.15, by a vote of 32 to 4, Arkansas, Colorado, New Jersey, and Delaware voting no, voted in favor of allowing the sitting delegates from New York to retain their seats.

The Committee on Resolutions elected Henry Watterson, of Kentucky, chairman. The committee gave a hearing to the advocates of woman suffrage. Susan B. Anthony, Mrs. Matilda Joslyn Gage, Mrs. Lillie Deveraux Blake, and Mrs. Marxweather, of Tennessee, spoke. Henry Watterson presided, and expressed himself as very favorable to their request for recognition in the platform. Several other members avowed themselves in their favor.

The committee did not reassemble until late in the evening, with Henry Watterson as chairman, and John P. Irish, of Iowa, as secretary.

The representatives of the different States then, under a resolution, submitted the resolutions which they desired to be incorporated in the platform, and one or more were submitted from most of the States. They were all referred to a sub-committee of nine, appointed by the Chair, and consisting of the following persons: Messrs. Watterson, chairman; Wells, of Connecticut; Borksdale, of Mississippi; Myers, of Oregon; Fuller, of Illinois; Ireland, of Texas; Irish, of Iowa; Cassidy, of Pennsylvania, and How-

34

ells, of Georgia. The committee then adjourned to nine o'clock the following morning, and at half-past eleven the sub-committee began its task of sifting and classifying the resolutions referred to it.

SECOND DAY'S SESSION, JUNE 23, 1880.

On Wednesday the Convention was called to order, by Judge Hoadley, at 10.45 A. M., and prayer was offered by Rev. Dr. Taylor, of Covington, Ky. After the prayer, and the presentation of the report of the Committee on Permanent Organization, which we have given previously, commenced the first fight of the Convention, namely, that on the contested seats of New York, and this lasted from shortly after eleven o'clock until after one o'clock P. M.

The majority and minority reports of the Committee on Credentials were then read. The majority report favored the admission of the two delegations from the State of Massachusetts, the united delegation to cast the vote to which the State is entitled; that in the case of Pennsylvania, the sitting delegates were entitled to retain their seats; and that in the case of the New York contest, the sitting delegates also be recognized.

The minority report dealt only with the New York contest, and recommended that the Faulkner branch be allowed to cast fifty votes, and the Shake-speare Hall branch twenty votes, in the Convention; each division to determine its own methods of counting such votes.

By a vote of 316 yeas to 295 nays, the previous question was called, and twenty minutes allowed the sitting delegates, and forty minutes the contestants, to discuss the matter.

The discussion which followed is hardly of sufficient importance to occupy our space, the point at issue not being vital in view of the fact that it was well understood that Ex-Governor SAMUEL J. TIL-DEN had sent a letter of declination, and was not a candidate before the Convention. The following gentlemen advocated Tammany's claims: George W. Miller and Judge Amasa J. Parker of Albany, and Governor Hubbard of Texas. John R. Fellows of New York, Rufus W. Peckham of Albany, and P M. B. Young of Georgia, followed for the majority report, which was finally adopted by a vote of 457 to 205½: so the sitting members from New York retained their seats, and the Tammany delegates were complimentarily invited to the floor.

This matter having been settled, the report of the Committee on Permanent Organization was adopted, and, in accordance with it, Governor Stephenson was duly installed as permanent President of the Convention. On assuming the chair, he made an excellent address, in which he referred to the days of Thomas Jefferson, when then, as now, there were men ready to trample upon the popular will; there are men, he said, " who would now attempt, and have succeeded, in deposing those who were elevated to high offices from enjoying the high confidence given to them." He continued: " We enter upon the twenty-fourth Presidential election since the organization of the Government. You put forward your declaration of political faith, as it always has been, as it still is. We believe that this is a limited Government, and that no power not granted by the Constitution can be exercised by that Government. We believe in a free press. We believe in a popular education. We believe and declare that this people will stand no taxation not demanded by an economical administration of the Government. But, above all, we believe representation rests on suffrage, and that every suffrage must be preserved sacred that every man casts, and must be counted; and that the people who receive the majority of these votes must and shall be the officers."

In conclusion, he said: " Let your nominees receive your support, and there will be triumphal joy from every delegate and every Democrat."

At the conclusion of Governor Stephenson's speech, Henry Watterson, of Kentucky, Chairman of the Committee on Resolutions, announced that they were not then ready to report, and they were promptly excused by the Convention. After a resolution of thanks to Judge Hoadley, the temporary Chairman, had been warmly and unanimously adopted, the Convention, on the motion of Mr. Breckinridge, of Kentucky, proceeded to the nomination of candidates. The first name presented was that of Judge Field, the nomination being made by Mr. McElrath, of California, and seconded by Mr. Alva Adams, of Colorado. Honorable Thomas F. Bayard was then named, amid a storm of applause, by Attorney-General George Gray, of Delaware, who supported the presentation in an able speech. Colonel Morrison, of Illinois, was named by Mr. Marshall, of that State. Ex-Governor Hendricks, of Indiana, was then put in nomination by Senator Dan Voorhees, and the "Tall Sycamore of the Wabash" eloquently presented the claims of his candidate, and, *en passant*, remarked: "I know the accomplished jurist of California. I know the able and distinguished Senator from Delaware. I know the gallant, iron-hearted, brave man from Illinois, Colonel Morrison. I know them all. I am proud to do them honor. Every name thus far is worthy of this great presence; and yet I venture in this comparison to announce the name of Thomas A. Hendricks." He was interrupted for some moments by enthusiastic cheering; and, when it subsided, he continued in a ringing speech, provoking from time to time a renewal of the cheering. Mr. Sulstonstall, of Massachusetts, then made an excellent speech to second the nomination of Senator Bayard. New York, by the silent head-shake of Chairman Manning, indicated that it had no candidate to present. Senator Thurman, of Ohio, was next nominated by Mr. John McSweeny, of that State, and the applause which greeted this presentation was intensified by a humorous imitation of Roscoe Conkling's Chicago effort, in the following:

> If you ask what State he came from,
>   Our sole response shall be,
> "He comes from Ohio-o,
>   And his name is Allen G."

Shouts of laughter welcomed this happy hit, and the Ohio delegation gave him three hearty cheers when he resumed his seat.

Then came *the* sensation of the day, when Hon. Daniel Dougherty, of Philadelphia, presented the name of

WINFIELD SCOTT HANCOCK,

of Pennsylvania, in the following polished specimen of cultivated oratory.

"I rise to nominate one whose name would reconcile all factions, whose election would crush the last embers of sectional strife and be hailed as the dawning of the day of perpetual brotherhood. With him we can fling away our shields and wage an aggressive war. We can appeal to the supreme tribunal of the American people against the corruption of the Republican party and their untold violations of constitutional liberty. With him as our chieftain the bloody banner of the Republicans will fall from their palsied grasp. Oh! my countrymen! in this supreme moment, when the destinies of the Republic are at stake, when the liberties of the people are imperilled, I rise to present to the thoughtful consideration of this Convention the name of one who, on the field of battle, was styled 'the Superb,' yet who has won a nobler renown as the military Governor, whose first act, on assuming command of Louisiana and Texas, was to salute the Constitution by proclaiming, amid the joyous greetings of an oppressed people, that the military, save in actual war, shall be subservient to the civil power. The plighted word of the soldier was proved in the statesman's acts. I name him whose name will suppress every faction, will be alike acceptable to the North and South, and will thrill the land from end to end. The people hang breath- less on your deliberation. Take heed! Make no mis- step! I nominate one who can carry every Southern State, and who can carry Pennsylvania, Indiana, Connecticut, New Jersey, and New York — the soldier-statesman with a record as stainless as his sword is keen — WINFIELD SCOTT HANCOCK, of Pennsylvania. If elected, he will take his seat."

The applause which followed this speech lasted fully five minutes. Then came another burst of cheering when General WADE HAMPTON, of South Carolina, took the platform to speak in support of Senator BAYARD, as a second seconder. In closing a capital address, he said:

"When the Greeks were returning from a great victory, the generals were called upon to vote for the two men whom they thought most worthy of honor, and the name of Pericles was found on every ballot. So the name of THOMAS F. BAYARD is always placed, if not first, at least second, and we choose to take the second man."

Governor Hubbard, of Texas, then seconded the nomination of General HANCOCK. He said it was peculiarly fit that Texas and Louisiana should respond to HANCOCK's nomination, because, when the war closed, there came down through the South a race of carpet-baggers, like the Vandals of old, preying on her wasted substance, and the jails and bastiles were filled with prisoners by order of the military governors, and then, in that darkness of the night, there came a voice, saying, "The war has closed; unbar your dungeons and open your forts." That man was HANCOCK. "It is an easy thing," he said, "to be a summer friend. The world and Hades are full of them. But this man knew that he was in the power of the Republican party, and his official head was cut off. That is a man to whom it will do to intrust the standard of our party."

Mr. Stringfellow, of Virginia, seconded Judge Field, and Mr. Goode, of Virginia, seconded Senator Thurman. Then Mr. J. W. Daniels, of Virginia, took the stand for General HANCOCK, and made a stirring speech, closing with a reference to the blue and the gray joining in one hurrah for the nominee.

The roll of States being concluded, Mr. Breckinridge moved to proceed to a ballot; but Judge Hoadley submitted a motion to adjourn, which was, however, voted down by a vote of 395 yeas to 317 yeas: so the roll-call proceeded.

There was prolonged applause when Kentucky

cast 5 votes for Samuel J. Tilden, and finally the result was announced, as follows:

	Delegates.		Delegates.
Hancock	171	Randall	6
Bayard	153½	Loveland	5
Payne	81	McDonald	3
Thurman	68½	McClellan	3
Field	65	Parker	1
Morrison	62	Black	1
Hendricks	50½	Jewett	1
Tilden	38	English	1
Ewing	10	Lothrop	1
Seymour	8		

Total delegates voting.. 729½

Absent. 8½

Total delegates.. 738

It should be here mentioned that each delegate, under the Democratic rules, has only half a vote. There were 369 full votes in the Convention; number necessary to a choice, under the two-thirds rule, 246, or the assent of 492 delegates. Of the scattering votes cast, no heed need be taken, for it was evident that there were but two actual candidates in the field.

The Convention then, at 6.07 P. M., adjourned until 10 o'clock on Thursday morning.

THIRD DAY'S SESSION, JUNE 24, 1880.

When Thursday dawned, with a lowering sky and a sultry atmosphere, it looked upon many who had not troubled the realms of sleep to any great extent. As the hour for re-assembling drew near, the delegates slowly filed into their places, there was an evident feeling that the struggle was over, the excitement of suspense was past. The door-keepers retained the platform and press tickets, and everything around gave evidence of a speedy winding up of business. Beneath all this, however, there was a suppressed enthusiasm, only kept in bounds by fatigue and a desire not to hinder the march of events. President Stephenson called the Convention to order at 10.35 A. M., and prayer was offered by Rev. Dr. Taylor, of the Methodist Episcopal Church, South.

Mr. Peckham, of New York, on behalf of the delegation from that State, referred to the votes cast yesterday for the Hon. Samuel J. Tilden, and stated that the delegation had received a letter from that gentleman renouncing all claims and all candidacy. He desired to place the letter at the disposal of the Convention, and to state that the New York delegation had agreed upon Speaker Randall as their candidate. On a *viva voce* vote, the Convention declined to have the letter read. A resolution introduced by Mr. Thomas, of Kentucky, denouncing as unconstitutional and unrepublican any State law affecting a citizen on account of religious or non-religious views, was referred, and the roll-call for the second ballot was proceeded with, resulting as follows:

	Delegates.		Delegates
Hancock	320	Hendricks	31
Randall	128½	English	15
Bayard	113	Tilden	6
Field	65½	Parker	2
Thurman	50	Jewett	1

Total delegates voting...................................... 736
Delegates absent 2

Total delegates... 738

Some difficulty arose when Ohio was called, and finally the entire 44 votes were cast for Thurman. Meanwhile, before the official announcement was made, State after State began to change their votes to HANCOCK, Wisconsin leading off with 20, and New Jersey following with 18. Malcolm Hay, of Pennsylvania, then cast the entire vote of Pennsylvania for Hancock amid prolonged cheering. After all the changes had been made, the result on the amended roll-call was as follows: HANCOCK, 705; Hendricks, 30; Tilden, 1; Bayard, 2.

Mr. Mack, of Indiana, moved to make the nomination unanimous, and spoke in favor of his motion. Speaker Randall and Senator Wallace of Pennsyl vania, General Wade Hampton of South Carolina, and Judge Hoadley of Ohio then followed in eloquent support of Mr. Mack's motion.

The Chair then put the motion as follows: "The motion has been made that WINFIELD SCOTT HANCOCK be declared unanimously elected the Democratic President of these United States. (Great laughter and applause.) Those in favor will say aye. (Shouts of ayes.) You who are opposed will say no. The motion is unanimously adopted, and HANCOCK is elected."

For a moment or two the humorous blunder of the closing sentence was not noticed, but when the Convention finally caught the full effect of the remark, the tumultuous applause and laughter broke forth again. The appearance of a transparency with the legend, "For President, WINFIELD SCOTT HANCOCK," and the tunes "Dixie" and "Hail Columbia," with which the band and the organ enlivened the scene, set the entire assemblage on platform, floor, and in the galleries wild with enthusiastic excitement. When order was restored, the tall form of Senator Voorhees was noticed above the excited throng, and obtaining the ear of the Convention, he spoke boldly for the Democracy of Indiana in favor of General HANCOCK. He claimed that the record

35

of the nominee was not alone to be found on battle-fields, for he had uplifted the down-trodden civil authorities, he had made a second Declaration of Constitutional liberty, and set an example for his own, and our future generations of obedience to that great framework devised by our fathers, and pro-tected by their bravery, and enjoyed by us.

He was followed by Mr. Breckinridge, of Kentucky, who also enthusiastically ratified the nomination. Just at this point John Kelly, of New York, ac-companied by Augustus Schell, Amasa J. Parker, George C. Green, and Samuel North — the committee appointed by the anti-Tilden delegation to appear be-fore the Convention in behalf of HANCOCK — came upon the platform. Mr. Kelly made a speech, in which he asked that all discordant feelings be buried, and promised to aid the ticket. Mr. Fellows, of New York, responded, and at the conclusion of his speech he and Kelly shook hands, formally and impressively, the band playing "Auld Lang Syne" and the entire audience cheering. Susan B. Anthony next attracted the attention of the Chair, and presented a printed appeal of the Women's Suffrage Association, which was read.

Mr. Watterson, Chairman of the Committee on Resolutions and Rules, then reported the following

PLATFORM.

The Democrats of the United States, in convention assembled, declare:

First.—We pledge ourselves anew to the constitutional doctrines and traditions of the Democratic party as illustrated by the teaching and example of a long line of Democratic statesmen and patriots, and embodied in the platform of the last National Convention of the party.

Second.—Opposition to centralization, and to that dangerous spirit of encroachment which tends to consolidate the powers of all the departments in one, and thus to create—whatever be the form of government—a real despotism. No sumptuary laws; separation of Church and State, for the good of each; common schools fostered and protected.

Third.—Home rule; honest money, consisting of gold and silver, and paper convertible into coin on demand; the strict maintenance of the public faith, State and national, and a tariff for revenue only.

Fourth.—The subordination of the military to the civil power, and a general and thorough reform of the civil service.

Fifth.—The right to a free ballot is the right preservative of all rights, and must and shall be maintained in every part of the United States.

Sixth.—The existing administration is the representative of conspiracy only, and its claim of right to surround the ballot-boxes with troops and deputy marshals to intimidate and obstruct the electors, and the unprecedented use of the veto to maintain its corrupt and despotic power, insults the people and imperils their institutions.

Seventh.—The great fraud of 1876–77, by which, upon a false count of the electoral votes of two States, the candidate defeated at the polls was declared to be President, and, for the first time in American history, the will of the people was set aside under a threat of military violence, struck a deadly blow at our system of representative government. The Democratic party, to preserve the country from the horrors of a civil war, submitted for the time, in firm and patriotic faith that the people would punish this crime in 1880. This issue precedes and dwarfs every other. It imposes a more sacred duty upon the people of the Union than ever addressed the conscience of a nation of freemen.

Eighth.—We execrate the course of this administration in making places in the civil service a reward for political crime, and demand a reform by statute which shall make it forever impossible for the defeated candidate to bribe his way to the seat of a usurper by billeting villains upon the people.

Ninth. — The resolution of Samuel J. Tilden not again to be a candidate for the exalted place to which he was elected by a majority of his countrymen, and from which he was excluded by the leaders of the Republican party, is received by the Democrats of the United States with sensibility, and they declare their confidence in his wisdom, patriotism, and integrity, unshaken by the assaults of a common enemy; and they further assure him that he is followed into the retirement he has chosen for himself by the sympathy and respect of his fellow-citizens, who regard him as one who, by elevating the standards of public morality, and adorning and purifying the public service, merits the lasting gratitude of his country and his party.

Tenth. — Free ships and a living chance for American commerce on the seas and on the land. No discrimination in favor of transportation lines, corporations, or monopolies.

Eleventh. — The amendment of the Burlingame treaty. No more Chinese immigration, except for travel, education, and foreign commerce, and therein carefully guarded.

Twelfth. — Public money and public credit for public purposes solely, and public land for actual settlers.

Thirteenth. — The Democratic party is the friend

35 *

of labor and the laboring man, and pledges itself to protect him alike against the cormorants and the commune.

Fourteenth. — We congratulate the country upon the honesty and thrift of a Democratic Congress, which has reduced the public expenditure $40,000,-000 a year; upon the continuation of prosperity at home and the national honor abroad; and, above all, upon the promise of such a change in the administration of the Government as shall insure us genuine and lasting reform in every department of the public service.

This platform having been unanimously adopted, the Convention proceeded to a roll-call for the nomination of a Vice-President. Mr. Pettis, of Alabama, presented the name of W. H. English, of Indiana, which was speedily made unanimous, and the main business of the Convention was at an end. The roll was then called by States for nominations for the National Committee.

By this time all were anxious to get away, and the usual resolutions complimentary to the President and officers of the Convention were submitted and adopted without delay. At seven minutes past three o'clock, on the motion of Mr. Preston, of Kentucky, the Democratic National Convention of 1880 adjourned *sine die*

APPENDIX TO CINCINNATI CONVENTION, No. 1.

First Ballot by States, June 23, 1880.

States.	Delegates.	Votes.	Field.	Bayard.	Morrison.	Hendricks.	Thurman.	Hancock.	Payne.	Tilden.
Alabama	20	10	5	7	...	...	1	7		
Arkansas	12	6	12							
California	12	6	6	...	...	1	3			
Colorado	6	3	1	...	...	...	...	...	2	
Connecticut	12	6	...	4	...	3	2			
Delaware	6	3	...	6						
Florida	8	4	...	8						
Georgia	22	11	8	5	...	1	...	8		
Illinois	42	21	...	...	42					
Indiana	30	15	...	...	...	30				
Iowa	22	11	...	3	6	2	...	7	2	
Kansas	10	5								
Kentucky	24	12	2	6	...	2	7	1	...	5
Louisiana	16	8	...	...	...	...	...	16		
Maine	14	7	...	...	...	...	...	14		
Maryland	16	8	...	16	...	...	...	...	...	2
Massachusetts	26	13	...	11½	...	1½	½	6		
Michigan	22	11	4	2	...	...	...	5	1	1
Minnesota	10	5	...	...	...	...	...	10		
Mississippi	16	8	2	8	...	...	...	5	...	1
Missouri	30	15	...	4	4	3	...	12	...	7
Nebraska	6	3	...	...	...	...	...	...	6	
Nevada	6	3	3	...	...	...	...	...	...	3
New Hampshire	10	5	1	3	...	...	2	4		
New Jersey	18	9	...	10	...	4				
New York	70	35	...	...	...	...	...	...	70	
North Carolina	20	10	...	7	...	1	...	9	...	1
Ohio	44	22	...	...	...	...	44			
Oregon	6	3	4	...	...	...	...	...	...	2
Pennsylvania	58	29	1	1	...	1	...	28	...	15
Rhode Island	8	4	1	2	...	...	...	2	...	1
South Carolina	14	7	...	14						
Tennessee	24	12	2	9	...	...	1	11		
Texas	16	8	...	5	...	1	1	9		
Vermont	10	5	...	...	...	...	...	10		
Virginia	22	11	9	10	...	...	...	3		
West Virginia	10	5	...	...	...	...	7	3		
Wisconsin	20	10	2	6	10	...	...	1		
Totals	738	369	65	153½	62	50½	68½	171	81	38

APPENDIX TO CINCINNATI CONVENTION, No. 2.

Second Ballot by States, June 24, 1880.

States.	Delegates.	Votes.	Field.	Bayard.	Hendricks.	Thurman.	Hancock.	Randall.	English.	Tilden.	Parker.	Jewett.
Alabama	20	10	4	5	...	...	11					
Arkansas	12	6	12									
California	12	6	5	...	1	...	5					
Colorado	6	3	6									
Connecticut	12	6	...	1	...	...	...	...	11			
Delaware	6	3	...	6								
Florida	8	4	...	8								
Georgia	22	11	10	5	...	...	7					
Illinois	42	21	...	...	...	...	42					
Indiana	30	15	...	...	30							
Iowa	22	11	...	1	...	...	9	12				
Kansas	10	5	...	...	...	...	10					
Kentucky	24	12	4	7	...	2	8	...	...	3		
Louisiana	16	8	...	...	...	...	16					
Maine	14	7	...	...	...	...	14					
Maryland	16	8	...	16								
Massachusetts	26	13	1½	7	...	...	11	3½	...	2		
Michigan	22	11	...	4	...	...	14	1	2	1		
Minnesota	10	5	...	...	...	...	10					
Mississippi	16	8	2	8	...	...	6					
Missouri	30	15	...	2	...	...	28					
Nebraska	6	3	...	...	...	...	...	6				
Nevada	6	3	4	...	..	1	...	1				
New Hampshire	10	5	...	...	...	...	5	5				
New Jersey	18	9	...	4	...	...	7	4	...	...	2	1
New York	70	35	...	...	...	...	...	70				
North Carolina	20	10	...	...	...	...	20					
Ohio	44	22	...	...	...	44						
Oregon	6	3	6									
Pennsylvania	58	29	...	1	...	...	32	25				
Rhode Island	8	4	...	...	...	...	6	1	1			
South Carolina	14	7	...	14								
Tennessee	24	12	2	8	...	...	14					
Texas	16	8	...	5	...	...	11					
Vermont	10	5	...	...	...	...	10					
Virginia	22	11	7	8	...	...	7					
West Virginia	10	5	...	1	...	2	7					
Wisconsin	20	10	2	2	...	1	10	...	5			
Totals	738	369	65½	113	31	50	320	128½	19	6	2	1

CHAPTER XL.

WILLIAM H. ENGLISH, OF INDIANA.

Nominated for Vice-President of the United States by the Cincinnati Convention of 1880 — Sketch of his Life — A Native Indianian — Early Career — Political Record — Services in Congress — The Kansas-Nebraska Bill — Commercial Life.

WILLIAM H. ENGLISH was born August 27, 1822, at Lexington, Scott County, Indiana, when that was a wild frontier region. His father, Elisha G. English, was pioneer emigrant from Kentucky. Young ENGLISH attended the common schools of his native village, spent three years at South Hanover College, studied law, and was admitted to the bar when only eighteen years old, also to practise in the Supreme Court of the United States when only twenty-three. He entered politics early, being a delegate to the Democratic State Convention several years before he came of age, or in the hard-cider-and-log-cabin campaign of 1840. He stumped Indiana for the Democratic ticket, and when Harrison died, and Tyler succeeded him, young ENG-

LISH was appointed postmaster at Lexington. In 1843 he was elected Clerk of the Indiana House of Representatives, and after Polk's election, in 1844, received a treasury appointment at Washington. He opposed Taylor's election in 1848, and just before his inauguration, Mr. ENGLISH resigned his treasury position in a letter that was widely published. The family was always Democratic, his father and one uncle being vice-presidents and two other uncles being delegates in the National Democratic Convention of 1848. These four English brothers, all Democrats, were members of the respective Legislatures of four different States at the same time. Mr. ENGLISH was Clerk of the United States Senate Claims Committee in 1850, and Secretary of the Indiana Constitutional Convention of the same year. In 1851 he was chosen a member, and then Speaker, of the State Legislature, when only twenty-nine years old.

With the close of the long session of the Legislature of 1851, in which Mr. ENGLISH had earned golden opinions of men of all parties, he was justly regarded as one of the foremost men of their State, and the Democrats of his district, with great unanimity, selected him for their standard-bearer in the race for Congress. In October, 1852, when just

thirty years of age, he was elected to the United
States House of Representatives by 488 majority.
Mr. ENGLISH entered Congress at the commencement of Mr. Pierce's administration, and gave its
political measures a warm and generous support.

Mr. ENGLISH served four terms in Congress — in
all eight years — immediately preceding the war,
and that during the entire period as stormy as the
National Legislature ever experienced. The Kansas-
Nebraska bill and questions growing out of its introduction were among the most prominent and important measures that were ever submitted to Congress.
With these measures he was conspicuously identified,
and the comprehensive statesmanship then displayed
gave him a national reputation which subsequent events
have not obscured. Mr. ENGLISH, at the time the
Kansas-Nebraska bill was introduced, was a member
of the House Committee on Territories, which was
charged with the consideration of the subject. Passing by the question of area and other questions of
secondary importance, the real question at issue was,
"Popular Sovereignty," — the right of the people
to determine for themselves the character of their
Territorial and State institutions; and this great question, which underlies the Democratic idea of government, was first sharply defined in the discussion of

the " Kansas-Nebraska bill," for the organization of the Territories bearing these names, and now sovereign and prosperous States. Mr. ENGLISH, for prudential reasons, did not concur with the majority of the Committee on Territories in bringing forward the Kansas-Nebraska bill, but a majority of the committee decided to report it, whereupon Mr. ENGLISH, on the 31st of January, 1854, made a minority report. Both the House and Senate bill, at the time Mr. ENGLISH made his minority report, contained a provision " that the Constitution and all laws of the United States which are not locally inapplicable shall have the same force and effect within the said Territory as elsewhere in the United States," and then followed this important reservation:

" Except the eighth section of the act preparatory to the admission of Missouri into the Union, approved March 6, 1820, which was superseded by the principles of the legislation of 1850, commonly called the compromise measures, and is hereby declared inoperative."

Mr. ENGLISH proposed to strike out this exception and insert the following:

" Provided that nothing in this act shall be so construed as to prevent the people of said Territory, through the properly constituted legislative authority, from passing such laws in relation to the institution of slavery, not inconsistent with the Constitution of the United States, as they may deem best adapted to their locality and most conducive to their happiness and welfare; and so much of any existing act of Congress as may conflict with the above right of the people to regulate their domestic institutions in their own way be, and the same is, hereby repealed."

The agitation of the slavery question continued and culminated in Congress upon the proposition to admit Kansas into the Union under what was known as the Lecompton Constitution, which did not prohibit the institution of slavery, and it was at this period of Mr. ENGLISH's Congressional history that he acquired his widest reputation as a statesman. He was firmly opposed to the admission of Kansas under the Lecompton Constitution until that instrument had been ratified by a vote of the people, and so true was he to his convictions that he opposed the policy of the administration of his own party upon the measure. It was the turning-point in the history of the country, and the position assumed and maintained by Mr. ENGLISH in that long and exciting contest was the crowning glory of his Congressional life. He was "anti-Lecompton" from principle and not from hostility to the administration; opposition did

36

not intimidate him, dangers did not affright him. He shrank from no duty, and while his utterances were bold, they were consistent with the right, with duty, and with the best interests of the country.

The Senate saw proper to pass a bill admitting Kansas, under the Lecompton Constitution, without limit or condition; but this bill, although it commanded the favor of the President and his Cabinet, failed to receive the sanction of the House of Representatives. The House, on the other hand, passed a bill as a substitute for that of the Senate, but this the Senate would not accept nor the Executive approve. Thus was an issue formed between great co-ordinate branches of the Government, whose joint and harmonious action could alone remove the dangerous question and give peace to the country.

In this stage of the proceedings, when the whole country had about abandoned the hope of a settlement of the disagreement between the Houses, and the angry contest was likely to be adjourned, for further and protracted agitation, before a people already inflamed with sectional animosities, Mr. ENGLISH took the responsibility of moving to concur in the proposition of the Senate asking for a committee of free conference. The excitement upon the occasion had scarcely ever been equalled in the House of Representatives. Upon adopting this motion, the vote was 108 to 108, but the Speaker voted in the affirmative, and the motion carried. From this committee Mr. ENGLISH reported what is known as the "English bill," which became the law after a struggle of unparalleled bitterness. Under this law, the question of admission under the Lecompton Constitution was, in effect, referred back to the people of Kansas, and they voted against it, just as Mr. ENGLISH and almost every one else expected they would do. On the final vote, which admitted Kansas as a State, he was still a member, and voted for her admission.

After the passage of the "English bill," a very determined effort was made to prevent Mr. ENGLISH's re-election to Congress, but he was returned by a larger majority than ever. There had been no change in the boundaries of his district, but his career in this, as in everything else, had been upward and onward, his majority gradually increasing at each election from 400 in 1852 to 2000 in 1858; and though he had defeated Buchanan's favorite measure, the President wrote a letter to him, saying, " I omit no opportunity of expressing my opinion of how much the country owes you for the 'English' amendment. Having lost the bill of the Senate, which I preferred, the country would have been in a sad condition had it not been relieved by your measure. It is painful even to think of what would have been the alarming condition of the Union had Congress adjourned without passing your amendment. I trust you will have no difficulty in being renominated and re-elected. If I had a thousand votes, you should have them all with a hearty good-will." As the war approached, Mr. ENGLISH openly disavowed all sympathy for the rule-or-ruin element of the Democracy, and tried to conciliate the factions. Addressing the Southern Democratic Congressmen, one day, he said, "Looking at this matter from the particular standpoint you occupy, it is to be feared you have not always properly appreciated the position of the Free-State Democracy or the perils which would environ them in the event of a resort to the extreme measures to which I refer. Would you expect us, in such an event, to go with you out of the Union? If so, let me tell you frankly, your expectations will never be realized. Collectively, as States, it would be impossible, and as individuals, inadmissible; because it would involve innumerable sacrifices and a severance of those sacred ties which bind every man to his own immediate country, and which, as patriots, we never would surrender." He now retired from Congress, and, declining the command of an Indiana regiment offered him by the great war-Governor of Indiana, Oliver P. Morton, still advocated the Union cause.

At the close of the Thirty-sixth Congress, and when in the full meridian of success, never having been defeated before the people, and with a fair prospect of being advanced to still higher political honors, he retired from Congress and active political life as an office-holder. As Chairman of the Committee on Resolutions at the Convention of 1864, which nominated his friend, Michael C. Kerr, for Congress from his old district, Mr. ENGLISH prepared and reported a resolution, which was adopted, declaring:

"That we are now, as we ever have been, unqualifiedly in favor of the Union of the States under the Constitution, and stand ready, as we have ever stood heretofore, to do everything that loyal and true citizens should do to maintain that Union under the Constitution, and to hand it down to our children unimpaired, as we received it from our fathers."

To these sentiments of loyalty to the Union, Mr. ENGLISH firmly and consistently adhered throughout the struggle. His fidelity never wavered, nor did

36 *

426 LIFE OF W. II. ENGLISH, OF INDIANA.

his doubts.ever gain an ascendency over his convictions that the Union would be preserved.

At the close of his useful and honorable Congressional services, Mr. ENGLISH was confronted with the fact that a new departure in his business life was inevitable. At this juncture he concluded to embark in the business of banking, and, in connection with J. F. D. Lanier, of New York, and George W. Riggs, of Washington City, he established, in the spring of 1863, the First National Bank of Indianapolis. This bank was among the first organized in the United States under the national system, and the very first to get out its circulation. Mr. ENGLISH's connection with this bank brought him into great prominence as a financier, and in this position, as in other places of great responsibility, he displayed consummate ability. During the period of his connection with the First National Bank, the question of national finances excited the profoundest solicitation, and engaged the attention of the best thinkers in the country. During the entire period of that discussion, Mr. ENGLISH's views were well understood. No man's opinions were less equivocal. His knowledge of business, of finances, and of the needs of the country was comprehensive. He was opposed to inflation, and as certainly opposed to extreme and hasty legislation looking to forced resumption. With re gard to gold and silver as the standards of value, and to the absolute necessity of ultimate resumption, no man in the country was more pronounced in his declarations, — as a result, his financial record is without a blemish. Mr. ENGLISH presided over this bank over fourteen years, to the entire satisfaction of the stockholders, and then, in 1877, in the full meridian of financial success, he resigned the Presidency and retired from active business, as he had years before retired from active politics as an officeholder when in the full tide of political success. Faithful to every trust, he retained the good opinion of his associates then, as he had of his constituents when he retired from Congress. He took part in political organization at home, but declined to run for office, his banking business occupying his attention. He has a fine residence in Indianapolis, and is a widower with two grown children. His son, W. E. English, is a member of the Indiana Legislature, where the English family rival the Bayards in winning family honors. His daughter is married and lives in Louisville. Mr. ENGLISH is described as above the average height, with an erect, well-made figure. His head is of good size, with regular features. The forehead is high and broad. He is dignified and gentlemanly in his manners, and has a pleasing address with all persons. His whole contour of face and person would at once attract favorable attention in any gathering.

Such is the man who was selected by the Democratic party in Convention at Cincinnati on June 24, 1880, for the second place on their Presidential ticket. A man who has gained unqualified success in every phase of his life; a man who has earned and retained the confidence of all with whom he has had social, political, or commercial relations; a man of action rather than of speech, for, though a good debater, he is remarkable rather for hard logic and practical common sense than for the flowers of rhetoric or the ponderous periods of oratorical display. Energy of character, firmness of purpose, and an unswerving integrity are his chief characteristics. In personal intercourse he is inclined to be retiring and reserved, which might be attributed to haughtiness or pride by a stranger, but to an acquaintance or friend he is open, candid, and affable. In the private and social relations of life he stands "without blemish and above reproach." As a business man he has most valuable qualities. Without being too cautious, he is prudent and conservative.

CHAPTER XLI.

CONCLUSION.

WITH a feeling of regret, we approach the conclusion of a congenial task, and write the closing passages of a biography of one of Nature's noblemen; for it may truly be said of WINFIELD SCOTT HANCOCK that such he is. A pure, honorable man; a Cœur de Lion in battle; a Bayard in chivalry; a Chesterfield in politeness; and, above all, an American citizen-soldier, revering the principles of the immortal Declaration of Independence, obedient to their commands, jealous of their safety, and determined that they shall be respected. Of the people and with the people, it is fitting that by the people he should be honored. Of the soldiers and with the soldiers, it is but natural that by the soldiers he should be esteemed almost to adoration, for he invariably identified himself with their interests or their sufferings, and, with sympathies easily aroused, ever strove to alleviate their misfortunes with a personal zest, and thus making himself as much the

(429)

friend as the Commander, ensured at once their love and their obedience. To this is due that almost reckless bravery of his men, leading them to prefer death on the field sooner than merit a reproachful glance from those blue eyes which could light up so eloquently over an act of valor.

In appearance, General HANCOCK is commanding, being not less than six feet two inches in height, well formed, with a graceful carriage, and his handsome features improved, if that were possible, by the silvery moustache, which tells something of the thirty-five years of military life and its hardships. Weighing about two hundred and forty pounds, he is a fine specimen of mature American manhood. His only son, Russell Hancock, a worthy son of a worthy sire, is an enterprising planter in Mississippi.

Before closing, we must advert to a misstatement which, from some hostile source, has recently been promulgated, to the effect that General HANCOCK is inimical to the present administration. It is quite true that he believed Mr. Tilden had been elected, and so told General SHERMAN; but, acquiescing in the decision of the Electoral Commission, he was one of the first Major-Generals to pay his respects to President HAYES, modestly inscribing in the visitor's book, "WINFIELD SCOTT HANCOCK, Major-General

U. S. A., by invitation of General SHERMAN."
Law had spoken, and HANCOCK, the soldier-citizen,
saluted the law.

Had we space, we might fill many pages with the
complimentary telegrams from all sources on his
presidential nomination; with the eloquent speeches
of ex-Governor Hendricks, of Senator Thurman, of
the plucky general and ex-governor Wade Hampton;
with the enthusiastic endorsement of General and
Governor GEORGE B. McCLELLAN, of General AL-
FRED T. PEARSON, and hundreds of others, Republican and Democratic alike; but we must conclude,
and most appropriately, we think, with the reply of
General SHERMAN to an interviewer: "I am not
much interested in politics; but *if you will sit down
and write the best that can be put in the English language of General HANCOCK as a soldier and as a
gentleman, I will sign it without hesitation.*"

A volume could say no more, and we will not.

THE END.